T0400013

Diversity in Local Political Practice

In what ways do local authorities respond to the increasing socio-cultural heterogeneity of urban populations? While other studies have often focused on policy declarations, the eight chapters in this book provide rich evidence on the content and implementation of local policies. Furthermore, several chapters offer theoretical insights into the factors driving or hindering policies that acknowledge socio-cultural heterogeneity and ensure more equality and inclusive public services.

The general focus of the book is on cities in France and Germany, that is, two major immigration countries in Europe – countries in which local authorities have a relatively strong position within the state structure. The contributions analyze how local actors use their powers to ensure more equal public employment, adapt cultural offers and recreational facilities to the demands of a diverse population, and/or to fight discrimination. Further chapters investigate who takes part in formulating policies and seek to explain why cities take different decisions about strategies and practices. As a whole, the book contributes to the comparative study of societal diversity and local politics in France and Germany, and will be of interest to academics, researchers and advanced students of sociology, public policy, law, and political science.

This book was originally published as a special issue of *Ethnic and Racial Studies*.

Karen Schönwälder is Research Group Leader at the Max Planck Institute for the Study of Religious and Ethnic Diversity in Göttingen, Germany, and Professor of Political Science at Göttingen University.

Ethnic and Racial Studies

Series editors:
Martin Bulmer, *University of Surrey, UK,*
John Solomos, *University of Warwick, UK*

The journal *Ethnic and Racial Studies* was founded in 1978 by John Stone to provide an international forum for high quality research on race, ethnicity, nationalism and ethnic conflict. At the time the study of race and ethnicity was still a relatively marginal sub-field of sociology, anthropology and political science. In the intervening period the journal has provided a space for the discussion of core theoretical issues, key developments and trends, and for the dissemination of the latest empirical research.

It is now the leading journal in its field and has helped to shape the development of scholarly research agendas. *Ethnic and Racial Studies* attracts submissions from scholars in a diverse range of countries and fields of scholarship, and crosses disciplinary boundaries. It is now available in both printed and electronic form. Since 2015 it has published 15 issues per year, three of which are dedicated to *Ethnic and Racial Studies Review* offering expert guidance to the latest research through the publication of book reviews, symposia and discussion pieces, including reviews of work in languages other than English.

The *Ethnic and Racial Studies* book series contains a wide range of the journal's special issues. These special issues are an important contribution to the work of the journal, where leading social science academics bring together articles on specific themes and issues that are linked to the broad intellectual concerns of *Ethnic and Racial Studies*. The series editors work closely with the guest editors of the special issues to ensure that they meet the highest quality standards possible. Through publishing these special issues as a series of books, we hope to allow a wider audience of both scholars and students from across the social science disciplines to engage with the work of *Ethnic and Racial Studies*.

Most recent titles in the series include:

Diversity in Local Political Practice

Edited by
Karen Schönwälder

Routledge
Taylor & Francis Group

LONDON AND NEW YORK

First published 2021
by Routledge
2 Park Square, Milton Park, Abingdon, Oxon OX14 4RN

and by Routledge
52 Vanderbilt Avenue, New York, NY 10017

Routledge is an imprint of the Taylor & Francis Group, an informa business

Introduction, Chapters 1, 3, 7 © 2021 Taylor & Francis
Chapter 2 © 2020 Christine Lang. Originally published as Open Access.
Chapter 4 © 2020 Michalis Moutselos. Originally published as Open Access.
Chapter 5 © 2020 Miriam Schader. Originally published as Open Access.
Chapter 6 © 2020 Maria Schiller, Julia Martínez-Ariño and Mireia Bolíbar. Originally
published as Open Access.
Chapter 8 © 2020 Ines Michalowski and Max Behrendt. Originally published as
Open Access.

British Library Cataloguing in Publication Data
A catalogue record for this book is available from the British Library

ISBN 13: 978-0-367-69634-4 (hbk)
ISBN 13: 978-1-003-14263-8 (ebk)

Typeset in Myriad Pro
by Newgen Publishing UK

Publisher's Note
The publisher accepts responsibility for any inconsistencies that may have arisen
during the conversion of this book from journal articles to book chapters, namely
the inclusion of journal terminology.

Disclaimer
Every effort has been made to contact copyright holders for their permission to
reprint material in this book. The publishers would be grateful to hear from any
copyright holder who is not here acknowledged and will undertake to rectify any
errors or omissions in future editions of this book.

Contents

Citation Information

The chapters in this book were originally published in *Ethnic and Racial Studies*, volume 43, issue 11 (July 2020). When citing this material, please use the original page numbering for each article, as follows:

Chapter 5

Chapter 6

Chapter 7

Chapter 8

For any permission-related enquiries please visit:
www.tandfonline.com/page/help/permissions

Notes on Contributors

Max Behrendt, WZB, Social Science Research Centre, Berlin, Germany.

Laure Bereni, CNRS–Centre Maurice Halbwachs, Paris, France.

Mireia Bolíbar, Department of Political and Social Sciences, Universitat Pompeu Fabra, Barcelona, Spain.

Renaud Epstein, Sciences Po Saint-Germain (CESDIP), Saint-Germain-en-Laye, France.

Anouk Flamant, Department of Political Science, EA Grhapes, Laboratoire Triangle, INSHEA, Suresnes, France.

Christine Lang, Max Planck Institute for the Study of Religious and Ethnic Diversity, Göttingen, Germany.

Julia Martínez-Ariño, Department of the Comparative Study of Religion, University of Groningen, Netherlands.

Ines Michalowski, Department of Sociology, University of Münster, Germany; WZB, Social Science Research Centre, Berlin, Germany.

Michalis Moutselos, Department of Social and Political Science, University of Cyprus; formerly at the Max Planck Institute for the Study of Religious and Ethnic Diversity, Göttingen, Germany.

Miriam Schader, Max Planck Institute for the Study of Religious and Ethnic Diversity, Göttingen, Germany.

Maria Schiller, Department of Public Administration and Sociology, Erasmus University Rotterdam, Netherlands.

Karen Schönwälder, Max Planck Institute for the Study of Religious and Ethnic Diversity, Göttingen, Germany; University of Göttingen, Germany.

Alexandre Tandé, Independent Scholar, Brussels, Belgium; formerly at the Max Planck Institute for the Study of Religious and Ethnic Diversity, Göttingen, Germany.

Manon Torres, INED–Centre Maurice Halbwachs, Paris, France.

INTRODUCTION

Diversity in local political practice

Karen Schönwälder

ABSTRACT
This article frames and introduces the contributions to a special issue. Their focus is on France and Germany, not only two major immigration countries in Europe, but also countries where local authorities have a relatively strong position within the state structure. While other studies have often focused on policy declarations, the eight articles in this special issue provide rich evidence on the content and implementation of policies. Furthermore, several articles offer theoretical insights into the factors driving or hindering policies that acknowledge socio-cultural heterogeneity, ensure more equality and inclusive public services. Results of a project at the Göttingen Max Planck Institute for the Study of Religious and Ethnic Diversity are presented together with other contributions. The introduction concludes with reflections on the difficulties of "intercultural" communication among scholars and comparison of France and Germany.

Cities have traditionally been described as being marked by heterogeneity. Such heterogeneity takes different shapes. Even within the homogenizing framework of a nation state, cities may be more or less segregated along lines of wealth and ethnicity, have a more or less varied cultural life, and more or less welcoming public spaces, to name just a few potential differences. In what ways are such differences shaped by the interventions of urban actors? And how do such actors intervene to make differences, for instance of physical ability or cultural backgrounds, matter – or not – for the life chances and everyday lives of their city's residents?

This special issue presents articles aiming to contribute to a more precise picture of urban interventions into the contours and relevance of societal diversity. Some of the contributions emerged as parts of an umbrella project at the Göttingen Max Planck Institute for the Study of Religious and Ethnic Diversity. Contributions by colleagues from other institutions complement this selection.[1]

The focus of this set of articles is on France and Germany, two major immigration countries in Europe. Germany and France are the leading powers of the European Union and countries traditionally shaped by immigration. In both countries, local authorities have a relatively strong position within the state structure (Wollmann and Bouckaert 2006, 27). They are thus able to intervene, in relevant ways, in the shape and relevance of diversity. In Germany, municipalities perform a wide range of tasks. They represent the state at the local level and implement national as well as regional laws, but also have autonomous functions. Land use, cultural policies, childcare, some aspects of social welfare provision, support for associations, and the promotion of the economy fall within their competences (Bogumil and Holtkamp 2006).

In centralized France, the local level has altogether had a functionally weaker position, but cities have traditionally been well represented at the national level. "Owing chiefly to the influence that the *cumul de mandats* gives powerful mayors in national politics, French local authorities have traditionally tended to be politically strong but (until well into the 1980s) functionally weak." (Kuhlmann 2006, no page; Wollmann et al. 2010, 26–33). However, decades of decentralization measures have strengthened local government in France. Municipalities have responsibilities with regard to town planning, culture and education. Local councils and in particular large municipalities also develop policies in fields formally assigned to the regions (Borraz and Le Galès 2005, 13, 15).

Where and how local actors intervene

This special issue is motivated by the belief that our understanding of how localities and local actors shape the life chances of immigrants and other disadvantaged groups of the population still has gaps. While there is a considerable body of scholarship on immigration-related discourses and positions (e.g. Scuzzarello 2015), other interventions of local actors and their effects have been less studied. Furthermore, while scholars have emphasized the important role of cities in immigrant policies and their commonalities, we should aim to develop a more precise understanding of this role by considering the specific competencies of local government and how they vary across states. Local government takes on distinct roles in different policy fields. It may be a relatively independent actor, a mediator and moderator, or a dependent executor of national law.

- In some policy fields, major decisions are taken at the local level. Local councils and local governments, for instance, determine spatial structures and thus influence patterns of residential segregation and public space. Whether central city areas are inhabited by mixed populations or not,

whether disadvantaged parts of the population live in areas that are particularly polluted is, if not determined by, at least influenced by decisions
of the council. The cultural life of a German or French city is strongly
influenced by local decisions over programme orientations and funding
for theatres, museums, and other institutions (Tandé 2020). The opportunity to practise sports and use leisure facilities may depend on local regulations (see Michalowski and Behrendt 2020) and on local decisions about
access to public sports grounds for different clubs.

- Local actors may also get involved in policy fields where their formal competences are weak. Education in Germany, for instance, falls within the
competences of the regional states, but local governments may become
active to further the cooperation between schools and employers (Aybek
2014). Such activities can improve the employment chances of disadvantaged youths. Further, local authorities are major employers and thus
actors that co-determine opportunities for work and access to careers.
While in both Germany and France, local public employment follows
more general public service regulations, local authorities can take measures
that influence fairness of access (Lang 2020; Mezziani-Remichi and
Maussen 2017). As Räuchle and Schmiz (2018, 7) recently argued, "municipal politics play a crucial role for migrant economies." The extent to which
residents of a city experience discrimination can be influenced by active
local policies scandalizing such discrimination and providing support to
victims (Flamant 2020).

- In implementing national immigration law, local authorities may have
some leeway to interpret the law and determine how exactly they
implement it. Whether residents are met with a welcoming attitude in
the offices of the municipalities, or encounter distrust, is importantly
influenced by mayors and other leading civil servants. German municipalities have been shown to differ, for instance, with regard to whether and
how soon refugees are granted a work permit (Schader 2020). Mayors in
France may have handled their duty to report fake marriages or to issue
certificates of "decent housing", decisive for the immigration of family
members, in different ways (Nicholls and Uitermark 2017, 191).

Other local actors, beyond the council, mayor and administration, contribute to a local political culture and influence power structures. Such a local
culture affects the practices of the administration as well as the policies of
council and government. It further presents a more or less encouraging
context for minority political articulation and participation.

While local authorities and other local actors thus clearly have an important
role, scholars disagree on whether the powers of the local state have grown or
diminished in the past decades. In the immigration literature, we often find an
enthusiastic emphasis on increased local powers in Europe. Some scholars

suggest that the autonomy of cities has grown due to European Union policies that encouraged city networks and provided additional funds (Borkert and Caponio 2010, 9; Gesemann and Roth 2009, 21–2). Others even identify a "local turn" in immigrant integration policy. In contrast, another strand of scholarship points at the loss of power through EU-enforced liberalization, the privatization of public services and the budget crisis of many cities (Bogumil and Holtkamp 2006, 77; Heeg and Rosol 2007). And yet, there are many ways in which politics and policies in cities influence the lives of immigrants and other minorities. Local decisions not only determine the extent to which residents have equal access to some resources and services, they also contribute to the societal standing of minorities. The public presence of minorities through prominent buildings or festivals, their visibility in a city's cultural and political life, conveys recognition and thus contributes to the status of minority members (Morris 2009; Phillips 1995). The urban culture of cooperation importantly influences how minority claims can be articulated.

The Göttingen "CityDiv"-project underlying several contributions to this special issue started from the assumption that the development of socio-cultural heterogeneity in French and German society and the presence of "diversity" as a positive narrative in national politics and public life present conditions that influence responses to immigration and immigration-related change. Certainly, immigration itself is a major source of socio-cultural differentiation. But it is not the only one. Immigrants have brought with them and developed differing lifestyles, languages, value systems and religious practices, but the pluralization of the forms of life, of cultural preferences and norms also results from other developments, such as rising levels of education and individualization processes. The declining relevance of the once standard heterosexual family with children, all living in one household, and the broadening scope of what life in old age means, illustrate the trend towards more varied forms of living within many highly industrialized, democratic societies.

Furthermore, some differences that were long forced to the background of public social life are now visible and have vocal advocates demanding recognition, participation in the life of cities and their share of the resources. In the 2000s, it has become common in Western Europe that mayors and other prominent politicians take part in Gay Pride events, thus underlining the legitimacy of such minority claims. The UN Convention on the Rights of Persons with Disabilities, in force since 2008, has strengthened the rights of disabled people to participate in all spheres of social life and put pressure on public institutions to ensure the preconditions for inclusion. Disabled people themselves have also organized more publicly and increasingly demand visibility and access to all services and resources. As the public life of cities is increasingly marked by a multi-facetted heterogeneity, immigration becomes just one aspect of a more complex social reality.

Sometimes, a positive image of "diversity" is used to capture such multiple features of contemporary societies. The usage and meaning of this term differs across Europe. And yet, not least due to the presence and politics of large global businesses, positive diversity campaigns are a familiar discursive framework that may be taken up by urban actors and impact on their policies. Scholarship is divided as to the relevance and character of these developments. Is "diversity" just a management rhetoric without positive (or negative) impact on the lives of minorities? What do we find if we look beyond the rhetoric and search for de facto responses to socio-cultural heterogeneity regardless of their labels?

In German localities, "diversity"-framings have increasingly entered into immigrant integration policies (Pütz and Rodatz 2013). Mayors of big cities routinely celebrate the diversity of their cities' populations. Urban actors in big cities are altogether convinced of the relevance of diversification and embrace its positive effects (Moutselos et al. 2020). Furthermore, as a recent analysis by the "CityDiv"-project team demonstrated, cities also implement a range of policy instruments aiming to accommodate and recognize the socio-cultural diversity of cities. They include, for instance, changes to recruitment practices, image campaigns and concepts for local museums or libraries. Maybe more surprisingly, such policy instruments are not only common across big German cities, but were also found to exist in the big French cities (Martínez-Ariño et al. 2018). Apparently, the French Republican ideology of equal citizens does not preclude difference-conscious policies. Christophe Bertossi has pointed at the "variations and malleability of the French model" (2012, 252) and criticized "the degree of normative density scholars assign to" it (2012, 249). Similarly, Christopher Downing (2015, 1557) has pointed at "the various formations and applications of difference-orientated policies in French cities". The *label diversité*, a reward issued by a French government agency to various organizations, including local authorities, is one example illustrating the recognition of difference, or diversity, in French society (Bereni, Epstein, and Torres 2020). We refer to "diversity policies", or "diversity policy instruments", regardless of whether the actors involved use the term "diversity". This is an analytical term, distinct from diversity concepts for instance in business strategies. Unlike terms such as "multiculturalism", it captures responses to disadvantage more broadly, and not only for ethnic minorities, including measures "aiming to adjust the public administration and its services to a heterogeneous population and to publicly acknowledge the socio-cultural diversity of the population" (Martínez-Ariño et al. 2018, 2).

In a comparative light, it turns out that explicit references to "diversity" in the public discourse serve different functions in different contexts. While in Germany the term is associated with a positive affirmation of immigration-related change, in France its function has been ambiguous. In French politics, *diversité* has been used as a concept allowing explicit reference to ethnic difference (Escafré-Dublet and Simon 2009, 138). However, as Bereni, Epstein, and Torres (2020) argue, it may have "lost that meaning in later years". And often diversity is also seen as a concept that makes equality conditional on individual performance, a neoliberal logic incompatible with demands for equality (Sénac 2012, 260–1). In cities in the Netherlands, "diversity" has functioned as a counter-concept to multiculturalism, and sometimes an individualized perception of social positions serves to depoliticize issues of inequality (Hoekstra 2015). Researchers should closely study how an affirmation of diversity is linked with particular policies, rather than assuming that it generally serves neo-liberal or social justice-oriented purposes. Furthermore, both may not be clear-cut alternatives. As the CityDiv-team could show in a recent study of German urban actors' positions, market-oriented perceptions of diversity often go along with support for justice-oriented interventions, such as accommodating the disabled and representing societal diversity in municipal councils (Moutselos et al. 2020).

Another key theme addressed by the Göttingen project – and a number of articles in this collection – are the changing structures of local politics and their implications for the representation of immigrant concerns in urban politics. While other studies have investigated representation in elected councils, that is urban government (e.g. Bloemraad and Schönwälder 2013), a further area that deserves more interest is the broader development of "governance". In the past two decades, as several scholars have pointed out, we have witnessed the development of "new forms of governance and participatory politics on the local scale" (Blokland et al. 2015, 662; see also Guarneros-Meza and Geddes 2010). Already in 2005, Borraz and Le Galès (2005, 24–5) pointed out that "new forms of non-electoral participation are emerging". The term governance aims to capture the increasingly blurred boundary between state, market and civil society actors in policy-making. Further, as Giersig (2008, 55) underlines, "governance points to a diversification and proliferation of policy-making coalitions that only in part consist of representatives of the state".

Local political cooperation can help empower disadvantaged groups of the population, help incorporate them in mainstream politics or, rather, exclude such groups and contribute to their marginalization. Funding for associations, their involvement in larger fora, participation in governance structures and local decision-making, the election of minority representatives to political office may convey confidence, allow an articulation of group-specific claims and support an implementation of group interests. At the same time, political incorporation can also come at a price. As Nicholls and Uitermark argue (2017, 234, 33–4), movement organizations and spokespersons may "come to serve rather than challenge the status quo" and "effectively become outposts of the state within urban civil society".

If new forms and fora of deliberation and decision-making in local politics become more common, it is imperative to assess empirically how they reflect power structures and impact on the position of minorities. To what extent are immigrant representatives or advocates of immigrant and minority interests present in such coalitions? In one rare optimistic piece, Korteweg and Triadafilopoulos (2015, 663) argue that, in European municipalities, "immigrant groups are regularly integrated into policymaking and implementation efforts on issues ranging from youth criminality to language learning and lagging labour-market participation", an involvement they term "multicultural governance". Can other studies confirm this tentative finding? Drawing on more systematic empirical evidence, Schiller, Martínez-Ariño, and Bolíbar (2020) find support for this broad assessment for German and French cities.

The contributions to this special issue

The eight articles in this special issue provide rich evidence on the local political practice of diversity. While other studies have often focused on policy declarations, the content and implementation of policies is central here. Furthermore, several articles offer theoretical insights into the factors driving or hindering policies that acknowledge diversity and serve to reduce discrimination, ensure more equality and appropriate public services.

The first two contributions examine how local authorities respond to initiatives from the national and local state. Labels or prizes issued by a public institution or a foundation have become common instruments for furthering broader societal aims, such as openness to diversity, family-friendly employment conditions, etc. Thus, Germany has a *Charta der Diversität* and France the *Label Diversité*. Bereni, Epstein, and Torres (2020) examine the motivations and strategies of the very small number of French local and regional authorities who so-far received the label. Do such instruments actually help change practices or do they just provide cover for not doing so? The authors argue that local actors actively used the national instrument for their own purposes by interpreting it in a specific way. The *Label Diversité* provided an opportunity, albeit taken up by only very few local authorities (four by mid-2019). In one case examined here, it was associated with the "institutionalization and managerialization of pre-existing antidiscrimination policies". In two other cases, it resulted in "a process of deracialization of these policies". Interestingly, pragmatic rather than ideological considerations seem central when human resources officials, seeking indicators to measure performance, favour interventions where such indicators are available, i.e. gender, age and disability – but not ethnicity or ascribed "race". Local conditions more generally, the mayors as potential policy entrepreneurs, and the Human Resources departments in the urban administration are identified as crucial for the varying outcomes.

German local administrations can, to some extent, draw on such statistics, but Lang (2020) equally points out how organizations resist innovations that do not align with what they perceive as their core functional needs. Her contribution examines the implementation of a German regional-state initiative to promote the "intercultural opening" of public administrations. Looking at three local administrations, she discusses what factors caused differences in the extent to which the regional policy was implemented. Once again, the existence of such differences, ranging from "practically unaltered continuity of established hiring routines" to "structural changes with substantial effects on staff composition", underlines the significant room for manoeuvre that local political and administrative actors can exploit. The employment of persons with an immigrant background is at the centre of this investigation. Unlike in France, reference to migration background is not a taboo in German politics and administrations, although a belief in the fairness of existing, allegedly "colourblind" procedures is common. Three factors are found to determine the local responses: political leadership, the fit of new initiatives with functional requirements, in this case in the recruitment of personnel, and the population structure of the locality, where high immigrant shares can increase the urgency of the issue.

In Anouk Flamant's study cities do not respond to a national initiative but instead, they change their policies on their own accord. Three named French cities, Lyon, Strasbourg, and Nantes, following elections in the early 2000s, introduced new organizational units in order to implement changed immigrant policies. The directions of the changes differed, and Flamant investigates why this was the case. Differences concern the conceptualization of policy as related to equality more generally, to antidiscrimination, integration, or citizenship – important differences as Flamant stresses. Thus, reference to citizenship tended to imply a focus on political participation, while "integration" likely signalled a perception of immigrants themselves as responsible for their socioeconomic incorporation. Policy instruments and aims also varied. Four factors are found to account for the different urban policies: the power of the leading politicians, the experiences and convictions of leading civil servants, the influence of civil society actors, in this case immigrant advocacy groups, and the influence of European Union initiatives. Participation in EU-programmes and networks may play a particular role in French local developments, as thereby a big political player introduced the recognition of (ethnic) minorities into a context where this was, and still is, heavily contested.

In France in particular, in a sharply divided polity, as Paul May points out, the theme of multiculturalism is "a structural element of the left–right ideological divide" (2016, 1349). Pro-active policies with regard to diversity are often put into place by Left-leaning governments (see Martínez-Ariño et al. 2018). As in Thatcherite Britain, during the Sarkozy presidency in particular, they sometimes became instruments of protest against a right-wing government. Moutselos (2020) is interested in the exceptions. His study contrasts, on the one hand, a city governed by a conservative major which still implements policies of minority recognition and, on the other, a Socialist-dominated city that stays distant from any diversity or explicit ethnic minority policy, but furthers social equality. Drawing on theories of the policy process, he tests the role of policy entrepreneurs and advocacy coalitions for promoting change. In Marseille, the existence of an established policy network, or coalition of actors advocating a recognition of minority presence, enabled the continuation of diversity policies under conservative rule, albeit without a focus on anti-discrimination measures. In contrast, in Grenoble, a stronghold of the political Left, municipal policies are marked by an absence of presentations of the city's diversity, and politicians refrain from co-operating with ethnic or religious groups. Traditional colour-blind universalism, in a Socialist-dominated form, goes along with social policies for disadvantaged, often heavily immigrant-populated, neighbourhoods, with anti-discrimination policies and support for immigrant associations. Thus, the two cities represent a multicultural recognition policy, on the one hand, and a colourblind anti-discrimination policy, on the other.

Both Moutselos as well as Schader point out how a crisis (or critical juncture) can provide the impetus and political space for reforms. In the study of Schader (2020) the impulse for change was an external shock - the mass refugee arrival in central Europe in 2015. Taking a stance against a common perception, she insists that the events did not cause German urban bureaucratic machineries to fail in their duties. Instead, she outlines how a situation that required improvization and extraordinary efforts could, in some cases, provide a push for reforms. At least two of the three investigated urban administrations restructured their immigration-related services and built up more comprehensive departments handling previously separated tasks. As Schader argues, the alleged "crisis" thus provided the stimulus for a much-needed adjustment of administrative arrangements to the realities of diverse population structures and requirements.

What role do immigrants and ethnic minorities themselves play in the development and implementation of policies affecting them? Flamant's article (2020) identifies immigrant advocacy groups as one factor impacting on the direction and shape of urban policy. In her case studies, foreigners' councils are the organizational form through which their advice is communicated to the city government. Schiller, Martínez-Ariño, and Bolíbar (2020) provide a birds'-eye-view of the place of immigrant advocacy actors within urban networks for 40 French and German cities and qualitative evidence from selected cities. Based on the Max-Planck CityDiv-survey, they show that such actors now have a well-founded place within the networks of a broad spectrum of the cities' corporate and collective actors. At the same time, they find indicators suggesting that participation in governance networks mainly takes place with regard to immigrant integration issues, and to a lesser extent in other fields of urban policy. As they further suggest, such networks often go back to the existence of organized forms of co-operation in urban fora, roundtables, councils, or similar gatherings. Drawing on qualitative fieldwork in selected cities, the study develops a number of hypotheses regarding mechanisms through which such fora enhance cooperation.

The two final contributions to this special issue investigate specific policy fields: Tandé (2020) explores an aspect of the cultural policies of cities, the development of public libraries in France. Cultural policies are one of the main responsibilities of local authorities, both in France and in Germany. In France, libraries are traditionally seen as helping to transmit high culture and the French language. However, increasingly they are also confronted with demands of a diversifying population, for whom libraries may also provide access to information, meeting spaces, or even serve to represent cultural plurality. Like other articles in this collection, he points at the variety of policy responses and the agency of the officials. Tandé's contribution underlines that even in centralist and often assimilationist France, local organizations respond in flexible and varying ways to the pluralization of urban populations.

Sports and leisure facilities are another area largely controlled by local authorities. Michalowski and Behrendt (2020) present results of a survey examining to what extent religious minority demands have become an issue for pools in German localities, and how they accommodate such demands. Their study forms part of a growing literature examining the renegotiation of secularity and religion in organizations. Body practices are a particularly sensitive issue. Not surprisingly, Muslim concerns and issues of clothing and gender separation predominate. More surprisingly, perhaps, the authors find that most pools have rather smoothly introduced regulations providing e.g. for the use of unconventional bathing suits. Such regulations are, maybe surprisingly, at best loosely related to the concerns of citizens and pool users.

Altogether, the contributions to this special issue illustrate what different shapes diversity policy in practice can take. Further, several contributions provide insights into actors and conditions that further, hinder and crucially shape such policies. In producing these results, we also learned about some difficulties of "intercultural" communication among scholars. French scholars are often centrally concerned with the question of whether broader aims like "diversité" or "equality" serve the interests of ethnic minorities and often fear – or assume – that inclusion in a broader policy context will "dilute" or undermine the interests of ethnic minorities. "Diversity" itself is a negatively loaded term, and French scholars seem to prefer terms such as anti-discrimination or equality policies. This is not just a terminological difference. Implied is a low regard for policies of recognition and presence – expressed e.g. in cultural policies or image campaigns. In German academic contexts, the recognition aspect of diversity policies seems to be accorded more importance, and diversity framings are, at least potentially, often also seen as possibly benefitting immigrant populations. In the end, these are of course empirical questions that we should further pursue. Studies on the effects of diversity, anti-discrimination, or multi-cultural policies are still scarce. We should make sure that terminological differences do not stand in the way of that effort.

Note

1. Thanks to further colleagues who took part in discussions of previous versions of the articles, in particular the participants of a workshop in 2018: Mathias Rodatz, Nicolaus von Puymbroek, Christian Jacobs, Marlon Barbehön, Christopher Downing, Vivian Lowndes, Claire Bullen, Christine Lelevrier and Angeline Escafré-Dublet.

Disclosure statement

No potential conflict of interest was reported by the author(s).

References

Aybek, Can M. 2014. *Migrantenjugendliche zwischen Schule und Beruf: Individuelle Übergänge und kommunale Strukturen der Ausbildungsförderung.* Wiesbaden: VS Verlag.

Bereni, Laure, Renaud Epstein, and Manon Torres. 2020. "Colour-blind Diversity: How the 'Diversity Label' Reshaped Anti-discrimination Policies in Three French Local Governments." *Ethnic and Racial Studies.* This issue.

Bertossi, Christophe. 2012. "French Republicanism and the Problem of Normative Density." *Comparative European Politics* 10 (3): 248–265. doi:10.1057/cep.2012.6.

Bloemraad, Irene, and Karen Schönwälder, eds. 2013. "Immigrant Incorporation in Urban Politics [Special Issue]." *European Political Science* 12 (4): 448–454.

Blokland, Talja, Christine Hentschel, Andrej Holm, Henrik Lebuhn, and Talia Margalit. 2015. "Urban Citizenship and Right to the City: The Fragmentation of Claims." *International Journal of Urban and Regional Studies* 39 (4): 655–665. doi:10.1111/1468-2427.12259.

Bogumil, Jörg, and Lars Holtkamp. 2006. *Kommunalpolitik und Kommunalverwaltung: Eine policyorientierte Einführung.* Wiesbaden: VS Verlag.

Borkert, Maren, and Tiziana Caponio. 2010. "Introduction: The Local Dimension of Migration Policymaking." In *The Local Dimension of Migration Policymaking,* edited by Tiziana Caponio, and Maren Borkert, 9–32. Amsterdam: Amsterdam University Press.

Borraz, Oliver, and Patrick Le Galès. 2005. "France: The Intermunicipal Revolution." In *Comparing Local Governance: Trends and Developments*, edited by Bas Denters, 12–28. Basingstoke: Palgrave Macmillan.

Downing, Joseph. 2015. "European Influence on Diversity Policy Frames: Paradoxical Outcomes of Lyon's Membership of the Intercultural Cities Programme." *Ethnic and Racial Studies* 38 (9): 1557–1572. doi:10.1080/01419870.2014.996241.

Escafré-Dublet, Angéline, and Patrick Simon. 2009. "Représenter la diversité en politique: une reformulation de la dialectique de la difference et de l'égalité par la doxa républicaine." *Raison politiques* 35 (3): 125–141. doi:10.3917/rai.035.0125.

Flamant, Anouk. 2020. "The Local Turn in Integration Policies: Why French Cities Differ." *Ethnic and Racial Studies*. This issue.

Gesemann, Frank, and Roland Roth. 2009. "Kommunale Integrationspolitik in Deutschland - Einleitende Bemerkungen." In *Lokale Integrationspolitik in der Einwanderungsgesellschaft*, edited by Frank Gesemann, and Roland Roth, 11–29. Wiesbaden: VS Verlag.

Giersig, Nico. 2008. *Multilevel Urban Governance and the "European City": Discussing Metropolitan Reforms in Stockholm and Helsinki*. Wiesbaden: VS Verlag.

Guarneros-Meza, Valeria, and Mike Geddes. 2010. "Local Governance and Participation under Neoliberalism: Comparative Perspectives." *International Journal of Urban and Regional Research* 34 (1): 115–129. doi:10.1111/j.1468-2427.2010.00952.x.

Heeg, Susanne, and Marit Rosol. 2007. "Neoliberale Stadtpolitik im globalen Kontext." *PROKLA* 37 (149): 491–509. doi:10.32387/prokla.v37i149.495.

Hoekstra, Myrte. 2015. "Diverse Cities and Good Citizenship: How Local Governments in the Netherlands Recast National Integration Discourse." *Ethnic and Racial Studies* 38 (10): 1798–1814. doi:10.1080/01419870.2015.1015585.

Korteweg, Anna C., and Triadafilos Triadafilopoulos. 2015. "Is Multiculturalism Dead? Groups, Governments and the 'Real Work of Integration'." *Ethnic and Racial Studies* 38 (5): 663–680. doi:10.1080/01419870.2014.907925.

Kuhlmann, Sabine. 2006. "Local Authorities between the State and the Market: An International Comparison of Local Government Systems and Reforms." *German Journal of Urban Studies/Deutsche Zeitschrift für Kommunalwissenschaft* 45 (2).

Lang, Christine. 2020. "Workforce Diversity Policies in Practice: Drivers and Barriers in Local Administrations." *Ethnic and Racial Studies*. This issue.

Martínez-Ariño, Julia, Michalis Moutselos, Karen Schönwälder, Christian Jacobs, Maria Schiller, and Alexandre Tandé. 2018. "Why Do Some Cities Adopt More Diversity Policies than Others? A Study in France and Germany." *Comparative European Politics*. Advance online publication. doi:10.1057/s41295-018-0119-0.

May, Paul. 2016. "French Cultural Wars: Public Discourses on Multiculturalism in France (1995–2013)." *Journal of Ethnic and Migration Studies* 42 (8): 1334–1352. doi:10.1080/1369183X.2015.1093412.

Mezziani-Remichi, Yasmina, and Marcel Maussen. 2017. "Recruitment in Public Administrations: Diversity Policies and Selection Practices in a French City." *Journal of Ethnic and Migration Studies* 43 (10): 1679–1695. doi:10.1080/1369183X.2017.1293591.

Michalowski, Ines, and Max Behrendt. 2020. "The Accommodation of Muslim Body Practices in German Public Swimming Pools." *Ethnic and Racial Studies*. This issue.

Morris, Lydia. 2009. "Civic Stratification and the Cosmopolitan Ideal." *European Societies* 11 (4): 603–624.

Moutselos, Michalis. 2020. "What Explains Diversity-policy Adoption? Policy Entrepreneurs and Advocacy Coalitions in Two French Cities." *Ethnic and Racial Studies*. This issue.

Moutselos, Michalis, Christian Jacobs, Julia Martínez-Ariño, Maria Schiller, Karen Schönwälder, and Alexandre Tandé. 2020. "Economy or Justice? How Urban Actors Respond to Diversity." *Urban Affairs Review* 56 (1): 228–253.

Nicholls, Walter J., and Justus Uitermark. 2017. *Cities and Social Movements: Immigrant Rights Activism in the United States, France, and the Netherlands, 1970–2015.* Oxford: Wiley Blackwell.

Phillips, Ann. 1995. *The Politics of Presence. The Political Representation of Gender, Ethnicity, and Race.* Oxford: Oxford University Press.

Pütz, Robert, and Mathias Rodatz. 2013. "Kommunale Integrations- und Vielfaltskonzepte im Neoliberalismus: Zur strategischen Steuerung von Integration in deutschen Großstädten." *Geographische Zeitschrift* 101 (3-4): 166–183.

Räuchle, Charlotte, and Antonie Schmiz. 2018. "Migrant Economies: Opportunity Structures and Potential in Different City Types." *Ethnic and Racial Studies.* Advance online publication. doi:10.1080/01419870.2018.1506143.

Schader, Miriam. 2020. "Externalisation or Imitation: The 2015–16 Asylum-Seeker Immigration as a Catalyst for Local Structural Change." *Ethnic and Racial Studies.* This issue.

Schiller, Maria, Julia Martínez-Ariño, and Mireia Bolíbar. 2020. "A Relational Approach to Understanding Local Immigrant Policy-making: Collaboration with Immigrant Advocacy Bodies in Cities in Germany and France." *Ethnic and Racial Studies.* This issue.

Scuzzarello, Sarah. 2015. "Policy Actors' Narrative Constructions of Migrants' Integration in Malmö and Bologna." *Ethnic and Racial Studies* 38 (1): 57–74. doi:10. 1080/01419870.2013.848287.

Sénac, Réjane. 2012. *L'invention de la diversité.* Paris: Presses Universitaires de France.

Tandé, Alexandre. 2020. "Cultural Policies in Support of Commonality or of the Recognition of Difference? The Case of Public Libraries in French Cities." *Ethnic and Racial Studies.* This issue.

Wollmann, Hellmut, Enzo Balboni, Jean-Pierre Gaudin, and Gérard Marcou. 2010. "The Multi-level Institutional Setting in Germany, Italy, France and the UK: A Comparative Overview." In *The Provision of Public Services in Europe: Between State, Local Government and Market,* edited by Hellmut Wollmann, and Gérard Marcou, 15–48. Cheltenham, UK: Edward Elgar.

Wollmann, Hellmut, and Geert Bouckaert. 2006. "State Organisation in France and Germany: Between 'Territoriality' and 'Functionality'." In *State and Local Government Reforms in France and Germany. Convergence and Divergence,* edited by Vincent Hoffmann-Martinot, and Hellmut Wollmann, 11–13. Wiesbaden: VS Verlag. doi:10.1007/978-3-531-90271-5.

Colour-blind diversity: how the "Diversity Label" reshaped anti-discrimination policies in three French local governments

Laure Bereni, Renaud Epstein and Manon Torres

ABSTRACT
Drawing on the qualitative study of three French local governments (Paris, Nantes and the Seine-Saint-Denis department), this article examines the implementation of local anti-discrimination policy during the 2010s. To what extent have these local governments, particularly eager to assert "diversity" values, renegotiated the dominant, colour-blind perspective prevailing at the national level? To address this question, we examined how they used a policy instrument called the "Diversity Label". We found that in the three cases, the commitment to the label reinforced both the *institutionalization* and the *managerialization* of anti-discrimination policy. Yet, in Nantes and Paris, it also led to a *deracialization* of anti-discrimination policy – i.e. to the obliteration of its ethno-racial dimension. The Seine-Saint-Denis department, where the majority group tends to become a minority, appears as a contrasting case, as ethno-racial concerns have remained central. This study reveals the unlikely conditions under which French local governments differ from national colour-blindness.

Compared to other countries of immigration that have embraced multiculturalism and/or race-conscious anti-discrimination policies, France has been studied as an emblematic case of colour-blindness (Favell 1998; Bleich 2000; Sala Pala 2010; Mazouz 2017).[1] This perspective, strongly ingrained in the ideology of "republican universalism", finds its legal roots in Article 1 of the 1958 French Constitution: the Republic "guarantees equality before the law for all citizens, regardless of descent, race, or religion", and has been endorsed by the leading anti-racist organizations since the early 1970s (Bleich 2000; Lamont, Morning, and Mooney 2002). Colour-blindness informs four dimensions of French public discourse and public policy toward ethno-racial minorities. Firstly, it pervades an assimilationist perspective on immigration, in which immigrants and their descendants are expected to integrate into the cultural values and behaviours of the majority, or at least to confine their cultural specificities to the private sphere (Schnapper 1998). Secondly, colour-blindness manifests itself in the reluctance to recognize ethno-racial discrimination as a distinct social problem –what Fassin and Fassin (2006) refer to as a "denial". Since the end of the 1970s, postcolonial immigrants and their descendants have remained mostly addressed through the well-established paradigms of integration, social insertion and urban cohesion (Kirszbaum 2004; Dikec 2007; Mazouz 2017; Cerrato Debenedetti 2018; Escafré-Dublet and Lelévrier 2019). Thirdly, colour-blindness translates into the legal restrictions on the collection of ethnic and racial statistics, a subject that has repeatedly triggered heated controversies since the late 1990s (Peer and Sabbagh 2008; Simon 2008). Finally, the republican ideology of colour-blindness results in the absence of any form of positive action explicitly based on ethno-racial grounds, although preferential treatments based on other grounds, notably gender and place of residence, have gained legitimacy since the yearly 2000s in the political and employment fields (Calvès 2016).

Yet, the principles of republican universalism have encountered numerous challenges in the last twenty years. Firstly, in France like in other European countries, under the pressure of EU 2000 anti-discrimination directives, a more extensive and protective legal anti-discrimination framework has been established since the early 2000s. Secondly, by the second half of the decade, France has witnessed the development of a discourse celebrating the benefits of diversity, especially in the workforce, echoing a globalized diversity discourse born in the US in the 1980s (Kelly and Dobbin 1998; Bereni 2009). The "promotion of diversity" was initially brought to the public agenda by business elites, through the introduction of a "Diversity Charter" (*Charte de la diversité*) (2004) asserting a corporate commitment "in favour of ethnic, cultural, and social diversity within [their] organization".[2] This diversity framing was quickly adopted by the national government, as illustrated by the creation in 2008 of the state-monitored "Diversity Label" (*label diversité*), a public award granted to private and public employers that develop "good practices" with regard to "the prevention of discrimination and the promotion of diversity", primarily in their management of human resources (HR). Thirdly, policy orientations and instruments set up at the national level within the framework of the republican principles have not systematically been replicated identically at the local level. Studies conducted in various European countries found that national frames of reference regarding diversity and equality of treatment can be reshaped by urban governments (Poppelaars and Scholten 2008; Dekker et al. 2015; Schiller 2015), and this was the case in France (Flamant 2017; Meziani-Remichi and Maussen 2017; Cerrato Debenedetti 2018; Martínez-Ariño et al. 2018). In particular, while the issue of combating ethno-racial discrimination faded away from the national agenda in the late 2000s, the picture was different at the local level. Against a background of hardening public attitudes towards immigrants and their descendants under the right-wing presidency of Nicolas Sarkozy (2007–2012), this issue gained some prominence on the local political agendas especially in large cities governed by centre-left coalitions (Martínez-Ariño et al. 2018).

This article examines the implementation of anti-discrimination policy by French local governments during the 2010s. In a country dominated by a colour-blind doctrine and in the context of the weakening of this policy at the national level, to what extent have local governments, and more particularly those eager to assert "diversity" values, renegotiated the dominant national perspective on ethnic and racial issues?

To address this question, we explored how three local governments used a specific public policy instrument, the Diversity Label. Launched in 2008 by the French government, the label quickly became a pillar of the national anti-discrimination policy in employment, albeit of modest scope. At the end of 2019, more than a decade after its creation, 108 large organizations were label holders, including 33 public bodies. At this date, the label covered around 500,000 public sector employees.[3] Seeking to boost the diffusion of the label in the public sector from the start of the 2010s, the French state encouraged local government bodies[4] to adopt it, with relatively little success. By the end of 2019, only 6 local governments (5 cities and 1 department) had received the Diversity Label– including Nantes (2012), Conseil départemental de Seine-Saint-Denis (2016) and Paris (2019)[5]– while a few others were considering applying for it.

The article investigates three cases of local governments, which were considered, when fieldwork was conducted (2013–2019), as particularly advanced in terms of anti-discrimination policies: Nantes and the Seine-Saint-Denis department, both label holders, and Paris, which was in the last stages of the label application process in 2018–2019. Did the Diversity Label act as a lever for addressing ethno-racial discrimination and shifting away from the national colour-blind framework at the local government scale?

In the three cases, we found that the Diversity Label led to the *institutionalization* of anti-discrimination policies, and simultaneously reinforced the *managerialization* of these policies (Dobbin 2009; Edelman 2016): while local anti-discrimination programmes had been so far directed towards *external* targets (local communities, civic organizations and firms), the label led to an increasing focus on *internal*, organizational processes, with a growing influence of HR management ideas. Yet, the cases differ in terms of how race and ethnicity were addressed. In Nantes and Paris, the commitment to the Diversity Label led to a *deracialization* of anti-discrimination and diversity policies – that is, to the obliteration of their specifically ethno-racial dimension (Doytcheva 2015) –, in line with a broader national pattern. The Seine-Saint-Denis department appears as a contrasting, exceptional case. In this highly segre-gated suburban space, where the majority group tends to become a minority – 50 per cent of minors are of foreign descent (Beauchemin, Hamel, and Simon 2018) – ethno-racial concerns remained at the core of anti-discrimi-nation policy. Studying this contrasting case reveals the unlikely conditions for French local governments to address straightforwardly ethno-racial issues in their diversity policies.

Genesis and development of a multilevel anti-discrimination policy

National level

Despite the rising presence of postcolonial immigrants and their descendants since the 1960s,[6] the existence of ethno-racial discrimination was recognized belatedly and precariously in France (Heargraves 2015; Mazouz 2017). In the aftermath of the 2000 EU anti-discrimination directives, the rules on the burden of proof were adjusted to be more favourable to plaintiffs, the list of legal discrimination grounds was progressively expanded (to 25 at the time of writing), and an independent agency[7] was created to facilitate the enforce-ment of anti-discrimination rights (Chappe 2011). The EQUAL Program, launched by the EU in 2000, provided a framework and financial support for the emergence of "experimental" anti-discrimination initiatives. involving public and private, local and national actors. Several of these plans targeted ethno-racial discrimination specifically (Cerrato Debenedetti 2018).

At the same time, the diversity discourse, introduced by business circles, gained prominence in the public debate. It initially appeared as an attempt to shift away from the colour-blind republican paradigm, and to put the issue of ethno-racial minorities (called "visible minorities") at the core of public attention (Bereni 2009; Doytcheva 2015).

The riots that engulfed hundreds of relegated suburban neighbourhoods in November 2005 completed the process of bringing the issue of ethno-racial discrimination on to the national agenda. In March 2006, the "Equal opportunity" law (*Egalité des chances*) was presented as a response to the dis-criminations that affected the people living in those neighbourhoods and implicitly targeted young people of postcolonial descent.

Yet, by the end of the 2000s, the issue of ethno-racial discrimination lost importance on the national agenda (Simon 2015). The traditional paradigms of integration, social insertion and urban cohesion regained the upper hand (Safi 2017; Cerrato Debenedetti 2018). In the workplace, "anti-discrimination" and "diversity" policies became increasingly detached from the ethno-racial significations that pervaded their initial formulations (Doytcheva 2015; Mazouz 2017). On the one hand, these policies referred to an individual-approach to equal treatment – a "liberal" (as opposed to structural) conception of anti-discrimination (Stryker 2001). On the other hand, they increasingly targeted other disadvantaged groups, such as women, disabled or senior workers, rather than ethnic and racial minorities.

Local level

The decline of national policies targeting ethno-racial minorities at the turn of the 2010s was partly counterbalanced by the development of such policies at the local level, especially in the largest and most diverse cities (Cerrato Debenedetti 2018). Local governments' attention to immigrants and their descendants was hardly new. A number of initiatives had been carried out by municipalities during the 1980s and 1990s to manage the "reception" and "integration" of immigrants, promote "intercultural dialogue", or support area-based "social development programmes" in deprived neighbourhoods, where post-colonial immigrants and their descendants were concentrated (Kirszbaum 2004; Dikec 2007; Downing 2016). By the early 2000s, the local implementers of these policies were increasingly encouraged by the French government and European institutions to take the anti-discrimination legal framework into account, which they did by integrating it into existing urban policy and integration programmes (Kirszbaum 2004; Flamant 2017). The 2008 municipal election campaign witnessed an unprecedented politicization of the issue of the "diversity" of the lists of candidates (Avanza 2010). In many big cities and suburban municipalities, socialist party candidates highlighted the issues of discrimination and diversity to show their opposition to Nicolas Sarkozy, who had adopted the National Front's themes during the 2007 presidential campaign and, once elected, gave priority to asserting "national identity" that was deemed to be threatened by immigration.

In the immediate aftermath of the 2008 municipal elections, which saw centre-left coalitions triumph in more than two-thirds of municipalities with more than 100,000 inhabitants, deputy mayors and policy officers were appointed to "fight against discrimination" in many of these cities.[8] By 2008, anti-discrimination officers in several municipalities held training sessions on discrimination for a variety of local professionals, launched awareness-raising campaigns, put structures to provide legal support in place, and so forth.

All of these local policies targeting ethno-racial minorities shared some common features with the national, republican framing: they addressed their targets only implicitly and indirectly, relying on proxies such as place of residence, immigrant background, social deprivation. Besides, officers in charge of anti-discrimination policies remained relatively marginal within the local administrations, their initiatives remaining mainly symbolic and decoupled from organizational routines. Yet, at the turn of the 2010s, in the context of a declining concern for ethno-racial issues at the national level, local governments – more particularly large cities – asserted themselves as major promoters of antidiscrimination policies, primarily focusing on post-colonial immigrants and their descendants. Against a background of cities acquiring increasing autonomy from the state (Le Galès 2011; Epstein 2013), the commitment of some mayors and urban governments to fighting discrimination supported the hypothesis that national colour-blindness could be inflected at a local level.

Case selection and methods

The Diversity Label

In order to test this hypothesis, we examined the implementation of the Diversity Label in three local governments. The introduction of such a label reflects a broader evolution of French regulatory framework, which has increasingly involved non-state actors in the design and implementation of public policies (Bergeron, Castel, and Dubuisson-Quellier 2014). Introduced by the French state in 2008, the label rewards employers demonstrating "good practices" with regard to the "prevention of discrimination and promotion of diversity", mostly in RH processes. Applicants are subject to a "quality management audit" by an independent certification body (AFNOR, French Standardization Association) which checks, on site, their "compliance" with the label's specifications. To receive the label, applicants must set up an diagnosis of their major "discrimination risks", carry out an assessment of their HR procedures, implement staff training and awareness sessions with regard to discrimination, set up an "internal" (targeting employees) and "external" (targeting the local communities) communication policy, and establish an internal grievance procedure. The final decision of awarding the label is made by a "National Diversity Label commission", composed of representatives of the State, labour unions, employers' organizations, and human resources experts. The label is delivered for 4 years, renewable, with an on-site audit by the AFNOR every two years. This soft policy instrument, based on the voluntary participation of applicants, has become one of the main policy tools for fighting discrimination in the workplace since the end of the 2000s (Bereni and Epstein 2015). While the Diversity Label has often been branded as rewarding organizations that go "beyond" legal requirements, it essentially leads organizations to signal their compliance with the non-discrimination legal framework. The Diversity Label does not impose any monitoring or affirmative action programmes. Recipients are held by an obligation of means (setting up management procedures), rather than outcomes (redressing inequalities).

Although the Diversity Label was originally designed for large private sector companies, this instrument was quickly promoted among public sector employers. Keen to be seen as an exemplary and modern employer, in the context of bureaucratic reforms inspired by New Public Management (Bezes 2017), the French government committed several major ministries to applying for the label, and repeatedly incentivized local governments to adopt it. For multiple reasons – political, financial, technical, etc. (Bereni and Epstein 2015) – and despite the incentives, the label met with less success in local governments than in national-government bodies.

Data and methods

In order to explore if and how the Diversity Label reshaped local anti-discrimination policies, we investigated 13 local governments from 2013 to 2018. The article draws on data from two distinct qualitative studies. Laure Bereni and Renaud Epstein conducted the first study in 2013–2014 (Bereni and Epstein 2015). It mostly consisted of 18 interviews with officers and elected officials in Nantes (one of the few holders of the Diversity Label at the time), and 12 interviews with anti-discrimination officers working in 11 other local governments (including Seine-Saint-Denis). A corpus of internal documents was collected in each local government. Three interviews updating the study were held in 2018 with professionals in charge of anti-discrimination policies in Nantes and Seine-Saint-Denis, which by then had been awarded the label. Second, the article also draws on an in-depth, ethnographic study of Paris application for the Diversity Label, carried out by Manon Torres since 2017, based on participant observation over more than a year within municipal departments, and on 10 interviews with various actors engaged in implementing these policies. The 43 interviews that make up the corpus were fully transcribed and analysed inductively.

Case studies: Nantes, Paris, Seine-Saint-Denis

The three local governments selected for the case studies differ in several ways. Firstly, compared to Paris or to the Seine-Saint-Denis department that count respectively 2.1 and 1.6 million inhabitants, Nantes is a medium-sized city (the 6th largest in France, with 300 000 inhabitants). Secondly, the three local governments do not have the same legal competencies. The Seine-Saint-Denis department is in charge of social and health welfare for families, the elderly, the disabled, as well as secondary schools. As all municipalities, Nantes has a wider range of competencies including urban planning, housing, transportation, social support for families and youth, primary education, culture and sport. The city of Paris is both a municipality and a department, with a single council – a unique case in France –, and is granted both municipal and departmental competencies. Thirdly, regarding public policies and public service innovations, Paris and Nantes are frequently recognized as "trendsetting cities" (Bereni and Epstein 2015); their governments' initiatives are held up as examples to follow at the national or European level, in areas as varied as sustainable development, urban regeneration, technological innovation or culture. Conversely, the Seine-Saint-Denis department is rarely praised as a model. It suffers from a poor reputation nationwide, as it has become a symbol in recent years of France's troubled suburbs.

Yet, these three local governments have shared features: they are ruled by center-left coalitions (led by Socialist Party representatives); and they clearly state their commitment to the values of diversity, cosmopolitism, reception of foreigners, and equal opportunity. In Nantes and Paris, the Diversity Label crowned already established anti-discrimination initiatives. With respect to ethno-racial diversity, which can only be measured approximately because of the lack of ethno-racial data, the three territories have a presence of immigrants and people of foreign descent (notably from non-European countries) at least equal to the national average, although this share highly varies among the three cases: the proportion of immigrants in Nantes is just above the national average, while it is twice the national average in Paris, and three times the national average in the Seine-Saint-Denis department(see Table 1).

Compared to other large French cities, Nantes experienced a quite recent wave of postcolonial immigration. At the 1999 census Nantes's immigrants made up only 3.6 per cent of its population. Seventeen years later, it had almost caught up with the national average, with 9.6 per cent of immigrants (84 per cent of whom were born outside Europe). These are concentrated in the city's social housing neighbourhoods, where the proportion of immigrants in the population ranges from 22 per cent to 32 per cent for the most deprived of these neighbourhoods. While immigration is a recent phenomenon in Nantes, it echoes its slave-trading history, which has become the subject of local commemorative policies culminating with the opening of a Slavery abolition memorial in the early 2010s.

Paris has long been a city of immigration. Its population comprises 14.4 per cent foreigners and 20.3 per cent immigrants (of whom 75.8 per cent were born outside Europe). The city's mayor elected in 2014 is the daughter of European immigrants, who regularly reminds people that she was granted French citizenship only as a teenager. In the month following her election, she instructed the deputy mayor in charge of "gender equality and the fight against discrimination" to draw up a "comprehensive plan to combat discrimination", which implied among other things to apply for the Diversity Label. At

Table 1. Proportion of foreigners, immigrants, and non-EU immigrants (2016 census).

	Foreigners	Immigrants	Non-EU immigrants
France	6.7%	9.4%	6.5%
Nantes	7.6%	9.6%	8.1%
Paris	14.4%	20.3%	15,4%
Seine-Saint-Denis	23.6%	30.0%	25.3%

the time the research was being conducted (2017–2019), Paris was about to submit its application for the Diversity Label, as well as for the equality Label, another government certification label which focuses more specifically on workplace equality between women and men.[9]

The Seine-Saint-Denis department not only differs from Nantes and Paris in terms of legal status, but also from a socio-spatial standpoint: located on the outskirts of Paris, it is the poorest metropolitan department, with the largest number of deprived neighbourhoods where populations with an immigrant background are concentrated. 40 per cent of the department's inhabitants live in an area targeted by urban policy initiatives, six times more than the national average. The population of the department comprises 23.6 per cent foreigners, 30 per cent immigrants (of whom 84.3 per cent are from outside Europe), and a significant proportion of immigrants' descendants (28 per cent of adults aged 18–50, and 50 per cent of under-18s) (Beauchemin, Hamel, and Simon 2018). The Seine-Saint-Denis department is an untypical case regarding the presence of ethnoracial minorities. It is, moreover, routinely racialized in French public and media discourse, e.g. primarily described as an area of immigrants and people of colour, and often stigmatized as such.

Institutionalization and deracialization of diversity policies: Nantes and Paris

In the two cities, the Diversity Label led, on the one hand, to the institutionalization and managerialization of pre-existing anti-discrimination policies. On the other hand, it resulted in a process of deracialization of these policies.

Institutionalization and managerialization

Since the Socialist Party took over the town hall in 1989, Nantes has been strongly committed to the fight against racism, the integration of immigrants, and the social development of neighbourhoods where these are concentrated. However, it was only following the suburban riots of November 2005 that the issue of discrimination made it to the local political agenda. In the following months, at the instigation of its socialist mayor, Jean-Marc Ayrault, one of the country's leading opposition figures, and after having put in place a "benchmark for local policies for fighting discrimination in Europe", the city implemented an anti-discrimination policy comprising both "external" (targeting the territory) and "internal" (targeting city employees) components. The former was entrusted to a deputy mayor and an "integration" policy officer, both with an activist background, who occupied marginal positions in the municipality and had only a limited budget at their disposal. As a result, the external component was operationalized only to a limited extent, which consisted essentially of actions to raise public awareness. The policy's internal component was entrusted to a policy officer who was attached to the HR department, but worked closely with her colleagues in charge of the external component. This resulted in the setting up of an internal diagnostic process; the signing of a "Charter for Diversity and Gender Balance in the Workplace", which symbolically marked the municipality's commitment in this regard; the creation of an internal grievance procedure; and the formation of an "internal consultative committee for diversity and gender balance", which brought together officers from different departments, union representatives, and elected representatives.

The anti-discrimination policy gained new momentum in January 2011, when the mayor announced his decision to apply for the Diversity Label and obtain it by the end of the year. The mayor's commitment produced an unprecedented mobilization of the municipal bureaucracy around the theme of discrimination and diversity under the guidance of a HR department whose leadership had been reshaped and reaffirmed. Unlike their predecessors, the new HR leaders, imbued with New Public Management ideas, firmly made the case for setting up an anti-discrimination policy. They saw the Diversity Label as a tool to centralize and formalize HR management procedures that, until then, had been largely informal, decentralized, and influenced by political patronage. Applying for the label thus made it possible to establish more transparent processes, reducing the risks of workplace discrimination, while at the same time giving HR officers the opportunity to extend their jurisdiction (Abbott 1998) within the administration. Nantes's involvement in the Diversity Label resulted in an anti-discrimination policy increasingly focused on managerial issues within the Nantes administration, separated from and to the detriment of external actions targeting local stakeholders (businesses, schools, cultural and sport clubs, NGOs, etc.).

In Paris, the Diversity Label also resulted in the institutionalization and managerialization of pre-existing anti-discrimination programmes. The city had put in place a unit dedicated to promoting gender equality in the early 2000s, and had appointed an anti-discrimination officer, mostly concerned with ethno-racial discrimination, by the late 2000s. Following the 2014 municipal election, the Diversity Label project was first entrusted to the deputy mayor in charge of "gender equality and the fight against discrimination". Yet, two years later, when the plan for applying for the label was officially launched, the project was transferred to another deputy mayor in charge of "human resources and the modernization of public services". Simultaneously a "diversity coordinator" was appointed within the HR service. The "Integration and Equality" division, responsible for implementing anti-discrimination policies, was only involved as an "observer" in the label project. Such a transfer of political and administrative jurisdiction was not without consequences for the framing of the Diversity Label: as in Nantes, it was seen as a "lever for HR professionalization and for collective performance"[10] and part of a wider dynamic of managerial reform.

Diversity without race

Beyond these institutionalization and managerialization processes, the involvement of Nantes and Paris in the Diversity Label led to the deracialization of anti-discrimination policies – by which we mean the marginalization, and even the erasure, of their ethno-racial dimension. Admittedly, the label itself, reflecting the multi-ground framework of French anti-discrimination law, hardly encouraged candidate organizations to tackle the ethno-racial issue head-on. However, the Diversity Label could have been interpreted in a singular manner by local governments already engaged in fighting against racial discrimination.

In Nantes, the rise of ethno-racial concerns began in the early 2000s. As in other large French cities at the time (Meziani-Remichi and Maussen 2017), the urban policy department took steps to ensure access to municipal jobs for the descendants of immigrants living in disadvantaged neighbourhoods. In particular, they took the opportunity of the *"emplois jeunes"* –a national programme that subsidized employers willing to hire young people alienated from employment– to press the Nantes administration for recruiting young people of foreign descent living in the most deprived neighbourhoods. These initiatives, under condition that they were not explicitly based on ethno-racial categories, enjoyed the support of the city council. But it was not until the suburban riots of November 2005 that the fight against ethno-racial discrimination in municipal employment was explicitly put on the political agenda. Three months after the riots, on the mayor's initiative, Nantes co-sponsored a forum entitled "Diversity in employment: what commitments and what means to fight discrimination based on people's descent?" in the presence of the deputy minister responsible for promoting equal opportunities (*égalité des chances*), Azouz Begag. In the aftermath of the event, Nantes adopted a "diversity and gender balance" (*diversité et mixité*) action plan, promoting anti-discrimination principles within the Nantes administration. Yet, the implementation of anti-discrimination initiatives encountered resistance from HR officers. The latter mostly expressed a strong loyalty to the colour-blind competitive examination (*concours*, a standardized professional entrance examination), which they thought guaranteed full "republican equality" in the selection process for public administration jobs.

> I remember a fierce battle we had with HR after the opening of a new pool. We told the Deputy Mayor in charge of personnel that it was unthinkable not to do neighbourhood recruiting. He fully agreed. Yet, on the HR side, we hit a deadlock. Public entrance examinations are an equalizer, they said. Why would we be giving preference to the neighborhood inhabitants? (Municipal officer)

By the time Nantes applied for the Diversity Label a decade later, the new HR leadership had rallied to the cause of antidiscrimination. Yet, the seizure of anti-discrimination issues by the HR department favoured the rise of a formal, colour-blind approach to equality. The Diversity Label officer, who reported to the head of HR, self-identified as a HR professional rather than as an anti-discrimination specialist. She expressed her willingness to break with the "activist" approach and with the focus on ethno-racial issues that had characterized the city officers previously in charge of anti-discrimination issues. In line with the HR leadership's managerial vision of the Diversity Label, she envisioned it as a tool aimed at guaranteeing the principle of equal treatment between individuals, rather than as a means to redress structural inequalities between majority and minority groups.

The marginalization of ethno-racial concerns in Nantes was also the result of the growing weight of other domains of the municipal equality policy. Beyond the rise of formal equality principles in HR procedures, applying for the label favoured, in Nantes, the development of initiatives specifically aimed at gender equality and the integration of disabled workers. These two components of the diversity policy corresponded to category-based national policies that were more prescriptive and could be monitored with indicators[11], unlike the ethno-racial component.

In Paris, the involvement in the Diversity Label was associated to a similar deracialization of the local anti-discrimination policy. The label's specifications require candidate employers to carry out an internal diagnostic procedure. This initial diagnosis aims at identifying the "risks of discrimination in their various activities" (recruitment, promotion, remuneration, training, communication, relations with suppliers, etc.), and allows for determining what aspects will be prioritized in the diversity policy.[12] In Paris, the "risk evaluation table" designed by a specialized consultant hired by the HR department listed the discrimination grounds on which the city needed to focus to prepare its application for the Diversity Label: age, gender, sexual orientation, disability, union membership, and place of residence.

Interestingly, the "descent" (*origine*) criterion was not included in the list of the "main discrimination risks". Asked about this absence, the diversity officer mentioned the internal resistance to the recognition of racism and ethno-racial discrimination as an organizational issue.

- Are there things that came up from the audit on issues of racism?
- No. Some people would say: "it seems to me that I didn't get such-and-such a job because I am black or whatever". These are just impressions, which maybe aren't fully accurate? Anyway there is no means to measure this. And then, really, the principle of equality in public recruitment masks the issue. The argument that cannot be fought is: "Well, the public recruitment exams are open to everyone. If they don't pass the exams, they can't be selected".

Unlike her counterpart in Nantes, this diversity officer demonstrated particular concern with ethno-racial discrimination, an issue she had dealt with in a previous job. However, even for this officer, the issue seemed to be both "taboo" within the city administration and in the realm of subjective "impressions", and therefore difficult to objectify and deal with. In accordance with the internal diagnosis, the action plan set up by the city of Paris to apply for the Diversity Label focused on three discrimination grounds: disability, sex and age. Like in Nantes, priority was given to disadvantaged groups that, unlike ethnic minorities, are the target of proactive public policies that can be informed by statistical indicators.

The unlikely ethno-racial marking of French local anti-discrimination policies: the contrasting case of the Seine-Saint-Denis department

In the Seine-Saint-Denis department, which has a particularly high proportion of ethno-racial minorities in its population compared with the rest of France, the effects of the Diversity Label differed from those observed in Paris and Nantes in two respects: first, the label was used as a lever to build a comprehensive anti-discrimination policy, both with internal and external components and second, it did not lead to the fading away of the ethno-racial aspect of anti-discrimination policy.

In his inaugural speech after his election in 2015, the socialist president of the Seine-Saint-Denis department announced that fighting against discrimination would constitute a priority of his mandate, which was to be achieved by obtaining the Diversity Label. An "Equality and Diversity" unit was then set up to prepare the application for the label, which was obtained in 2016. This office was attached to a renewed "Management, Human Resources, and Diversity" Division, one of the main divisions of the HRD. However, unlike in Paris and Nantes, this attachment to the HRD did not lead to a separation between the internal and external components of the anti-discrimination policy. As the Equality and Diversity officer put it during an interview, even though the label "deals with the internal", it "provides a framework for accustoming [the department's bureaucracy] to the issue of the fight against discrimination". A year after being awarded the label, the Equality and Diversity office produced a "departmental plan for fighting discrimination" based on an "overall diagnosis of discrimination across the entire territory", with the aim of making local public services "exemplary". In other words, the Diversity Label acted in the Seine-Saint-Denis department as a lever for putting anti-discrimination policies on the agenda, and deploying them both internally and externally.

Moreover, the Seine-Saint-Denis department contrasts with the two other cases studied because of the importance given to the ethno-racial dimension of discrimination. Admittedly, the Diversity Label had, in some respects, a deracializing effect on anti-discrimination policies, as it was the case in the cities of

Paris and Nantes. The "diagnosis of the risks of discrimination" made by a specialized consultant as part of the application for the label highlighted the fact that, among the 37 per cent of city officers who said they had been "witnesses or victims of discrimination", "descent" was the first ground cited.[13] Yet the five "action plans according to specific grounds based on the identification of risks"[14] drawn up by the Equality and Diversity unit on the basis of this diagnosis focused on sex, (real or presumed) religious affiliation, disability, state of health, and age; none concerned descent. When asked about the disappearance of this criterion, the Equality and Diversity officer argued that discrimination based on descent was a "strong feeling" among employees, "but not a management risk". In her narrative, the experience of ethno-racial discrimination was a problem of "racism between colleagues", an issue that, she said, "is not part of the discrimination risks" assessed in the process of the application for the Diversity Label. In her view, the problem of ethno-racial discrimination was an interpersonal problem rather than a matter of HR management processes. This justified *not* making such discrimination ground the subject of a dedicated "action plan" within the framework of the label.

Nevertheless, ethno-racial concerns were still much more explicit in the Seine-Saint-Denis department than in the cities of Nantes and Paris. Relying on the results of the diagnosis carried out for applying to the Diversity Label, which were confirmed by later internal inquiries, the Equality and Diversity office launched an awareness-raising programme targeting employees and managers on ethno-racial discrimination, distinct from the Diversity Label action plan targeting the "risks of discrimination" in HR processes. The fight against ethno-racial discrimination appeared even more central in the anti-discrimination initiatives directed towards the territory. This was stated as a priority issue for the Seine-Saint-Denis department, whose communication strategy aimed to reversing the stigma of racialization: "for the Department's President, diversity is one of the main features of the Seine-Saint-Denis", and "diversity is an asset", said the president's assistant in an interview (2018). In the department's official communications, the connection was routinely made between "diversity" and "the fight against [by implication ethno-racial] discrimination": "Although diversity is part of the richness of [the Seine-Saint-Denis], too often it is at the cost of the daily experience of discrimination by its inhabitants. The department is therefore duty bound to send out a clear signal in seeking to be exemplary as an employer", the department's diversity officer stated, in a document promoting the Diversity Label in the mid-2010s.

Discussion and conclusions

Our article shows the paradoxical effects of the Diversity Label at the subnational level: it both institutionalized and often deracialized anti-discrimination policy. In doing so, we contribute to the literature on diversity policies implemented by local governments in France and in other countries in several respects.

First of all, our research confirms certain findings of this literature – notably, that the composition of the coalitions in power in local governments is a major determinant of the implementation of anti-discrimination and diversity policies, as demonstrated by the quantitative study carried out by Martínez-Ariño et al. (2018) in 20 large French cities. Indeed, in 2019, 5 out of 6 local governments that have been awarded the Diversity Label are governed by centre-left and green coalitions. Moreover, the studies that we conducted in 9 other cities between 2013 and 2018 show that only authorities headed by a Socialist considered applying for the Diversity Label. Three of these, which had taken preliminary steps to do so, abandoned the plan after the defeat of the outgoing administration in the municipal elections of 2014. Interviews with a diverse range of actors confirmed the strongly politicized nature of the issue of the fight against (ethno-racial) discrimination at the local level. Yet, although centre-left local governments focused on the issue during the Sarkozy presidency, the election of a Socialist president and parliamentary majority in 2012 neither had the effect of putting it back on the national agenda, nor did it result in its disappearance from the local government agendas. Our investigation thus confirms that local governments can exercise some autonomy on diversity issues: policy orientations in this field depend on local factors (social, political and institutional) and not only on national policies.

However, our in-depth, qualitative investigation of three cases has also brought to light dimensions overlooked by studies on a more macro scale and based on quantitative methods. Especially, our approach made it possible to thoroughly examine local policies that fall under the umbrella term of "anti-discrimination" or "diversity", and the salience of ethno-racial issues within them. We found that the introduction of local government policies under these headings does not necessarily lead to this type of discrimination being addressed, even though these policies were initially put on the agenda to address ethno-racial discrimination. Indeed, when the issue of "fighting against discrimination" was put on the government's agenda at the end of the 1990s (Heargraves 2015), and when the term "diversity" found its way into the French business world in the mid-2000s, these terms were mostly referring to post-colonial immigrants and their descendants. The terms "diversity" and "anti-discrimination" were then euphemisms for ethno-racial issues, in a context where no legitimate vocabulary existed for referring to racial minorities. But in following years, at the national level, these terms gradually lost their ethno-racial connotations. To an increasing extent, they were used to designate the multi-ground legal framework of equal treatment and referred, in practice, to categories targeted by specific public policies such as disability and gender equality. Our investigation shows that this process of deracialization of diversity, which has been observed in other social settings (Lemercier and Palomares

2012; Doytcheva 2015; Mazouz 2017; Bereni 2020), could also be observed in local governments during the 2010s, despite an unprecedented politicization of anti-discrimination at this level. The decline of public policies targeting ethno-racial discrimination at the national level, the impossibility of collecting ethno-racial data, and the persistence of competing paradigms in policies aimed at immigrants and their descendants acted as powerful curbs on the recognition of ethno-racial discrimination as specific problem at the local level – including for local governments that were the most "committed" to "diversity".

Our investigation also suggests, through the analysis of the untypical case of the Seine-Saint-Denis department, that the proportion of immigrants and their descendants in the population does affect the possibility for local government to address straightforwardly ethno-racial discrimination in a colour-blind country. From this point of view, our study leads to temper the results of the quantitative investigation by Martínez-Ariño et al. (2018), which found that the proportion of foreign-born people has no effect, in France (in contrast to Germany, where it is the determinant variable), on the implementation of diversity policies. We find that the especially significant over-representation of ethno-racial minorities and the racial stigma attached to this suburban department seem to constitute a safeguard against the dynamic of deracialization of anti-discrimination policies observed in other local governments and at the national level.

Finally, our investigation is an invitation to closely examine the contextualized meanings of "diversity". This term refers to different realities in different contexts, and its meaning is flexible and ambivalent in a given context (Raco and Tasan-Kok 2019). It routinely refers *simultaneously* to differences founded on ethno-racial grounds and to "all individual differences", thereby diluting the ethno-racial dimension – and this even in contexts where ethno-racial issues are the core targets of public policies, as demonstrated by research on diversity management in the United States (Kelly and Dobbin 1998; Berrey 2015; Edelman 2016). We should therefore recognize the empirical ambivalence and pliability of the category of diversity, and shift away from normative definitions.

Notes

1. Several historical studies showed that the republican principle of colour-blindness co-existed with the use of ethno-racial categories in the colonized territories overseas (Larcher 2014).
2. https://www.charte-diversite.com/
3. https://www.fonction-publique.gouv.fr/label-diversite-dans-la-fonction-publique. It should be noted that these numbers do not take into account the hundreds of - mostly private – organizations that had been granted the label in the early 2010s, but did not apply for renewal after a 4-year period.
4. France has three layers of local government (*collectivités territoriales*): regions, departments, municipalities. In addition to that, an intermediate metropolitan layer is emerging between the local and the departmental levels in large urban areas.

5. The label was also granted to Lyon (2010), Dijon (2018), and Bordeaux (2019).
6. According to French administrative categories, an immigrant (*immigré*) is a person who is born a foreigner and abroad, and resides in France. Thus, an immigrant is not necessarily a foreigner: in 2013, 40% of immigrants were French (INSEE 2016). In 2008, immigrants made up 10 per cent of the population living in France, as well as people of immigrant descent (*descendants d'immigrés*) (Beauchemin, Hamel, and Simon 2018). 52 per cent of immigrants and people of foreign descent stem from a non-EU country, most frequently from countries that used to be under French colonial rule.
7. In 2011, the High Authority for the Fight against Discrimination and for Equality (HALDE) merged into a new Administrative Independent Authority, the Défenseur des Droits.
8. Workshop of the Inter-Réseau du Développement Social Urbain, 2011, « Les politiques d'égalité: concurrence des publics ou convergence des luttes ? », Poitiers, April 14–15.
9. In January 2019, seven local governments were holders of the Equality label.
10. Interview with the diversity coordinator of Paris, 2018.
11. Since 1987 the French state has required private and public employers above a certain size to hire a quota of 6 per cent disabled individuals. Employers that do not comply must pay financial penalties, which were substantially increased by a 2005 law. Alongside this, a gender equality policy has been in place since the early 1980s; it was strengthened during the 2000s. It is based on incentives for collective bargaining, reporting obligations, and gender quotas for senior official jobs in public administration.
12. AFNOR website.
13. Report "Le Département et ses agents face aux discriminations" [The department and its officers faced with discrimination], September 2017.
14. Ibid.

Disclosure statement

No potential conflict of interest was reported by the author(s).

Funding

This work was supported by the Alliance de recherche sur les discriminations (ARDIS)

References

Abbott, A. 1988. *The System of Professions. An Essay on the Division of Expert Labor.* Chicago: University of Chicago Press.
Avanza, M. 2010. "Qui représentent les élus de la 'diversité' ? Croyances partisanes et points de vue de 'divers'." *Revue française de science politique* 60 (4): 745–767.
Beauchemin, C., C. Hamel, and P. Simon. 2018. *Trajectories and Origins: Survey on the Diversity of the French Population.* Population Studies. New York: Springer.
Bereni, L. 2009. "'Faire de la diversité une richesse pour l'entreprise'. La transformation d'une contrainte juridique en catégorie managériale." *Raisons politiques* 35: 87–106.
Bereni, L. 2020. "La valeur professionnelle de l'identité. Racialisation, genre et légitimité managériale à New York et à Paris." *Sociétés contemporaines* forthcoming.

Bereni, L., and R. Epstein. 2015. "Instrumenter la lutte contre les discriminations: le 'Label Diversité' dans les collectivités territoriales. Rapport final." Alliance de recherche sur les discriminations (ARDIS).

Bergeron, H., P. Castel, and S. Dubuisson-Quellier. 2014. "Gouverner par les labels. Une comparaison des politiques de l'obésité et de la consommation durable." *Gouvernement et action publique* 3 (3): 7–31.

Berrey, E. 2015. *The Enigma of Diversity. The Language of Race and the Limits of Racial Justice*. Chicago: University of Chicago Press.

Bezes, P. 2017. "The Neo-managerial Turn of Bureaucratic States. More Steering, More Devolution." In *Reconfiguring European States in Crisis*, edited by D. King, and P. Le Galès, 251–278. Oxford: Oxford University Press.

Bleich, E. 2000. "Antiracism without Races: Politics and Policy in a 'Color-blind' State." *French Politics, Culture & Society* 18 (3): 48–74.

Calvès, G. 2016. *La Discrimination Positive*. Paris: PUF.

Cerrato Debenedetti, M.-C. 2018. *La lutte contre les discriminations ethnoraciales en France: De l'annonce à l'esquive*. Rennes: PUR.

Chappe, V.-A. 2011. "Le cadrage juridique, une ressource politique ? La création de la HALDE comme solution au problème de l'effectivité des normes anti-discrimination (1998-2005)." *Politix* 94: 107–130.

Dekker, R., H. Emilsson, B. Krieger, and P. Scholten. 2015. "A Local Dimension of Integration Policies? A Comparative Study of Berlin, Malmö, and Rotterdam." *International Migration Review* 49 (3): 633–658.

Dikec, M. 2007. *Badlands of the Republic: Space, Politics and Urban Policy*. Oxford: Blackwell Publishing.

Dobbin, F. 2009. *Inventing Equal Opportunity*. Princeton: Princeton University Press.

Downing, J. 2016. "Influences on State–Society Relations in France: Analysing Voluntary Associations and Multicultural Dynamism, Co-option and Retrenchment in Paris, Lyon and Marseille." *Ethnicities* 16 (3): 452–469.

Doytcheva, M. 2015. *Politiques de la diversité. Sociologie des discriminations et des politiques antidiscriminatoires au travail*. Bernes: Peter Lang.

Edelman, L. 2016. *Working Law: Courts, Corporations, and Symbolic Civil Rights*. Chicago and London: University of Chicago Press.

Epstein, R. 2013. *La rénovation urbaine: démolition-reconstruction de l'Etat*. Paris: Presses de Sciences Po.

Escafré-Dublet, A., and C. Lelévrier. 2019. "Governing Diversity Without Naming it: An Analysis of Neighbourhood Policies in Paris." *European Urban and Regional Studies* 26 (3): 283–296.

Fassin, D., and E. Fassin, eds. 2006. *De la question sociale à la question raciale ? Représenter la société française*. Paris: La Découverte.

Favell, A. 1998. *Philosophies of Integration: Immigration and the Idea of Citizenship in France and Britain*. London: St. Martin's Press.

Flamant, A. 2017. "L'incomplète construction des politiques municipales de lutte contre les discriminations raciales. Enquête dans les villes de Lyon, Nantes et Strasbourg (2001-2012)." *Revue internationale de politique comparée* 24 (3): 257–292.

Heargraves, A. 2015. "Empty Promises? Public Policy Against Racial and Ethnic Discrimination in France." *French Politics, Culture & Society* 33 (3): 95–115.

INSEE. 2016. *France, Portrait Social*. Paris: INSEE Editions.

Kelly, E., and F. Dobbin. 1998. "How Affirmative Action Became Diversity Management: Employer Response to Anti-discrimination Law, 1961 to 1996." *American Behavioral Scientist* 41 (7): 960–984.

Kirszbaum, T. 2004. "La discrimination positive territoriale: de l'égalité des chances à la mixité urbaine." *Pouvoirs* 111: 101–118.

Lamont, M., A. Morning, and M. Mooney. 2002. "North African Immigrants Respond to French Racism: Demonstrating Equivalence through Universalism." *Ethnic and Racial Studies* 25: 390–414.

Larcher, S. 2014. *L'autre citoyen : l'idéal républicain et les Antilles après l'esclavage*. Paris: Armand Colin.

Le Galès, P. 2011. *Le retour des villes européennes. Sociétés urbaines, mondialisation, gouvernement et gouvernance*. Paris: Presses de Sciences Po.

Lemercier, E., and E. Palomares. 2012. "La disparition. Le traitement de la 'question raciale' dans l'action publique locale de lutte contre les discriminations." *Revue Asylon(s)* 8. http://www.reseau-terra.eu/article1310.html.

Martínez-Ariño, J., M. Moutselos, K. Schönwälder, C. Jacobs, M. Schiller, and A. Tandé. 2018. "Why do Some Cities Adopt More Diversity Policies Than Others? A Study in France and Germany." *Comparative European Politics* 17 (5): 651–672.

Mazouz, S. 2017. *La République et ses Autres. Politiques de l'altérité dans la France des années 2000*. Lyon: Ens Lyon.

Meziani-Remichi, Y., and M. Maussen. 2017. "Recruitment in Public Administrations: Diversity Policies and Selection Practices in a French City." *Journal of Ethnic and Migration Studies* 43 (10): 1679–1695.

Peer, S., and D. Sabbagh. 2008. "French Color-Blindness in Perspective: The Controversy over 'Statistiques Ethniques' (Special Issue)." *French Politics, Culture and Society* 26 (1): 1–6.

Poppelaars, C., and P. Scholten. 2008. "Two Worlds Apart: The Divergence of National and Local Immigrant Integration Policies in the Netherlands." *Administration & Society* 40 (4): 335–357.

Raco, M., and T. Tasan-Kok. 2019. "Governing Urban Diversity: Multi-scalar Representations, Local Contexts, Dissonant Narratives." *European Urban and Regional Studies* 26 (3): 230–238.

Safi, M. 2017. "Promoting Diversity in French Workplaces: Targeting and Signaling Ethnoracial Origin in a Colorblind Context." *Socius* 3: 1–14.

Sala Pala, V. 2010. "Differentialist and Universalist Anti-discrimination Policies on the Ground: How Far they Succeed, Why they Fail. A Comparison between Britain and France." *American Behavioral Scientist* 53 (12): 1788–1805.

Schiller, Maria. 2015. "Paradigmatic Pragmatism and the Politics of Diversity." *Ethnic and Racial Studies* 38 (7): 1120–1136.

Schnapper, D. 1998. *Community of Citizens: On the Modern Idea of Nationality*. New Brunswick, NJ: Transaction Publishers.

Simon, P. 2008. "The Choice of Ignorance: The Debate on Ethnic and Racial Statistics in France." *French Politics, Culture, & Society* 26 (1): 7–31.

Simon, P. 2015. "La lutte contre les discriminations n'a pas eu lieu." *Mouvements* 83: 87–96.

Stryker, Robin. 2001. "Disparate Impact and the Quota Debate: Law, Labor Market Sociology, and Equal Employment Policies." *The Sociological Quarterly* 42 (1): 13–46.

Workforce diversity policies in practice: drivers and barriers in local administrations

Christine Lang Ⓥ

ABSTRACT
Employment in the municipal workforce is a key area in which cities shape the inclusion of their population of immigrant origin. While many European cities have developed policies aiming to foster the employment of staff of immigrant origin, little is known about the drivers and barriers of their implementation. Based on a comparative case study of local administrations in one German regional state and drawing on organizational theory, this article explores the role of organizational factors. It shows how the interplay of mainly two factors matters: support from the administrative leadership and the pragmatic recruitment rationalities of the human resources practitioners. Additionally, the findings suggest that the local identity as municipality more or less shaped by immigration also informs practices. The article argues that to understand the implementation of policies promoting workforce diversity organizational structures and rationalities must be considered.

Introduction

Employment in municipal administrations is a field where cities can significantly shape the inclusion and participation of their population of immigrant origin. Since municipal authorities are important local employers, access to the civil service is a crucial dimension of economic inclusion. Moreover, it implies participation in the implementation of policies that affect the life chances of residents, and it conveys a symbolic meaning. While a fairly representative civil service suggests openness and equal opportunities (Mosher 1982), an obvious underrepresentation of immigrant or minority residents may signal unequal chances and limited belonging. Municipal authorities importantly influence employment and career opportunities by way of the recruitment and selection procedures applied and by possibly adopting measures to foster the recruitment of underrepresented groups. Across Europe, cities have introduced policies to promote equal opportunities and diversity within municipal workforces, though in different forms and to different degrees (Spencer 2008). While in the UK and the Netherlands, respective policies date back to the 1980s and 1990s (Solomos 1989; Groeneveld and Verbeek 2012), they were introduced more recently in countries without a multicultural tradition such as Germany and France (Meziani-Remichi and Maussen 2017).

In Germany, cities began to develop policies aiming to promote the employment of people with a "migration background"[1] in the mid-2000s. At this time, many German cities reformulated their integration policies (Gesemann and Roth 2009) in the course of a reorientation of the national approach to immigration and integration (Schönwälder and Triadafilopoulos 2016). In the 2010s, the national government also adopted the aim to increase the share of employees with a migration background in public administration (Die Bundesregierung 2012). However, while we witness a wide diffusion of the policy objective, major differences exist between cities regarding the introduction of measures (Gesemann, Roth, and Aumüller 2012, 54). Further, we know little about their actual implementation. This reflects a more general scarcity of research on responses to diversity in public organizations (Bührmann and Schönwälder 2017), despite the growing body of research on local integration and diversity policies (e.g. Alexander 2007; Dekker et al. 2015; Martínez-Ariño et al. 2019).

This article examines the implementation of policies promoting employment of staff with a migration background in selected local administrations in Germany. By choosing cases located within the city–state of Berlin, I can compare the practices in different local administrations situated within the same political and institutional context. Among German states, Berlin is one case that has introduced policies to increase the share of employees with a migration background and did so relatively early. Policies focus on access of young people to vocational training, the key route into the middle grade of the civil service, where internal career opportunities allow access to the middle management. Yet, implementation differs strongly between the administrations of the districts (Bezirke), the local level in the city–state. While in some districts, hiring routines have continued practically unaltered and numbers of new staff members of immigrant origin remain low, others seem to have effectively implemented measures to foster their recruitment. What factors further or prevent the implementation of policies promoting the employment of immigrants and their descendants in local administrations?

Drawing on in-depth qualitative case studies and theoretical approaches from organizational sociology, I will argue that the interplay of mainly two factors matters: first, how the administrative leadership supports policies for a more diverse workforce but also general innovation of human resources strategies, second, whether targeting individuals of immigrant origin corresponds to the recruitment rationalities of the human resources practitioners. Further, the analysis indicates that a local identity as a district more or less shaped by immigration also informs practices. The article argues that to understand the implementation of workforce diversity policies,[2] we must consider the organizational structures and rationalities underlying recruitment-related decisions and administrative practices more generally.

In the following, I will first draw on literature from organizational research to develop hypotheses regarding the implementation of policies to increase workforce diversity. In the second section, I will introduce the empirical case and the data before turning to the presentation of the case studies in the next three sections. The final section summarizes and discusses the findings.

An organizational perspective on workforce diversity policies in practice

Research on equal opportunity and diversity policies in municipal authorities and other public organizations has regularly documented "implementation gaps" and the persistence of inequalities in minority members' access to positions (e.g. Young 1987; Liff and Dale 1994; Creegan et al. 2003; Naff and Edward Kellough 2003; Groeneveld and Verbeek 2012). A number of studies have further investigated the factors fostering diversity policy adoption in public and private sector organizations. While there is contradictory evidence regarding the relevance of external normative pressure (Pitts et al. 2010; Dobbin, Kim, and Kalev 2011), these studies indicate several internal factors that are beneficial to diversity policy implementation. They include the presence of women or minorities in leadership positions (Dobbin, Kim, and Kalev 2011; Cook and Glass 2015), structures allocating responsibility for change such as diversity plans or representatives (Kalev, Dobbin, and Kelly 2006), human resources professionals (Edelman 1992), and corporate culture (Dobbin, Kim, and Kalev 2011). However, while emphasizing the importance of internal factors, these mainly large-scale quantitative studies cannot explain how and why the factors assumed to matter operate in practice. Further research is thus required (Dobbin, Kim, and Kalev 2011, 405; Groeneveld and Verbeek 2012, 370).

This article focuses on the processes and practices within local administrations to advance our understanding of the ways in which internal organizational factors shape the implementation of workforce diversity policies. I suggest drawing on organizational sociology and combining two kinds of literature: neo-institutionalist approaches focussing on the link between organizations and their institutional environment and the systems theory approach emphasizing the internal characteristics of organizations.

Neo-institutionalist approaches in organizational sociology argue that organizations typically respond to institutional expectations – such as policy objectives to improve workforce diversity – by "decoupling" symbolic adjustments of the features displayed to the environment from actual practices (Meyer and Rowan 1977), for instance in separating "talk" from "action" (Brunsson 2006). Decoupling allows to balance the possibly contradictory requirements for organizational survival: securing legitimacy – understood as crucial imperative for organizations (Deephouse and Suchman 2008) – by demonstrating compliance with societal rules, expectations and beliefs while at the same time efficiently solving the internal practical problems (Meyer and Rowan 1977, 357). Decoupling particularly responds to inconsistent institutional environments, which organizations often face (Brunsson 2006, 8–9; Boxenbaum and Jonsson 2008, 86). Organizations that are primarily shaped by their institutional environment and rely on societal acceptance for survival, including public administrations, are described as particularly likely to employ strategies of decoupling (Scott and John 1991, 125; Brunsson 2006, 14). However, the literature also emphasizes that by expecting decoupling, we should not ignore that even symbolic adjustments might in the long-term entail changes of actual practices (Edelman 1992; Bromley and Powell 2012, 485).

While neo-institutional approaches focus on the relationship between organizations and their environments, the systems theory approach (Luhmann 2000; Nassehi 2005) draws attention to internal rationalities and structures shaping practices. It allows conceptualizing why organizations may respond differently to a similar environment. Adopting a radical constructivist perspective, the approach states that the organizational environment is no objective given or "independent reality" (Luhmann 2003, 33) but a product of the organizational structures and modes of observation. Accordingly, organizations do not adapt to given institutional contexts, but to the contexts that they construct or "imagine" internally (Luhmann 2000, 78). This shifts the focus to the organizational structures and their differences between organizations. The structures shape whether environmental irritations are perceived as relevant information requiring action, what kind of problems they raise and what kind of solutions are considered and put into practice. Three types of organizational structures, or "decision premises", are distinguished, which have both formal and informal dimensions (Luhmann 2000; Kühl 2013).[3] These are programmes defining the conditions and purposes for decision-making; communication channels, i.e. the organization of positions and responsibilities, which defines who takes what kind of decisions; and the personnel, i.e. staff members with their characteristics, which also structure the organizational communication.[4] Further relevant characteristics are the organizational culture – the institutionalized values, knowledge and habits that often unconsciously shape practices (Luhmann 2000, 240–249) – and the organizational identities, which might latently inform practices (Seidl 2003, 136). In the case of local administrations, the organizational identities can include features of the territory administered, i.e. the city or district (Lang 2019).

Combining these approaches to study the implementation of workforce diversity policies in local administrations, we may thus expect that decoupling and merely symbolic adjustments occur, but also that practices differ between administrations depending on their specific – and possibly differing – structures, cultures and identities. Before investigating the practices in three local administrations in Berlin, the following section will present the empirical case and data.

Empirical case and data

The analysis draws on empirical data gathered from 2012 to 2015 in the German state of Berlin. Berlin was among the first German states that introduced policies to foster the employment of staff with a migration background. It was chosen because the administrative context of the city–state – where the city of Berlin represents the regional state level and the districts the local level – allowed comparing responses to these policies in different local administrations situated in the same political, institutional and discursive context. This helps identify organizational factors shaping whether and how these policies are put into practice.

In 2005, the objective "to increase the share of employees with a migration background" in public administrations was added to the state's integration policies (Der Beauftragte des Senats von Berlin 2005). The underrepresentation of the immigrant population in the civil service had been subject of political debates since the 1990s, but it only entered the official political agenda following a change in the city–state government – from a conservative-led grand coalition to a coalition of Social Democrats and socialist Left – and the reorientation of national integration policies in the early 2000s. Policies primarily aimed to foster the labour market integration of a disadvantaged group, especially young people of immigrant origin, and to promote the "intercultural opening" of public administrations in order to improve service provision for the immigrant population. Promoting equal opportunities was secondary. This objective did not become more prominent before the 2010s and continues to be challenged by a strong discourse arguing that the principle of formal equal treatment already guaranteed equal opportunities.

The new policies mainly focussed on vocational training (Ausbildung), in Germany a highly institutionalized and recognized pathway into a large range of qualified occupations. The three-year training combines a traineeship in the employing organization with theory at vocational schools. Employment in the middle grade of the civil service (e.g. as administrative clerk) is conditional on completion of the specific vocational training; higher grades require university studies. Usually, trainees are offered continued employment after successful completion of the training. Internal careers can lead up to the middle management. The recruitment of trainees thus has long-term effects on the staff composition. During the time of my fieldwork, state and district administrations recruited between 500 and 700 new trainees every year. It was the main form of regular recruitment during a time of staff cuts from the late 1990s to the early 2010s.

Measures introduced by the state to foster the recruitment of staff with a migration background mainly included a campaign called *"Berlin braucht Dich!"* ("Berlin needs you!") launched in 2006 to promote vocational training in the civil service among young people of immigrant origin. It has evolved into a comprehensive programme that supports internship offers, provides promotion material and facilitates contacts between schools and employers. In 2007, the share of new staff members with a migration background was included in the state's "integration monitoring" as one indicator for the "intercultural opening" of public administrations (Der Beauftragte des Senats von Berlin 2007). The "Law on Participation and Integration", adopted by the city–state in 2010, provided a legal frame and announced targets, benchmarking and regular reporting (Abgeordnetenhaus von Berlin 2010). However, the announced target was politically contested for allegedly violating the principle of equal treatment. Moreover, in the administrative structure of the city–state the law cannot exert coercive but only "softer" normative pressure on the district authorities. The 12 districts of Berlin enjoy relative autonomy in the implementation of integration policies and in matters of staff recruitment. Official employee statistics in German public administrations do not record a "migration background".[5] But the migration background of newly-hired trainees has been registered each year since 2006, and differences between districts are noticeable. When fieldwork was conducted in 2012–15, few districts had regularly shown shares of new trainees with a migration background between 25 and 50 per cent since 2006, whereas the numbers in others had varied largely between the years, and some districts had rarely reported more than 10 per cent of trainees with a migration background (BQN 2014).

To study factors shaping the implementation of the described policies in local administrations, the article draws on qualitative material. The research concentrated on the recruitment of trainees for administrative professions as the policies' main focus. This also guaranteed comparability across administrations. The empirical material encompasses 60 semi-structured interviews with different actors involved in politics and practice of recruiting employees with a migration background on the district and city–state levels: HR officers, integration commissioners, heads of administrative departments, representatives from political parties and NGOs as well as trainees and employees of immigrant origin. Further, it comprises participant observation in the recruitment process (e.g. in the selection of applications, in interviews, and at job fairs), and analysis of political, administrative and media documents. The data were analysed based on grounded theory (Strauss and Corbin 1996), supported by the software MAXQDA. Categories included, among others, the recruitment practices and underlying logics of action, the problem perceptions, migration-related differentiations, organizational structures as well as features of the institutional and local environments (for more details see Lang 2019).

For the in-depth study, I selected three district administrations. Case selection was based on documents, first interviews and data on trainees with a migration background. The aim was to include most different cases regarding the responses to the city-state's policies and their effects on recruitment practices, in line with Mill's "method of difference" (George and Bennett 2005, 153). In administration A, the policies did not seem to have affected recruitment practices, and numbers of newly-hired trainees with a migration background had usually remained below 10 per cent. In administration B, a local target had been set, paralleled by rising numbers of trainees with a migration background, but the target was practically abandoned after few years and numbers dropped again. In administration C, several measures had been introduced to increase the share of trainees with a migration background and numbers had regularly figured around 25–35 per cent. All three cases had in common that the mayors were members of one of the governing parties in the city–state during their mandate (Social Democrats or socialist Left). Further, none of the personnel in leadership positions had a migration background. Therefore, neither political affiliations nor internal advocacy from minority members in managing positions (see Cook and Glass 2015) could explain differences.

The following analysis of factors affecting the implementation of policies to foster employment of staff of immigrant origin draws on the reconstruction of processes and practices in these three local administrations as they developed in the context of the policies introduced by the city–state.

Administration A: continuity of established routines

District A is situated in the former Western part of Berlin. It figures among the districts with the highest shares of inhabitants with a migration background (ca. 36 per cent in 2014 when fieldwork was conducted) with the largest immigrant groups stemming from Turkey, former Yugoslavia, the former Soviet Union and Poland. In terms of social composition, the district has middle-class and wealthy neighbourhoods as well as poorer neighbourhoods. When I started my fieldwork in the district administration, the recruitment routines seemed unaffected by the political objective to increase the share of employees with a migration background despite low numbers.

Yet, first initiatives to foster the recruitment of immigrant-origin staff date back to the mid-1990s. The longstanding foreigners' commissioner of the district (later relabelled "integration commissioner") had introduced the issue in the administration and cooperated with the vocational training unit, where she regularly asked whether trainees of immigrant origin had been recruited. Further, she advertised the vocational training opportunities in foreign-language newspapers. In the mid-2000s, when the objective to increase the share of employees with a migration background had become part of Berlin's integration policies, the commissioner initiated internal workshops and working groups to promote the intercultural opening of the administration. A mission statement on "intercultural opening" was developed. However, the commissioner's suggestion to include a target for the recruitment of staff with a migration background was rejected by the administrative officers involved. At the time of my research, the earlier measures and the mission statement seemed forgotten. As the head of the HR unit suggested:

> This was probably an attempt to create an awareness in this house, and I would simply say that it failed because of the merciless power of the work overload of everyday life. (interview, November 2013)[6]

The implementation of measures to foster employment of staff with a migration background was hampered by different interplaying factors. This was, first, a lack of interest in intercultural opening policies on the part of the district mayor. He argued that promoting the employment of immigrant-origin staff was the responsibility of the city–state rather than the district and the state should improve the attractiveness of the civil service by ceasing to cut-down positions (protocol integration committee meeting, 24 October 2012). The new integration commissioner was less assertive and connected than her predecessor. She did not continue advertising in migrant media and enquiring at the vocational training unit about trainees with a migration background. Lacking support from the mayor, the commissioner had a hard time trying to implement initiatives to promote awareness for intercultural opening. Several attempts to organize workshops for executive staff members failed. Frustrated, she refrained from further efforts (interview, November 2013).

Further, unlike most of Berlin's districts, the district did not have a formal integration or intercultural opening policy. The district's parliament, which controls the administration and can initiate administrative action, had not passed a resolution instructing the administration to develop or implement respective measures. For the chair of the parliament's integration committee, who strove to strengthen this policy field, this was in part due to the prevailing district identity:

> The district is relatively well saturated and bourgeois, and perceives itself as such, and that we now have 60-70% children with a migration background in

primary schools, [...] that is not yet there in people's minds! (interview, May 2013)

Her proposal to organize a local integration conference focussing on the inter-cultural opening of the administrative workforce was rejected in the local par-liament. Representatives of the majority parliamentary groups (Social Democrats and conservatives) argued that the district administration lacked the resources for such a conference, an argument which supported the mayor's view that integration policies were above all a matter of the city–state and not the district (protocol integration committee meeting, 27 August 2014). Intercultural opening had thus hardly become institutionalized in internal structures.

Moreover, the recruitment rationalities of the HR practitioners ran counter to measures to promote the employment of staff of immigrant origin. The recruitment procedure for the vocational training had not been changed for years and no-one challenged the established selection criteria (school grades and degrees, a written test on grammar, mathematics and general education plus an interview) as possibly creating structural disadvantages for candidates from outside the traditional target group. The trainee positions were not advertised, which was not conducive to fostering applications from young people from immigrant families, who often lack knowledge about employment opportunities in the civil service (Lang 2019). The above-men-tioned state campaign "Berlin needs you!" aimed at reducing these barriers e.g. by supporting internships. The organization carrying out the project reg-ularly asked all administrations for numbers of newly-hired trainees with a migration background. Like all public employers in Berlin, administration A officially participated in this campaign and delivered the requested numbers. However, this was "decoupled" (Meyer and Rowan 1977) from actual practices. The vocational training unit neither accepted interns, nor did it attend meetings of the campaign, and the (low) numbers of trainees with a migration background reported had no internal significance. As the head of the unit explained:

> They show up every few months and ask if we have opportunities to take interns. They then get the information for the respective time. But I can't say that this is really a topic. We do not talk about it. It doesn't really matter at all (interview, May 2013)

The persistence of established routines was due, on the one hand, to a per-ceived contradiction between the political objective to recruit more staff members of immigrant origin and the organizational recruitment rationalities. The vocational training officers did not feel responsible for implementing what they perceived as integration measures for young people with difficul-ties on the labour market who possibly did not fulfil the expectations on trai-nees. As the head of the unit put it:

In my view, there is a need, in any case, for the promotion of the persons concerned, but not regarding the question: Am I hiring them for the civil service, but
regarding the question: How do I manage to motivate them to bring the
required qualifications. (interview, May 2013)

This argumentation reflects the dominant framing of the policy as supporting
the labour market integration of a disadvantaged group. On the other hand,
the officers did not see a need to change their routines since, for them, they
still fulfilled their purpose to hire enough qualified trainees. Although the
number of applications for vocational training had considerably dropped
over the years, they still deemed it sufficient. The decrease in applications is
a trend across administrations, reflecting both demographic changes and
changing educational preferences among high school graduates (Autorengruppe Bildungsberichterstattung 2014). In administration A, this was not perceived as imminent problem. Additional advertisement strategies were not
considered.

Maintaining the established routines was further supported by the lack of a
human resource strategy. The administration faced an important increase in
vacancies due to an upcoming retirement wave affecting all administrations
in Berlin. The human resources officers complained that the mayor, who
was also the head of the personnel department, did not develop a plan on
how to deal with this challenge. While the head of vocational training
suggested increasing the number of trainee positions, the mayor decided
to reduce them because of difficulties to place trainees with the different
departments. In view of the planning uncertainties generated by missing or
contradictory decisions from "above", developing new recruitment practices
did not seem rational for the vocational training officers.

Summing up, several factors impeded the implementation of policies fostering workforce diversity and contributed to decoupling. Regarding the
organizational structures (see Luhmann 2000), these were the non-existence
of programmes on intercultural opening and future-oriented recruitment,
and a lack of interest in these issues by the mayor as the personnel in the relevant decision-making position. Moreover, the HR officers' perceptions of
recruitment needs and (lacking) benefits of addressing young people with a
migration background contributed to maintaining established routines.
Additionally, the local identity as district where immigration was not a prominent feature did not encourage action, a factor that turns out to be relevant in
the comparison with the other cases.

Administration B: temporary changes

District B is situated in the Eastern part of Berlin. Due to the different immigration history of the GDR, the share of population with a migration background
is significantly lower than in district A (ca. 17 per cent in 2014). The largest

immigrant groups here originate from former-Soviet-Union countries and Vietnam. In administration B, the introduction of policies to increase the share of staff members of immigrant origin entailed changes of practices; however, they were short-lived.

In the early 2000s, initiatives from the integration commissioner and the local immigrant advisory council were taken up by the district's mayor who installed a steering committee on intercultural opening, which involved the heads of different administrative departments. While, according to the former integration commissioner, this initially met with "enormous resistance" among the officers expected to participate, it proved productive and pushed the issue of the employment of staff with a migration background forward (interview, November 2013). The steering committee developed a local integration plan, which was adopted by the local parliament in 2006 and included a target for the recruitment of trainees with a migration background of 15 per cent, corresponding to the district's share of population with a migration background at the time. The vocational training unit was regularly asked to report on the progress. As different from administration A, the policy objective had thus become part of the organizational structures in form of a formal programme, a new "communication channel" – the steering committee – , and support by the relevant personnel, mainly the mayor.

This had an impact on recruitment practices. The vocational training unit actively tried to hire young people with a migration background to achieve the target. The officers established contacts to an association that offered courses for young women of immigrant origin preparing for vocational training in public administration and recruited several of the participants. Further, they sought to address the Vietnamese community, responding to the "political will" of the mayor, as the head of the unit reported (interview, May 2013), to specifically foster the employment of staff of Vietnamese origin. This was meant to help improve relations with the local Vietnamese public who allegedly felt uneasy in dealing with the administration. But the HR officers also ascribed positive cultural characteristics to the Vietnamese ("high performing", "comply with rules") that suited the general expectations on staff members. The training unit commissioned an expertise to find out how to increase the applications from young people of Vietnamese origin and presented the vocational training in Vietnamese associations. Moreover, to meet the target, the officers informally prioritized candidates with a migration background in hiring decisions. They invited candidates to interviews who had not passed the written test and gave bonus points for a "migration background" in the final ranking (interviews, May 2013, March 2014). This practice of "usable illegality" (Luhmann 1964, 304) allowed a short-term response to the political demands. The share of new trainees exceeded the target for several years. In contrast to administration A, the tight coupling of recruitment practices to the policy by the closely monitored target did not allow decoupling between symbolic adjustments and actual practice. However, while the expected numerical output was produced, this was decoupled from the regular recruitment routines, a form of decoupling that Bromley and Powell (2012) label "means-end decoupling".

The "migration boom" and "hype around the Vietnamese" as one officer described it (interview, March 2014) came to an end when the personnel in the decision-making positions changed. In 2011, a new mayor came into office who was not interested in intercultural opening. He initially planned to dissolve the steering committee and only maintained it after internal opposition, but the committee only met rarely. The head of the HR unit changed, too, and the successor pursued different foci. The target regarding trainees with a migration background continued to exist on paper but regular control had ceased. The structures established to promote recruitment were hollowed out, the tight coupling between policy and practice was loosened. At the time of my fieldwork, the target and the migration background of candidates hardly mattered anymore for the vocational training officers since the superiors did not ask for it. The numbers of new trainees with a migration background had dropped to one or two per year. Only few practices had remained. The officers still recorded the numbers of candidates and trainees with a migration background to be able to respond, "in case there's any interest in it again" (interview, March 2014), and the head of the unit pursued some promotion addressing the Vietnamese community, which she now described as based on personal motivation.

Further, the vocational training practitioners' recruitment rationalities contributed to abandoning attempts to hire more trainees of immigrant origin. Distinct from their counterparts in administration A, the officers perceived the need to develop new promotion strategies to counter the declining application numbers. But they also struggled with planning uncertainties and lacking support. The head of the HR unit, who considered the number of applications still sufficient, cut down resources for advertisement, which thwarted efforts for innovation. Furthermore, the promotion efforts did not target young people of immigrant origin anymore, since the former recruitment strategies enforced by the target had generated opposition from the vocational training officers. They complained that they had to hire candidates who did not meet the criteria just because of their "migration background" and that some of these candidates had not shown the expected performance. They now associated "migration background" with lacking suitability, generalizing negative experiences with few trainees into the now "justified" expectation that young people of immigrant origin would more likely cause problems. In their eyes, the political objective stood in fundamental conflict with their recruitment interests. The negative experiences had for them not only discredited the short-term hiring strategy as means to achieve the target but the policy itself. While the vocational training unit was initially rather active in the city-state's campaign "Berlin needs you!", the officers now openly shared their critique of the campaign's aim and had stopped attending meetings or offering internships. This withdrawal was further supported by the district's identity. The officers criticized that the campaign focussed on the "classic" immigrant districts in the Western part of Berlin and was not beneficial for their particular district context and immigrant groups, which they perceived to be less in need of integration measures. Like in administration A, participation in the campaign was now merely symbolic, decoupled from actual practices.

Administration C: long-term changes in recruitment practices

District C, situated in the Western part of Berlin, figures among the districts with the highest shares of inhabitants with a migration background, here combined with a large population of lower socio-economic status. Some of its neighbourhoods feature prominently in the public discourse on immigration-related problems. In administration C, the policy to increase the share of staff members of immigrant origin seemed successfully implemented. Since 2006, the share of new trainees with a migration background had regularly figured around 25–35 per cent.

Factors contributing to this were first, concrete initiatives by the local mayor, fostered by the district's identity as shaped by immigration. In 2005–2006, when the political objective to increase the share of employees with a migration background was included in Berlin's integration policies, the mayor initiated a cooperation with a local association that offered preparation courses for young women of immigrant origin, the same project through which administration B recruited trainees. The administration gave funding for the courses and reserved several trainee places each year for participants who successfully passed the recruitment procedure. Moreover, upon the mayor's initiative, the administration took an active role in the steering committee of the state's campaign "Berlin needs you!".

The mayor was the key actor in the district's integration policies and a visible figure in the German public debate on "integration problems" of the immigrant-origin population. His pivotal position was structurally anchored. In the district's parliament, an integration committee was only created when it became mandatory for all Berlin districts and it only had a consultative function. According to a long-standing member of the parliament, the parliament did not demand stronger institutionalization because the mayor "could not accept anyone beside him" (interview, June 2015). A formal programme for intercultural opening, like in administration B, did not exist. The mayor defended an explicitly "pragmatic" understanding of integration policy against "abstractly formulated concepts" (written response to a parliamentary interpellation, 5 May 2014). However, fostering the recruitment of staff with a migration background corresponded to the mayor's "pragmatic" approach, which was beneficial to the implementation of measures. The district's identity as one of Berlin's main immigrant districts further supported this. The long-standing head of the vocational training unit described how the decision to take a leading role in the "Berlin needs you!"-campaign had come about:

> That was clearly a political decision. [...] We have a rather high quota of people here who at least have a migration background, or actually do not have a German passport, and the mayor is well known in Germany, so it was clear that of course this district must actively sit at the table. (interview, November 2013)

Undertaking visible action responded to public expectations, which focussed more on district C as prominent immigrant district than on districts A and B. These expectations required responses to not endanger the administration's legitimacy.

The top-down introduced measures entailed structural changes in recruitment practices – in contrast to administration B – because they increasingly overlapped with the recruitment rationalities of the vocational training officers. The specific recruitment channel of the preparation courses was abandoned in 2010 for causing extra work and since not all trainees hired had fulfilled the expectations. However, the HR officers developed new recruitment strategies because they perceived a growing competition for qualified young people and thus the need to attract new target groups. This included, among others, young people of immigrant origin. In this district, in which an important share of school graduates now had a migration background, they were perceived as inevitable target group when the pool of potential trainees had to be increased. The new recruitment practices included a professionalized assessment procedure, active advertisement on job fairs and in local schools, and promotion material that aimed at presenting the administration as attractive and diversity-friendly employer. Considering young people of immigrant origin had become part of the regular recruitment practices. Different from administrations A and B, the efforts to modernize recruitment received support and resources from the mayor (also head of the personnel department), who was interested in the vocational training scheme and in developing strategies to tackle the upcoming HR challenges.

In contrast to the previous two cases, the vocational training officers of administration C actively participated in the campaign "Berlin needs you!" because it served an important function for their promotion activities. The officers used the tools, material and networks provided and continued as an active member of the steering committee. They no longer understood the campaign as a specific integration policy measure, as it was introduced, but as a regular promotion measure. As the head of the training unit put it:

Of course, with this I have promoted the town hall [...] as an employer brand. Because many people on the streets here don't even know about the vocational training here [...] and it's of course an advertising platform for us, to present ourselves as employers: 'Look, we have a great training, we have the opportunities after the training, look how great we are'. (interview, November 2013)

This re-interpretation as useful measure to tackle the perceived problems of staff recruitment is a major factor why in this case the measure was adopted. The focus on young people of immigrant origin became secondary; what mattered was the general visibility the administration could gain as employer.

Thus, the long-term changes of recruitment practices were the product of different interplaying factors. They include a mayor, who pursued active integration policies and supported future-oriented human resources strategies, and the recruitment rationalities of the HR officers, who strove to attract new target groups. Further, changes were supported by a local identity as "immigrant district". This fuelled public expectations, which required responses to secure legitimacy (Deephouse and Suchman 2008), and it informed the officers' perception that young people of immigrant origin were inevitable addressees of promotion activities.

Conclusion

This article set out to explore factors that affect the implementation of policies promoting the employment of staff of immigrant origin in local administrations. It focussed on internal organizational factors, which were investigated drawing on approaches from organizational sociology and reconstructing the practices in three local administrations in one German regional state (Berlin). The analysis shows how the interplay of different organizational structures and rationalities affects effective policy implementation. Particularly two factors proved to be relevant. First, support from the administrative leadership, mainly the mayors, played a crucial role. As the personnel in the relevant decision-making positions, they are part of the organizational "decision premises" (Luhmann 2000) structuring practices. Their interest and support were crucial for ensuring that measures were adopted and that further internal structures – formal programmes and communication channels (Luhmann 2000) – were developed and enforced. This not only included support for workforce diversity policies but also for the general innovation of human resource strategies. The analysis shows that if leadership support is lacking, formal structures may not be developed, and structures established to support the implementation of policies may be hollowed out. Second, the pragmatic recruitment rationalities at the operative level mattered. It was decisive whether the human resources practitioners perceived a need to change established routines to ensure recruitment of qualified employees in a changing labour market environment, and whether they perceived a benefit from attracting a new target group of immigrant origin. Where this was not (yet) the case, the new policies met with opposition and "decoupling" occurred (Meyer and Rowan 1977; Bromley and Powell 2012) between merely symbolic or short-term adjustments and the recruitment practices which continued unchanged. The political attempt to steer recruitment practices with a target for staff with a migration background even produced opposite effects and fuelled resistance against the policy. This echoes insights from the public administration literature indicating that targets as techniques to steer performance are likely to fail their objectives if they are not adequately designed (Hood 2006; Boswell 2018). Additionally, the comparison indicates that the local identity – as a district more or less shaped by immigration – may affect the adoption of measures. It becomes relevant as part of the organizational identity latently informing practices (Seidl 2003), and due to environmental expectations that may require action to secure legitimacy, a crucial imperative for organizations (Deephouse and Suchman 2008).

The findings contribute to the literature on drivers and barriers of diversity policy implementation by shedding light on the role of internal organizational structures and rationalities. They show that the implementation of diversity policies is contingent on organizational structures and on the administrative officers' perceptions of problems and requirements. This adds to previous studies arguing that it matters for effective implementation how policies are structurally anchored (Kalev, Dobbin, and Kelly 2006) by revealing how such structural characteristics operate in practice. Further, the findings suggest that we must consider the interplay of "top-down" and "bottom-up" processes to understand the (non-)implementation of diversity policies. While formal policies and legal frameworks are important to initiate change, they may not be sufficient for substantive, long-term changes. The pragmatic rationalities underlying recruitment-related decisions, and administrative practice more generally, also play a crucial role. The implementation of practices furthering the employment of staff of immigrant origin requires that the officers at the operative level perceive a genuine need for changing established routines in order to fulfil their job, in this case to ensure the availability of well-qualified personnel for a functioning administration. These general rationalities might be even more relevant for changes if staff of immigrant origin is absent from managing positions, where they could advance diversity policies and practices as previous studies suggest (Cook and Glass 2015).

Investigating the case of local administrations in a German city–state, this study looked at a specific political and administrative context in a federal system. The organizational factors highlighted here are likely also relevant in other municipal administrations. At the same time, in the investigated case, the role of some environmental factors could not be further explored. Normative expectations in the organizational field, for instance, also shape organizational structures and practices (e.g. Dobbin, Kim, and Kalev 2011). Further, institutional factors such as the directive powers of the superior state levels and the binding character of diversity policies are likely to matter which differ from country to country. Moreover, the study focussed on a particular period of time – the introduction of policies and first measures. While this guaranteed comparability across administrations, the analysis of long-term effects of these policies on recruitment practices, and the workforce more generally, is beyond the scope of the study. Further research could extend our knowledge by focussing on different local and national contexts and by investigating the interplay of external institutional and internal organizational factors. Additionally, more research is desirable on the long-term impact of workforce diversity policies at different hierarchy levels including managing positions.

Notes

1. "Migration background" (*Migrationshintergrund*) is the official statistical category: "A person has a migration background if he or she or at least one parent does not have German nationality by birth" (Statistisches Bundesamt 2018, 4).
2. I understand workforce diversity policies as interventions promoting the inclusion of underrepresented social categories in the workforce. In this article, the term relates to migration-related diversity and to policies aiming to foster employment of staff of immigrant origin.
3. The structures are conceived as dynamic, constantly reproduced or modified by the organizational operations.
4. The conceptualization of persons as organizational structures is based on the premise that communication and not action is the basic unit of organizations and social systems in general (Nassehi 2005, 181–182). Persons are a structuring element of communication as authors, addressees and topics of communication.
5. The German sample census estimates a share of 6.7% for public administrations in 2013 (Ette et al. 2016, 32). More detailed data on administrative levels and units is not available.
6. Translation of the interview quotes by the author.

Acknowledgements

I would like to thank Karen Schönwälder, the other contributors of the Special Issue "Diversity in local political practice" as well as the anonymous reviewers for their helpful comments on earlier versions of this paper.

Disclosure statement

No potential conflict of interest was reported by the author(s).

ORCID

Christine Lang http://orcid.org/0000-0002-0844-8681

References

Abgeordnetenhaus von Berlin. 2010. *Gesetz zur Regelung von Partizipation und Integration in Berlin*. Berlin: Abgeordnetenhaus von Berlin.

Alexander, Michael. 2007. *Cities and Labour Immigration. Comparing Policy Responses in Amsterdam, Paris, Rome and Tel Aviv*. London: Ashgate.

Autorengruppe Bildungsberichterstattung. 2014. *Bildung in Deutschland 2014. Ein indikatorengestützter Bericht mit einer Analyse zur Bildung von Menschen mit Behinderungen*. Bielefeld: W. Bertelsmann Verlag.

Boswell, Christina. 2018. *Manufacturing Political Trust. Targets and Performance Management in Public Policy*. Cambridge: Cambridge Univ. Press.

Boxenbaum, Eva, and Stefan Jonsson. 2008. "Isomorphism, Diffusion and Decoupling." In *The SAGE Handbook of Organizational Institutionalism*, edited by Royston Greenwood, Christine Oliver, Roy Suddaby, and Kerstin Sahlin, 78–98. London: SAGE.

BQN Berlin. 2014. *"Entwicklung des Anteils neuer Auszubildender mit Migrationshintergrund im Öffentlichen Dienst Berlins 2006–2013*. Berlin: BQN.

Bromley, Patricia, and Walter W. Powell. 2012. "From Smoke and Mirrors to Walking the Talk: Decoupling in the Contemporary World." *The Academy of Management Annals* 6 (1): 483–530.

Brunsson, Nils. 2006. *The Organization of Hypocrisy: Talk, Decisions and Actions in Organizations*. 2nd ed. Copenhagen: Business School Press.

Bührmann, Andrea D., and Karen Schönwälder. 2017. "Public Organisations and Diversity: Approaches to an Under-Researched Topic." *Journal of Ethnic and Migration Studies* 43 (10): 1635–1643.

Cook, Alison, and Christy Glass. 2015. "The Power of One or Power in Numbers? Analyzing the Effect of Minority Leaders on Diversity Policy and Practice." *Work and Occupations* 42 (2): 183–215.

Creegan, Chris, Fiona Colgan, Richard Charlesworth, and Gil Robinson. 2003. "Race Equality Policies at Work: Employee Perceptions of the 'Implementation Gap' in a UK Local Authority." *Work, Employment and Society* 17 (4): 617–640.

Deephouse, David L., and Mark Suchman. 2008. "Legitimacy in Organizational Institutionalism." In *The SAGE Handbook of Organizational Institutionalism*, edited by Royston Greenwood, Christine Oliver, Roy Suddaby, and Kerstin Sahlin, 49–77. London: SAGE.

Dekker, Rianne, Henrik Emilsson, Bernhard Krieger, and Peter Scholten. 2015. "A Local Dimension of Integration Policies? A Comparative Study of Berlin, Malmö, and Rotterdam." *International Migration Review* 3 (49): 1–26.

Der Beauftragte des Senats von Berlin für Integration und Migration. 2005. *Vielfalt fördern – Zusammenhalt stärken. Das Integrationskonzept für Berlin*. Berlin: Der Beauftragte des Senats für Integration und Migration.

Der Beauftragte des Senats von Berlin für Integration und Migration. 2007. *Vielfalt Fördern – Zusammenhalt stärken. Das Berliner Integrationskonzept*. Berlin: Der Beauftragte des Senats für Integration und Migration.

Die Bundesregierung. 2012. *Nationaler Aktionsplan Integration. Zusammenhalt stärken – Teilhabe verwirklichen*. Berlin: Presse- und Informationsamt der Bundesregierung.

Dobbin, Frank, Soohan Kim, and Alexandra Kalev. 2011. "You Can't Always Get What You Need: Organizational Determinants of Diversity Programs." *American Sociological Review* 76 (3): 386–411.

Edelman, Lauren B. 1992. "Legal Ambiguity and Symbolic Structures: Organizational Mediation of Civil Rights Law." *American Journal of Sociology* 97 (6): 1531–1576.

Ette, Andreas, Susanne Stedtfeld, Harun Sulak, and Gunter Brückner. 2016. *Erhebung des Anteils von Beschäftigten mit Migrationshintergrund in der Bundesverwaltung: Ergebnisbericht im Auftrag des Ressortarbeitskreises der Bundesregierung.* Wiesbaden: Bundesinstitut für Bevölkerungsforschung.

George, Alexander L., and Andrew Bennett. 2005. *Case Studies and Theory Development in the Social Sciences.* Cambridge, MA: The MIT Press.

Gesemann, Frank, and Roland Roth. 2009. "Kommunale Integrationspolitik in Deutschland - Einleitende Bemerkungen." In *Lokale Integrationspolitik in der Einwanderungsgesellschaft: Migration und Integration als Herausforderung von Kommunen,* edited by Frank Gesemann and Roland Roth, 11–29. Wiesbaden: VS Verlag.

Gesemann, Frank, Roland Roth, and Jutta Aumüller. 2012. *Stand der Kommunalen Integrationspolitik in Deutschland. Studie erstellt für das Bundesministerium für Verkehr, Bau und Stadtentwicklung und die Beauftragte der Bundesregierung für Migration, Flüchtlinge und Integration.* Berlin: Bundesministerium für Verkehr, Bau und Stadtentwicklung.

Groeneveld, Sandra, and Stijn Verbeek. 2012. "Diversity Policies in Public and Private Sector Organizations: An Empirical Comparison of Incidence and Effectiveness." *Review of Public Personnel Administration* 32 (4): 353–381.

Hood, Christopher. 2006. "Gaming in Targetworld: The Targets Approach to Managing British Public Services." *Public Administration Review* 66 (4): 515–521.

Kalev, Alexandra, Frank Dobbin, and Erin Kelly. 2006. "Best Practices or Best Guesses? Assessing the Efficacy of Corporate Affirmative Action and Diversity Policies." *American Sociological Review* 71 (4): 589–617.

Kühl, Stefan. 2013. *Organizations: A Systems Approach.* Surrey: Gower.

Lang, Christine. 2019. *Die Produktion von Diversität in Städtischen Verwaltungen. Wandel und Beharrung von Organisationen in der Migrationsgesellschaft.* Wiesbaden: Springer.

Liff, Sonia, and Karen Dale. 1994. "Formal Opportunity, Informal Barriers: Black Women Managers Within a Local Authority." *Work, Employment and Society* 8 (2): 177–198.

Luhmann, Niklas. 1964. *Funktionen und Folgen formaler Organisation.* Berlin: Duncker & Humblot.

Luhmann, Niklas. 2000. *Organisation und Entscheidung.* Opladen: Westdt. Verl.

Luhmann, Niklas. 2003. "Organization." In *Autopoietic Organization Theory: Drawing on Niklas Luhmanns Social Systems Perspective,* edited by Tore Bakken and Tor Hernes, 31–52. Oslo: Abstrakt, Liber.

Martínez-Ariño, Julia, Michalis Moutselos, Karen Schönwälder, Christian Jacobs, Maria Schiller, and Alexandre Tandé. 2019. "Why Do Some Cities Adopt More Diversity Policies Than Others? A Study in France and Germany." *Comparative European Politics* 17 (5): 651–672.

Meyer, John W., and Brian Rowan. 1977. "Institutionalized Organizations: Formal Structure as Myth and Ceremony." *American Journal of Sociology* 83 (2): 340–363.

Meziani-Remichi, Yamina, and Marcel Maussen. 2017. "Recruitment in Public Administrations: Diversity Policies and Selection Practices in a French City." *Journal of Ethnic and Migration Studies* 43 (10): 1679–1695.

Mosher, Frederick C. 1982. *Democracy and the Public Service.* 2nd ed. New York: Oxford Univ. Press.

Naff, Katherine C., and J. Edward Kellough. 2003. "Ensuring Employment Equity: Are Federal Diversity Programs Making a Difference?" *International Journal of Public Administration* 26 (12): 1307–1336.

Nassehi, Armin. 2005. "Organizations as Decision Machines: Niklas Luhmann's Theory of Organized Social Systems." *The Sociological Review* 53 (1): 178–191.

Pitts, David W., Alisa K. Hicklin, Daniel P. Hawes, and Erin Melton. 2010. "What Drives the Implementation of Diversity Management Programs? Evidence From Public Organizations." *Journal of Public Administration Research and Theory* 20 (4): 867–886.

Schönwälder, Karen, and Triadafilos Triadafilopoulos. 2016. "The New Differentialism: Responses to Immigrant Diversity in Germany." *German Politics* 25 (3): 366–380.

Scott, W. Richard, and W. Meyer John. 1991. "The Organization of Societal Sectors: Propositions and Early Evidence." In *The New Institutionalism in Organizational Analysis*, edited by Walter W. Powell and Paul J. DiMaggio, 108–140. Chicago: Univ. of Chicago Press.

Seidl, David. 2003. "Organisational Identity in Luhmann's Theory of Social Systems." In *Autopoietic Organization Theory. Drawing on Niklas Luhmann's Social Systems Perspective*, edited by Tore Bakken and Tor Hernes, 123–150. Oslo: Abstrakt, Liber.

Solomos, John. 1989. "Equal Opportunities Policies and Racial Inequality: The Role of Public Policy." *Public Administration* 67 (1): 79–93.

Spencer, Sarah. 2008. *Equality and Diversity in Jobs and Services: City Policies for Migrants in Europe*. Dublin: European Foundation for the Improvement of Living and Working Conditions.

Statistisches Bundesamt. 2018. *Bevölkerung und Erwerbstätigkeit: Bevölkerung mit Migrationshintergrund - Ergebnisse des Mikrozensus 2017*. Wiesbaden: Statistisches Bundesamt. Accessed July 10 2019. https://www.destatis.de/Migration/DE/Publikationen/Thematisch/Bevoelkerung/MigrationIntegration/Migrationshintergrund.html.

Strauss, Anselm L., and Juliet Corbin. 1996. *Grounded Theory: Grundlagen Qualitativer Sozialforschung*. Weinheim: Beltz, Psychologie-Verlags-Union.

Young, Ken. 1987. "The Space Between Words: Local Authorities and the Concept of Equal Opportunities." In *Racism and Equal Opportunity Policies in the 1980s*, edited by Richard Jenkins and John Solomos, 93–109. Cambridge: Cambridge University Press.

The local turn in integration policies: why French cities differ

Anouk Flamant

ABSTRACT

This article examines how three major French cities designed their immigrant incorporation policies in the early twenty-first century. While political and administrative structures are similar in these cities, the favoured approaches – integration, equality, diversity – and the importance assigned to the issue of migration differed. Four factors explain the local shape of immigrant incorporation policies: the relationship with national authorities, the mobilization of European opportunities, the capacities of civil society, and the career paths of policy officers. This qualitative research provides insights into the "local turn" of migration policy in practice. It further illustrates how French cities may overcome a national model, although their fight against ethno-racial inequalities remains weak and inconsequent.

Some contemporary western cities are characterized by ethnic diversity or, sometimes, "super-diversity" (Vertovec 2007). New movements of migration and, above all, the plurality of migrants' life experiences have prompted new forms of action on the part of cities. Several publications highlight the "local turn" of immigrant incorporation policy in Europe, stressing that cities actively intervene in migration issues as they are primarily affected by this phenomenon (Penninx et al. 2004; Alexander 2006; Caponio and Borkert 2010; Caponio, Scholten, and Zapata-Barrero 2018). This "local turn" scholarship insists on the necessity to widen perspectives and acknowledge that the governance of migration is a multi-level process, in which European institutions and cities play an important part (Scholten 2013; Schiller 2016; Scholten and Penninx 2016; Caponio, Scholten, and Zapata-Barrero 2017). Many researchers also argue that local policies are often incongruent with national models of integration (Jorgensen 2012; Dekker et al. 2015; Caponio, Scholten, and Zapata-Barrero 2018). Localist theses rely on two arguments. First, they highlight the capacity of cities to accommodate ethnic diversity and respond to problems with pragmatic measures (Poppelaars and Scholten 2008; Caponio and Borkert 2010). Secondly, they point to the disintegration of national models and the fact that local policies towards migrants are shaped by different policy settings and political perceptions (Alexander 2003; Garbaye 2005). Schiller (2015) even evokes a "paradigmatic pragmatism" to define how officials combine measures and refer to various paradigms without taking part in any political debate. However, scholarship so far is mainly based on official documents and policies and compares different major European cities. We know too little about why cities in the same country, confronted with ethnic diversity, adopt different rhetoric and tools. French cities, in particular, have received little attention as the assumption prevails that, here, a centralized state implements a strong assimilationist national model (Brubaker 1992). However, the French governance of immigrants has, since the end of the 1980s, also included urban programs tackling "integration" or "welcoming new migrants" (Flamant 2014). Furthermore, some French cities define their own policies towards immigrants, mobilizing several approaches such as "integration", "citizenship" or "non-discrimination".

The macro and quantitative research of Martinez-Ariño et al. (2018) on German and French cities reveal how the political orientation of municipalities influences the development of equality policies in French cities. My perspective differs in that, through a micro and qualitative analysis, I outline how and why the "local turn" of immigrant incorporation policy and the development of equality policies evolves in city-specific forms and I further specify the factors affecting that. First, I outline similar dynamics in French cities regarding the local governance of migration. The creation of new administrative units illustrates the development of equality discourses at the beginning of the 2000s. However, the policies and tools adopted differed. Second, I identity four factors that account for similarities and differences of city's immigrant incorporation policies: – relations with national governments, the capacity to seize European opportunities, the ability of civil society to influence the local agenda, and the career paths of local civil servants. Finally, I argue that local policies towards immigrants are fragile and tend to be diluted in an abstract and generic approach to equality that pays little attention to ethno-racial inequalities.

Local immigrant incorporation policies: theoretical approaches and discussions

Comparing three French cities, this article focuses on municipal policies regarding immigrants.[1] The existence of these policies cannot be understood solely as the result of pragmatic adjustments at the local level. Neither should we assume that cities necessarily respond in similar ways. On the contrary, I

argue that four factors account for similarities and differences in the governance of immigrants.

Over the past two decades, the study of integration policies has undergone
major changes. Researchers show a growing interest in understanding how
local authorities are key actors in defining and designing immigrant policy
(e.g. Caponio and Borkert 2010). Early publications focused on the way in
which local authorities, and cities, in particular, reinterpreted different national
models – assimilationist, multicultural, intercultural – , and as a consequence
produced new policies labelled as "equality" or "diversity" policies (Penninx
et al. 2004; Entzinger 2005; Schiller 2015). Many scholars identify a "local
turn" in immigrant incorporation policy (Scholten 2013) and point at the
"pragmatism" displayed by local authorities who are more in touch with
their constituents. To understand local policies, researchers insist on the
necessity to go beyond national models and consider the multi-level governance of migration, especially the relations between cities, national authorities
and European institutions (Poppelaars and Scholten 2008; Hepburn and
Zapata-Barrero 2014; Caponio, Scholten, and Zapata-Barrero 2018). At the
same time, as e. g. Lacroix and Desille (2018) remind us, we should not
naively see cities as the "welcoming" actors in conflict with more restrictive
national authorities, but acknowledge the influence a neo-liberal doctrine.

While scholarship has rightly emphasized the growing interest of cities in
migration issues, it has too narrowly focused on official discourses of cities
and European institutions. We still insufficiently understand why cities in
the same national universe adopt different perspectives on and instruments
for immigrant incorporation. In order to achieve that, it is necessary to
adopt a micro perspective. Fourot (2013), in her stimulating study about
Quebec, identifies four elements explaining local configurations: the relationship with the national and provincial government, the politico-administrative
structure, the dynamism of civil society, and the discourses on "integration".
Following her study, I aim to identify the major factors accounting for the
varying immigrant incorporation policies in different cities. I argue that
center-left French cities increasingly engage in immigrant policies as these
cities concurrently develop a similar administrative structure. However, they
differ in the measures adopted and in how they consider ethno-racial inequalities. Like Martinez-Ariño et al. (2018) on French and German municipal diversity policies, I recognize that the left-leaning position of French municipalities
plays an undeniable role in bringing about diversity-policy measures.
However, their quantitative research approach does not capture the actual
development of these diversity policies, their focus (gender, immigrants or
disabled people) and the specific approach (non-discrimination, integration
or diversity). Investigation of these questions is all the more interesting as it
contributes to the analysis of the renegotiation of the French "republican
model of integration"[2] since the adoption of a broader anti-discrimination

framework in accordance with EU directives (Calves 2016; Chappe, Eberhard, and Guillaume 2016) and since positive action has been taken on gender and disabilities (Bereni 2009). However, the colour blindness of the French "republican model of integration" (Sabbagh and Peer 2008; Simon 2008) makes positive action for ethno-racial minorities illegal. This article contributes to understanding how French local actors deal with the persistent national low concern of ethno-racial inequalities (Fassin and Fassin 2006) given the reality of immigration.

I identify four factors that explain similarities and differences between three French cities. The first factor is the nature of the relationship with national government and its measures towards immigrants. The second factor is the resources offered by the European institutions and city networks that contribute to defining and developing a municipal immigrant incorporation policy. Third, I underline the role of civil society as partner of municipal actors and, fourth, of the career paths of local civil servants implementing policies towards immigrants.

Data and methodology

This article is based on a doctoral thesis completed in 2014 on municipal policies towards immigrants in three French cities: Lyon, Nantes and Strasbourg (Flamant 2017). The study uses in-depth interviews with people involved in the implementation of immigrant incorporation policies. Interviews were conducted between 2011 and 2014 with elected officials of the municipalities (seven in total), local civil servants responsible for equality and integration policies (all eight were interviewed), and representatives of associations defending immigrants' rights (fourteen in total). Interviews focused on the relationship of municipal actors with national authorities and with other French and European cities, their understanding of integration policies and the kind of policies they implemented. Additionally, interviews dealt with the biographies of interview partners and the history of their municipal department. Interviews were supplemented by an analysis of municipal documents, including those kept in the municipal archives. Using a grounded theory approach, interviews and written documents were coded with PhpMyAdmin software. Lastly, participant observation in the meetings of the Council of Foreign Residents in Nantes and Strasbourg between 2010 and 2012 (four sessions in total), enabled me to study the relations between the city and local associations representing migrants.

Lyon, Nantes, and Strasbourg share several characteristics. First, all have a similar political history and forms of mayoral management. Marked by the arrival of new young mayors in 1989, these cities invested in urban marketing policies at the end of the nineties. Over the period 2001–2008, only Strasbourg was governed by a Conservative municipal majority, replaced in 2008 by Socialists, while Lyon and Nantes had Socialist mayors throughout. The cities are of regional importance and therefore able to challenge the primacy of the central state. Lyon is France's second-largest city, while Strasbourg is the capital of the Alsace region. Nantes is the largest city in western France. Lastly, the comparison undertaken is all the more relevant as the cities in question are "most similar cases" (Seawright and Gerring 2008) considering migration. None of them can be described as "refuge", "transit", or "gateway" city (Babels 2018) even if all have seen growth in their immigrant populations over the last two decades and a rising geographical diversity, mainly with people coming from sub-Saharan countries. Strasbourg has a larger "immigré" or foreign-born population[3] (21 per cent in 2015), than Lyon (13 per cent) and Nantes (9.5 per cent), as it houses the headquarters of several European and international institutions. As the three cities share similar political governance, I argue that their political orientation is not sufficient for understanding different outcomes in municipal policies.

Immigrant incorporation policies in Lyon, Nantes and Strasbourg (2001–2012)

Between 2001 and 2012, the cities of Lyon, Nantes, and Strasbourg developed initiatives to support immigrant populations. Local governance took a similar form: all three cities appointed deputy mayors for this purpose who slowly developed immigrant incorporation policies – like training for municipal staff in welcoming non-French speakers, new recruitment processes to make the municipal administration reflect the diversity of the territory or councils of foreign residents. While local discourses generally moved from integration toward equality and combating discrimination, the challenges and objectives tied to the various measures demonstrate the ability of cities to combine different approaches to migration. I outline the social backgrounds and the political weight of deputy mayors in the municipal majority to understand in what political context cities framed their immigrant incorporation policy. It contributes to understanding how they consider ethno-racial inequalities. Lyon adopted an equality-based model and did little to address the specific issue of immigrants. Nantes was characterized by a policy connecting the concepts of integration, citizenship, and non-discrimination to build its specific policy towards immigrants. Lastly, Strasbourg considered migration issues mainly through measures promoting their political integration and without a clear statement on ethno-racial inequalities.

The progressive institutionalization of the governance of immigrants

In 2001, the cities of Lyon and Nantes were governed by teams mainly composed of elected representatives of the Socialist Party and left-wing minority groups. Lyon had been experiencing a political shift toward the center-left, after having been governed by coalitions representing the right and center-right from the early 1950s. In Nantes, the same mayor had been re-elected since 1989 with a municipal assembly dominated by socialist members and minority left-wing representatives. In 2001, new municipal councilors were elected, including the *adjointe* in charge of the integration of immigrants. The case of Strasbourg is different as the municipal assembly shifted to the center-right in 2001 and back to the left in 2008. In all French cities, elected mayors are supported by deputy mayors, the *adjoints*, belonging to the same political coalition and in charge of particular issues defined by the municipal assembly. The deputy mayors also run administrative departments, along with top civil servants.

In all three cities, the election of new municipal councilors in 2001 led to the creation of new municipal "délégations"[4] focusing on immigrants. These decisions prove the cities' interest in migration issues as it is not a mandatory competence of French municipalities. The *adjoints* nominated as the heads of these *délégations* were all not powerful politically and had to struggle to avoid being perceived as the one embodying the "diversity" i.e. the nomination of people from minority groups as a guarantee to do politics in new ways (Avanza 2010). Neither of them could benefit from strong support from their political party as they either belonged to minority parties in the municipal coalition (Communist Party in Lyon and Nantes) or no political party at all (Strasbourg). Moreover, they were all young women (under forty) with little political experience. Two of them had migration backgrounds corresponding to what Avanza (2010) qualified as the "French typical ideal diversity": coming from the Maghreb and achieving high educational credentials with lower-class background. Finally, they had little administrative capacity at their disposal as no administrative department was dedicated to immigrant incorporation policy.

In Lyon, the municipal *délégation* was named "Integration and rights of citizens", in Nantes, "Integration and citizenship", and in Strasbourg "Integration". All municipal *délégations* referred to "integration" and none to "discrimination" illustrating the strong commitment to universalism and a reluctance to recognize ethnic groups (Amiraux and Simon 2006; Safi 2017) in spite of the national non-discrimination policy (Fassin 2002). In the case of Strasbourg, the *adjointe* assumed mainly a political role by receiving immigrants facing administrative difficulties while no concrete policy was implemented. In Lyon and in Nantes, the *adjointes* commanded more political capacities. They adopted the traditional rhetoric of the French Republic according to which the "integration" of individuals is produced by their political capacity. In that perspective, they considered voting rights as the major challenge for non-EU immigrants. As a consequence, they set up councils of foreign residents to facilitate the local political participation of immigrants. They also worked on the creation of specific administrative units dealing with inequalities immigrants faced (see below).

In 2008, after municipal elections, the three municipal *délégations* remained in place but with significant changes to their designations reflecting new approaches to immigrant incorporation policies. The notion of "integration" was replaced or complemented by the concepts of "citizenship", "fight against discrimination" or "equality". In Lyon, the *adjoint* was now in charge of "new ways of life and rights of citizens", in Nantes, it was "Integration, Equality, Citizenship" and in Strasbourg, one *adjointe* was in charge of "Citizenship, electoral affairs, and nationality affairs" and another of "urban development, fight against discrimination". Those changes signalled opposition to the national approach. The presidential campaign preceding the election of Nicolas Sarkozy in 2007 had been characterized by a discourse and policies in which the "integration" of immigrants was defined through the capacities of immigrants to respect French values such as secularity (Simon 2013). Contesting a perception of "integration" solely as an effort made by immigrants, all three municipal majorities insisted on the importance to also promote "citizenship" or to develop "non-discrimination" approaches in the governance of migration.

In Lyon, the *délégation* for "Culture, heritage and citizens' rights" went to a man in his sixties, of Armenian immigrant background, who held a central position in the city executive. Nevertheless, the political commitment to the governance of immigrants was weakened by the way in which the responsibilities of the *adjoint* were combined. Attaching the issue of "citizens' rights" to the portfolio of the deputy mayor in charge of "culture", a mainstay in city marketing policy, led to reduced investment in inhabitants' rights. Moreover, as immigrants' issues were included in "citizens' rights" a specific political commitment towards them was weakened.

In Strasbourg, two *adjoints* were in charge of immigrants and ethno-racial inequalities, one dealing with "citizenship", the other with "*politique de la ville*, discrimination, and youth policy". While they were relatively young (under forty), they had been strongly involved in the Socialist Party's youth organizations and held other local political mandates which gave them more power in the municipal majority. They adopted two kinds of discourses to promote immigrants' incorporation. The *adjointe* in charge of citizenship favoured a separation of "citizenship" and "nationality", the typical French integration model, that according to her "has run its course". As she argued "immigrants must be given the right to vote [locally]".[5] For her, this right was the main instrument for a political integration of immigrants, perceived as the major discrimination provoking social exclusion. The *adjoint* in charge of "*politique de la ville*, discrimination and youth policy" emphasized that the municipality had to address urban inequalities to facilitate the integration of excluded persons, including first and second generation of immigrants.[6] This municipal *délégation* linked spatial segregation and discrimination but without adopting a clear position on specific measures benefitting immigrants.

Lastly, in Nantes, the *adjointe* was reappointed and continued to emphasize "Equality" and "Citizenship". She also insisted that local citizenship should be encouraged. As in Strasbourg, she considered the right to vote in local elections, disconnected from French nationality, a crucial change needed to make immigrants feel members of the society. She also emphasized the necessity to fight ethno-racial discrimination, which threatened "equality" and thus the integration of immigrants.[7] However, with the arrival of a new city councilor in charge of equal treatment for city employees, she faced competition. The new policy frame proposed an equality policy targeting different groups (disabled people, women, seniors, ethnic minorities) mainly with municipal human resources measures. Whereas the appointment of two *adjoints* could have signalled a stronger engagement for immigrants, the split into two *délégations* lead to weaken a strong and generic policy on equality.

At first sight, the local political governance of immigrant issues was similar in all three cities. However, they adopted somewhat different perspectives on the mechanisms assumed to favour immigrants' incorporation. These different perspectives are embodied in the creation of new administrative units, *missions*, to deal with the governance of migration and to a larger extent with equality.

Municipal missions as instruments for different equality policies

The three *adjointes* created new administrative units, "missions", to support and implement their political programs. As Bezes (2009) demonstrates, this kind of administrative unit has spread in French administrations with the promotion of new public management. These administrative units are supposed to exist for a limited period and for a cross-sectorial issue with a strong political management ensured by the *adjoints*. In French cities, the "missions" mostly deal with environmental issues, urban policy (*politique de la ville*)[8] and immigrant incorporation policies. The creation of these *missions* also reflects the desire of the *adjoints* to be supported by a dedicated administrative unit.

Again, these similarities in the administrative local governance should not obscure the differences of the approaches towards immigrants – integration, equality, non-discrimination – reflected in the names given to the administrative units. In Lyon, the "Equality Mission" was created in 2005, whereas in Nantes, an "Integration mission" was formed in 2003 and renamed "Equality, Integration and Citizenship" mission in 2008. In Strasbourg, when the Left returned to power, two municipal *missions* were dedicated to "Local Democracy" (with a local civil servant dealing with the Council of Foreign Residents) and to "Preventing and Combating discrimination".

The city of Lyon chose to promote "equality" to honour the Republican promise of the equality of all individuals. In that context, the Equality Mission mainly promoted a non-discrimination policy in the recruitment process arguing that the urban administration should represent the "diversity" of the society and be a model for any other local actor.[9] Concretely, during two years, the Equality Mission proposed specific preparation-measures for public service examinations for minorities (women, people living in urban poor areas) and revised all recruitment processes to track possible discriminatory elements in the course of its candidature for the *"Label diversité"* (see Bereni, Epstein, Torres in this issue).[10] As Bereni and Epstein (2015) stress, this process eventually led to a reduced focus on ethno-racial discrimination in favour of other minority groups. More generally, while ethno-racial discrimination is mentioned in Lyon's framework documents[11], it is not a top priority for the civil servants of the Equality Mission. First, a focus on ethno-racial issues in their view contradicts the French principle of colourblindness.[12] Secondly, civil servants of the Equality Mission preferred to leave migration issues to the Mission for Cultural Cooperation whose main objective is to encourage the opening of cultural facilities to inhabitants living in deprived areas, often immigrants.[13] They continue a French tradition to deal with ethnic minorities only through positive action in some urban areas. Finally, ethno-racial discrimination was not central in discourses on "equality" or in measures promoting access to the local civil service for disadvantaged groups.

In contrast, in Nantes, the mission focused on immigrants, while weaving different approaches together. Some of the actions of the municipal mission were in line with the national measures for "integration" as they strongly supported French language courses, perceived as a major indicator of being "well integrated". Other measures reflected different perspectives on immigrant incorporation. The creation of the Council of Foreign residents pursued two objectives: disconnecting nationality from citizenship at the local level and training immigrants to participate in municipal consultative bodies where they were often underrepresented. The mission developed measures to combat discrimination, such as training civil servants to adopt non-discrimination attitudes when providing services. The coexistence of several frames – "integration", "equality", and "non-discrimination" – is characteristic of the political discourse and the tools adopted towards immigrants in Nantes. The head of the Mission considered it necessary for conducting an ambitious policy towards immigrants.

> Perhaps in the next term, [the new Equality Mission] will deal with fighting against discrimination, with diversity, and with equality, and it would be a mistake to drop the matter of integration. [...] Some cities have put everything into the fight against discrimination. It makes no sense; we are not going to explain the difference in the five-fold unemployment rate among non-EU foreigners solely by discrimination. There are many other factors as well.[14]

In Strasbourg, the division into two missions, one dedicated to citizenship and the other to combatting discrimination, reflected the perception that "integration" is possible through the promotion of a local citizenship whereas ethno-racial inequalities could be addressed through non-discrimination measures. However, as one community activist pointed out, the immigrant incorporation policy mainly relies on the Council of Foreign Residents, a narrow way to address the challenges faced by immigrants.[15] In fact, while the chief of the Preventing and Combating Discrimination Mission declared ethno-racial discrimination as equally important as gender or age, she admitted that no major action had been implemented other than supporting a working group dedicated to that thematic in the Council of Foreign Residents. She explained this choice by pointing out that the *politique de la ville* already dealt with ethno-racial inequalities,[16] albeit without saying so.

All three French cities investigated here introduced political and administrative responsibilities for the governance of immigrants. Political factors, in particular the left-wing orientations of the governing majorities are important to understand the investment in that topic but do not fully explain the divergent discourses and measures adopted by the municipal *délégations* and *missions*. The following section will turn to the factors explaining similarities and differences of the city's approaches.

Factors determining immigrant incorporation policies

As I argue below, similarity is mainly noticeable with regard to organizational aspects (municipal *délégations*, *missions*), and it is due to two principal external factors: the relationship with national authorities and the increasing opportunities offered by European Union authorities and European city networks. At the same time, the differences in the municipal policies can mainly be explained with reference to two factors: the capacities associations have to influence the city agenda and the career paths of local civil servants. In consequence, the attention to immigrant interests varied between the three cities and policies sometimes addressed ethno-racial inequalities, and sometimes did not.

European metropolis in opposition to their national governments

The creation of municipal *délégations* on "integration" and/or "equality" in Lyon and Nantes and the subsequent establishment of two city missions took place at a time when the central state, embodied by Interior Minister Nicolas Sarkozy, the later President, adopted an increasingly repressive migration policy (Carvalho and Geddes 2012). The discourse on "national identity" was marked by a focus on knowledge of and commitment to French Republican values (mainly secularity, equality between men and women) by newcomers or applicants for French nationality and on the fight against illegal migration. The turn to hardening migration policies and to presenting immigrants as threatening "national identity" led elected officials in some cities to adopting discourses and policies insisting on the recognition of immigrants as part and parcel of the society and on the existence of socio-economic inequalities that immigrants suffered from.

The *adjointe* in Nantes emphasized the need to support immigrants' rights given the "Le Pen-ization of minds".[17] Her opposition to national choices motivated the political leadership in Nantes to promote political equality and local citizenship to incorporate immigrants. The discourse on national identity served as an adversary and to justify the development of new tools. The council of foreign residents emphasized the legal discrimination immigrants faced and which they perceived as one major element of their social exclusion. In that perspective, it is not immigrants who have to make an effort to become incorporated, but the welcoming society.

In Lyon, elected representatives reunited members of local NGOs in 2002 in a working group to make recommendations for a better "social integration" in the city.[18] The members stressed the deficiencies of national policies in promoting equality for all and combating discrimination.[19] Above all, political leaders wanted to ensure a leadership role for Lyon at the national level on equality issues and to become one of the most active European cities on that topic.[20] The city was the first to apply for the national label "Diversity", a visible indicator of its commitment. Promoting equality and distinguishing oneself from the national rhetoric contributed to a global ambition of Lyon as a major innovative European metropolis.

In Strasbourg, the creation of the city mission was the combined result of a new majority opposing both the national government and the former right-wing municipal majority. The civil servant in charge of the Preventing and Combating Discrimination Mission stressed the political desire of the mayor to emphasize differences with the former political majority, especially on minorities. In that context, the mayor re-established a Council for Foreign Residents[21] in order to stress that, as in Nantes, the exclusion of immigrant from the right to vote was a major problem and not only the efforts made by immigrants to adopt French values. Equally, the *adjointe* in charge of citizenship argued that the ending of the Council of Foreign Residents reflected their unwillingness to work on ethno-racial inequalities and to promote the political integration of immigrants.[22]

The commitment of local politicians to equality and the creation of the municipal missions was part of a strategy of opposition to the national authorities in a context of restrictive migration policies and a "national identity" rhetoric. Cities affirmed, in similar ways, their independence from the national frame on immigrants' incorporation. These similar processes point to the politicization of the migration issue at the local level in left-wing cities when a conservative party governs at the national level. However, as outlined before, opposition was not always translated into concrete measures in favour of immigrants.

The role of European Union resources for the development of equality policies

The progressive institutionalization of urban immigrant policies was also the result of a "bottom-up Europeanization" of French municipalities. European funding opportunities and European city networks supported the measures of Lyon and Nantes in favour of immigrants and supported, to some extent and with different timing, the institutionalization of relevant municipal policies.

In Lyon, the European level played a role in the early design of the local equality policy as the creation of the Equality mission was inspired by a European city exchange project, "Multicultural cities and racial discrimination" (2001–2003), during which local politicians and members of the working group on integration met the Equality Mission team in Birmingham.[23] Moreover, the mobilization of the European Social Fund conditioned the recruitment of a civil servant dedicated to equality. Consequently, Europe was a dominant factor in the development of a policy, with a dedicated administrative unit, on equality in Lyon. Besides, the head of the Equality Mission was member of the working group "Migration & Integration" of the city network *Eurocities* between 2006 and 2010 and participated in a peer review project on the governance of migration. European involvement gave him resources to ensure political leaders that working on equality policy was a major topic of any European metropolis.

In Nantes, European discourse and funding was not at the beginning of the policy towards immigrants. However, both local politicians and civil servants consider the European investment in city networks as a major element in legitimizing their policies within the municipal administration (Flamant 2014). In Nantes, the *adjointe* in charge of integration took time to investigate other European cities before proposing a Mission dedicated to immigrants.[24] Participation in the working group "Migration & Integration" of *Eurocities* has also been a regular activity for the chief of the Equality and Integration Mission since 2007. With that participation, he said that he becomes familiar with European funding. Nantes managed to obtain funding from the European Fund of Integration in 2012 to produce a movie on the living conditions of elderly immigrants and to publish a leaflet on the services dedicated to immigrants in Nantes in four languages.

In Strasbourg, in spite of the geographical closeness of European institutions, the European scene was initially not considered by the new *adjointe*. She joined a network of cities and experts in 2010, the CLIP (*Cities for Local*

Integration Policies) network, in order to better develop local policy towards immigrants, but at first remained uncommitted.

While Europe was an external factor that supported the discourse and implementation of their immigrant incorporation policies, the timing of the three cities' European involvement differed. As Downing (2015) stressed for culture policies, the major difficulty for French cities at the European level is to work in a universe in which the policy frame is based on the recognition of ethnic minorities. In fact, the chief of the Equality Mission in Lyon ended his participation in the working group "Migration & Integration" because "the British approach to equality"[25] was too dominant in the exchanges between cities and incompatible with French universalism. As the municipality of Lyon progressively affirmed an equality policy characterized by ignoring ethno-racial discrimination, the civil servant faced difficulties in interacting with his European peers. In Nantes, the strong commitment of the Equality and Integration Mission to work on the migration issue facilitated their membership in the working group. Moreover, while recognizing the difference to the French approach to migration, the chief of the *mission* ensured that investing in the European level gives access to resources for designing and funding policies towards migrants that are not strongly supported at national level.[26] In the case of Strasbourg, the investment in the European scene is mainly the result of personal initiatives of the *adjointe* in charge of citizenship. She participated in European events to grasp some information on other municipal experience and bring back some new ideas.

For all three cities, the European level was a factor in defining and encouraging the development of their policies towards immigrants.

The ability of local associations to influence the municipal agenda

In all three places studied, a large number of immigrants' rights and community associations exist, mainly established since the 1980s (Flamant 2017, 62–64). However, their relations with the city administration differ, leading to different weight to their claims to consider immigrants as a specific target group. If they had little weight in municipal politics in Lyon because of internal conflict, they managed to be heard in Nantes and in Strasbourg and to participate in the implementation of municipal tools.

In Lyon, associations defending the rights of immigrants dominate as interlocutors of the city, while community associations enjoy little recognition. The associations representing immigrants have been in strong conflict with each other since the late 1990s about the approach to undocumented immigrants. These tensions restrict their ability to speak to city authorities with a united voice and to demand an active policy in favour of immigrants. Given this history and a focus on the recruitment process, the Equality Mission preferred to seek advice from academics specialized in law and human resources and to nominate them as members of its working groups on equality. The absence of activist familiar with the difficulties faced by immigrants in the municipal councils dedicated to equality contributed to the minimization of ethno-racial inequalities in the measures adopted. Thus, the Equality Mission does not consider this thematic a priority, and it is dealt with just within the *politique de la ville*.

The cooperation between associations and city governments in Nantes and Strasbourg was stronger as the capacity of civil society to be united enabled them to adopt a common discourse and to participate in developing munici-pal policy. In Nantes, the associations representing immigrants created umbrella organizations to combat at the local level the national migration policy and to campaign for local policies in favour of immigrants. The *adjointe* considered these activists as partners to contest national migration policies and hopes that, as a consequence, they will not contest the municipal measures.[27] The local administration sought the advice of these associations in designing the municipal integration policy. They insisted upon the neces-sity to go beyond criticizing the national agenda and to implement concrete measures at the municipal level. They supported the idea of a dedicated *mission* in the municipal administration and asked to be members of the Council for Foreign Residents. As actors in that Council, they were a driving force in extending the local policy to the welcoming of all documented and undocumented immigrants. Thus, the Council produced a leaflet containing the contacts of all associations dealing with immigrants in Nantes. Plus, they were committed to changing the representation of immigrants and helped with the organization of an exhibition on migration in Nantes. This rec-ognition enabled them to demand municipal subsidies to recruit a coordina-tor of all the associations involved in the defense of immigrants. The associations positioned themselves as the most qualified actors to assess the needs of immigrants and to design some tools to welcome immigrants.

Relations between immigrants' defense associations and the Strasbourg city administration were characterized by considerable conflict between 2001 and 2008 after the dissolution of the Council for Foreign Residents. When the Socialists returned to lead the city government in 2008, CARES[28] was asked by the deputy mayor in charge of citizenship to develop a new version of the Strasbourg Council of Foreign Residents. Cooperation with that umbrella association was at the heart of the policy towards immigrants. During the meetings of the Council, activists claimed to go beyond political integration and to consider discrimination first and second-generation immigrants suffered from. Finally, they inquired on housing and urban equality and managed to get one activist appointed as a member of the municipal commission that distributes social housing to ensure that immigrants are not discriminated against.[29] The involvement of these associations lead to the greater prominence of the fight against discrimination in the municipality and contributed to the creation of the Preventing and Fighting Mission in 2012.

If the associations were able to speak collectively, as in Nantes and in Strasbourg, they had the capacities to demand policies not only on the political integration of immigrants but on a welcoming policy and on the fight against discrimination. They managed to be actors of the municipal policies created, especially the councils of foreign residents, and sometimes to initiate local measures furthering immigrants' incorporation. They sided with local civil servants who saw immigrants as a core target of equality policies.

The career paths of local civil servants

The last factor impacting urban policies are the local civil servants in charge of them. While they are officially implementing measures promoted by *adjoints,* these civil servants have the opportunity to shape the agenda and to resist specific political constraints and orientations (Biland 2012). These political capacities of the local civil servants are all the more important in the case of migration as they had specific knowledge while their deputy mayor and the heads of the *missions* were new to the issue. In fact, the very small *mission* teams (3 members in Nantes, 6 in Lyon, 2 in Strasbourg) were headed by people who had dealt with the migration issue in their previous functions. In Nantes and in Strasbourg, the two mission heads had their first professional experience in the *politique de la ville*, in which several national policies dealing with the "integration of immigrants" were implemented. Furthermore, they had participated in the first national programs at the end of the nineties that slightly shifted from "integration" to "non-discrimination" These experiences were major factors leading these civil servants to connect discourses on integration, citizenship and non-discrimination and develop appropriate local measures such as the support for the Councils of Foreign residents or training on non-discrimination processes. This mixed approach is perceived as a way of dealing with all the challenges faced by immigrants. The local civil servant in Strasbourg and one of the Nantes civil servants were also activists in local associations defending immigrants. Against that background, they were reluctant to promote "diversity" or any measure tackling equality without focusing on immigrants as they perceived that as abandoning the issue of ethno-racial inequalities.

In contrast, the career paths of the local civil servants in Lyon are characterized by experiences in human resources more than in *politique de la ville*, by discourses on the recognition of diversity of individuals and not on structural ethno-racial inequalities and lack of experience in associations defending immigrants. For instance, the head of the Equality Mission led several projects for private companies in which he advocated the recognition of "diversity" and the promotion of all individual capacities. With this background, he promoted a generic approach to equality over a non-discrimination policy and relied on consultants specialized in the management of "diversity" in the working groups of the Equality Mission. He believes that the socio-economic disadvantages of immigrants should be dealt with by neighbourhood or cultural policies, while issues related to the reception and living conditions of immigrants are referred to as the city's social services. Ethno-racial inequalities are thus minimalized in Lyon's equality policy.

In all the three cases, local civil servants with their specific experiences influenced the choice of measures and the extent to which immigrants were considered a relevant target group.

Discussion and conclusion

This article demonstrates that while in all three French cities, immigrants were a target group of local policy, the shape of immigrant incorporation policy was not uniform. The issue of immigrant rights could be diluted, or even abandoned, in a generic and unspecific approach to equality policy that did not include specific measures for immigrants. By illustrating such different paths, this article enriches the literatures on the "local turn" of immigrant incorporation policies and provides insights into the treatment of ethno-racial inequalities in a colour blind country.

First of all, my research confirms that in the beginning of the 2000s some French cities, as in other European countries, developed a growing interest in dealing with integration issues and producing local answers to the challenge of ethno-racial diversity (Penninx et al. 2004). Moreover, this "local turn" was politicized in France as the development of a municipal policy towards immigrants mainly occurred in center-left cities, confirming the research of Martinez-Ariño and al (2018). However, dominant political orientations do not sufficiently explain how immigrants are governed locally. A comparison of similar cities in terms of political background in the same national context can demonstrate how similarities in the political and administrative structures to govern immigrants can be accompanied by strong divergence in the concepts favoured and in the consideration of the migration issue in their equality policy.

My investigation demonstrated the benefits of going beyond the discourses on "integration", "equality" or "non-discrimination" by analysing the way migration is dealt with in actual policies. I argue that four factors influence the design of the governance of migration: the relationship with the national governments, the European level through its funding and its peer exchanges, the capacities of civil society to bring and to keep migration on the municipal agenda and the career paths of local civil servants in charge of the municipal equality policy. The "local turn" in the governance of immigrants is neither an automatic nor a uniform process. Further research may want to clarify whether the same four factors are equally influential in other national contexts.

Third, my comparison underlines that the specific French unwillingness to recognize ethno-racial inequalities is an additional element that contributes to weakening any equality policy targeting immigrants. Nonetheless, the European level, especially transnational exchanges between cities, offers resources for local civil servants and local politicians to step outside their national constraints and to be an actor in international urban competition.

Finally, this article invites researchers to continue the investigation of the local governance of migration by considering especially local civil servants in charge of equality policies. New knowledge will be gained by considering the multi-level governance of immigrants together with the role of this specific group of civil servants in municipal policies. It will enable us to understand the fragile institutionalization of city policies that tackle ethno-racial inequalities.

Notes

1. I use the term "immigrants" throughout to refer to first-generation immigrants. French cities use the terms "immigré", "foreigner", "with a migrant background" for the first and sometimes second generation, which illustrates the difficulties in acknowledging ethnic minorities in the French Republic. I will specify when policies and tools focus on both generations of immigrants.
2. This model is supposed to be equal because of the officially proclaimed formal equality between individuals, regardless of gender, age, ethnicity or disabilities.
3. I refer to "foreign born" or *immigré* as defined in the national census. An *immigré* is a person who was born in a foreign country as a foreigner and who is living in France, with or without French citizenship.
4. A "*délégation*" in French cities is the topics an *adjoint* is responsible for during his or her political mandate.
5. Interview 1, deputy mayor for citizenship, Strasbourg, 2010.
6. Observation of the meeting of the Council of Foreign Residents, 2012.
7. Interview 2, deputy mayor for integration, equality, citizenship, Nantes, 2011.
8. The *politique de la ville* is the policy dedicated to the renewal of deprived urban areas. This positive action is a method to target ethnic minorities who are major inhabitants of these neighborhoods without naming them (Tissot 2007).
9. Lyon Municipal Archives, 2253 WP 11, Final report on the non-discrimination policy, 2008.
10. The label « Diversity » is a national label public and private companies can apply for to gain recognition for their efforts to promote diversity.
11. Equality Mission, Annual report on discrimination, 2013.
12. Equality Mission. Annual report on discrimination, 2013.
13. Interview 3, Head of the Equality Mission, Lyon, 2010.
14. Interview 4, Head of the Equality and Integration Mission, Nantes, 2011.
15. Interview 5, member of the council, Strasbourg, 2012.
16. Interview 6, Head of the Mission for Preventing and Combating discrimination, 2012.
17. Interview 2.
18. Lyon Municipal Archives, 2084 WP 1, Working document, Initiative Group for Integration in the City, 2002.
19. Report on housing, Initiative Group for Integration in the City, 2004.

20. Interview 7, member of the working group, July 2010.
21. Interview 6.
22. Interview 1.
23. Lyon Municipal Archives, 2084 WP 1, Working document, Initiative Group for Integration in the City, 2002.
24. Interview 2.
25. Interview 3.
26. Interview 4.
27. Interview 2.
28. La Coordination des Associations de Résidents Étrangers Strasbourgeois [Coordination of Associations of Foreign Strasbourg Residents] was created in 1989 to campaign for local voting rights for immigrants.
29. Interview 8, member of the council, Strasbourg, 2013.

Disclosure statement

No potential conflict of interest was reported by the author(s).

References

Alexander, Michael. 2003. "Local Policies Toward Migrants as an Expression of Host-Stranger Relations: A Proposed Typology." *Journal of Ethnic and Migration Studies* 29 (3): 411–430. doi:10.1080/13691830305610.

Alexander, Michael. 2006. *Cities and Labour Immigration: Comparing Policy Responses in Amsterdam, Paris, Rome and Tel Aviv*. London: Ashgate Publishing.

Amiraux, Valérie, and Patrick Simon. 2006. "There Are No Minorities Here: Cultures of Scholarship and Public Debate on Immigrants and Integration in France." *International Journal of Comparative Sociology* 47 (3–4): 191–215. doi:10.1177/0020715206066164.

Avanza, Martine. 2010. Qui représentent les élus de la « diversité »: Croyances partisanes et points de vue de « divers ». *Revue française de science politique* 60 (4): 745–767. doi:10.3917/rfsp.604.0745.

Babels. 2018. *Entre accueil et rejet. Ce que les villes font aux migrants*. Lyon: Le Passager clandestin.

Bereni, Laure. 2009. "Faire de la diversité une richesse pour l'entreprise." *Raisons politiques* 35 (3): 87–106. doi:10.3917/rai.035.0087.

Bereni, Laure, and Renaud Epstein. 2015. *Instrumenter la lutte contre les discriminations: le "Label Diversité" dans les collectivités territoriales*. Paris: Rapport ARDIS.

Bezes, Philippe. 2009. *Réinventer l'Etat: les réformes de l'administration française*. Paris: Presses de Sciences Po.

Biland, Émilie. 2012. "Les transformations générationnelles de la politisation dans les collectivités Territoriales." *Politix* 96 (4): 17–37. doi:10.3917/pox.096.0017.

Brubaker, Rogers. 1992. *Citizenship and Nationhood in France and in Germany*. London: Harvard University Press.

Calves, Gwenaelle. 2016. *La discrimination positive*. Paris: PUF.

Caponio, Tiziana, and Maren Borkert. 2010. *The Local Dimension of Migration Policymaking*. Amsterdam: Amsterdam University Press.

Caponio, Tiziana, Peter Scholten, and Ricardo Zapata-Barrero. 2017. "Theorizing the 'Local Turn' in a Multi-Level Governance Framework of Analysis: A Case Study in

Immigrant Policies." *International Review of Administrative Science* 83 (2): 245–250. doi:10.1177/0020852316688426.

Caponio, Tiziana, Peter Scholten, and Ricardo Zapata-Barrero. 2018. *The Routledge Handbook of the Governance of Migration and Diversity in Cities*. London: Routledge.

Carvalho, Joan, and Andrew Geddes. 2012. "La politique d'immigration sous Sarkozy. Le retour à l'identité nationale." In *Les politiques publiques sous Sarkozy*, edited by Jacques de Maillard and Yves Surel, 279–298. Paris: Presses de Sciences Po.

Chappe, Vincent-Arnaud, Mireille Eberhard, and Cécile Guillaume. 2016. "La Fabrique des Discriminations." *Terrains & Travaux* 29: 5–19. doi:10.3917/tt.029.0005.

Dekker, Rianne, Henrik Emilsson, Bernahrd Krieger, and Peter Scholten. 2015. "A Local Dimension of Integration Policies? A Comparative Study of Berlin, Malmö, and Rotterdam." *International Migration Review* 49 (3): 633–658. doi:10.1111/imre.12133.

Downing, Joseph. 2015. "European Influence on Diversity Policy Frames: Paradoxical Outcomes of Lyon's Membership of the Intercultural Cities Program." *Ethnic and Racial Studies* 38 (9): 1557–1572. doi:10.1080/01419870.2014.996241.

Entzinger, Han. 2005. "Politiques d'intégration en Europe : un modèle multidimensionnel." In *Les minorités ethniques dans l'Union européenne*, edited by Lionel Arnaud, 25–45. Paris: La Découverte.

Fassin, Eric. 2002. "L'invention française de la discrimination." *Revue Française de Science Politique* 52 (4): 403–423. doi:10.3917/rfsp.524.0403.

Fassin, Didier, and Éric Fassin. 2006. *De la question sociale à la question raciale ? Représenter la société française*. Paris: La Découverte.

Flamant, Anouk. 2014. "Droit de cité ! Construction et dilution d'une politique municipale d'intégration des étrangers" dans les villes de Lyon, Nantes et Strasbourg (1981–2012)." PhD diss., University of Lyon.

Flamant, Anouk. 2017. "Les cadres de l'action publique locale en charge des politiques d'intégration des étrangers." *Politique européenne* 57 (3): 84–115. doi:10.3917/poeu.057.0084.

Fourot, Aude-Claire. 2013. *L'intégration des immigrants: cinquante ans d'action publique locale*. Montréal: Presses de l'Université de Montréal.

Garbaye, Romain. 2005. *Getting Into Local Power: The Politics of Ethnic Minorities in British and French Cities*. London: Blackwell Publishing.

Hepburn, Eve, and Ramon Zapata-Barrero. 2014. *The Politics of Immigration in Multi-Level States*. Oxford: Palgrave Macmillan.

Jorgensen, Martin. 2012. "The Diverging Logics of Integration Policy Making at National and City Level." *International Migration Review* 46 (1): 244–278. doi:10.1111/j.1747-7379.2012.00886.x.

Lacroix, Thomas, and Alexandra Desille. 2018. *International Migrations and Local Governance*. Oxford: Palgrave Macmillan.

Martinez-Ariño, Julia, Michalis Moutselos, Karen Schönwälder, Christian Jacobs, Maria Schiller, and Alexandre Tandé. 2018. "Why Do Some Cities Adopt More Diversity Policies Than Others? A Study in France and Germany." *Comparative European Politics* 17 (5): 651–672. doi:(…)57/s41295-018-0119-0.

Penninx, Rinus, Karen Kraal, Marco Martiniello, and Steven Vertovec. 2004. *Citizenship in European Cities: Immigrants, Local Politics and Integration Policies*. Aldershot: Ashgate.

Poppelaars, Caelesta, and Peter Scholten. 2008. "Two Worlds Apart: The Divergence of National and Local Immigrant Integration Policies in the Netherlands." *Administration & Society* 40 (4): 335–357. doi:10.1177/0095399708317172.

Sabbagh, D., and S. Peer. 2008. "French Color Blindness in Perspective: The Controversy Over "Statistiques Ethniques": Introduction." *French Politics, Culture & Society* 26 (1): 1–6. doi:10.3167/fpcs.2008.260101.

Safi, Mirna. 2017. "Promoting Diversity in French Workplaces: Targeting and Signaling Ethnoracial Origin in a Colorblind Context." *Socius: Sociological Research for a Dynamic World.* doi:10.1177/2378023117728834.

Schiller, Maria. 2015. "Paradigmatic Pragmatism and the Politics of Diversity." *Ethnic and Racial Studies* 38 (7): 1120–1136. doi:10.1080/01419870.2014.992925.

Schiller, Maria. 2016. *European Cities, Municipal Organizations and Diversity. The New Politics of Difference.* London: Palgrave Macmillan.

Scholten, Peter. 2013. "Agenda Dynamics and the Multi-Level Governance of Intractable Policy Controversies: The Case of Migrant Integration Policies in the Netherlands." *Policy Sciences* 46 (3): 217–236. doi:10.1007/s11077-012-9170-x.

Scholten, Peter, and Rinus Penninx. 2016. "The Multilevel Governance of Migration and Integration." In *Integration Processes and Policies in Europe*, edited by Garcés-Mascarenas Blanca and Rinus Penninx, 91–108. Amsterdam: Springer.

Seawright, Jason, and John Gerring. 2008. "Case Selection Techniques in Case Study Research: A Menu of Qualitative and Quantitative Options." *Political Research Quarterly* 61 (2): 294–308. doi:10.1177/1065912907313077.

Simon, Patrick. 2008. "The Choice of Ignorance: The Debate on Ethnic and Racial Statistics in France." *French Politics, Culture & Society* 26 (1): 7–31. doi:10.3167/fpcs.2008.260102.

Simon, Patrick. 2013. "Contested Citizenship in France: The Republican Politics of Identity and Integration." In *Developments in French Politics*, edited by Alistair Cole, Alistair Meunier, and Vincent Tiberj, 203–217. Basingstoke: Palgrave Macmillan.

Tissot, Sylvie. 2007. *L'Etat et les quartiers: Genèse d'une catégorie de l'action publique.* Paris: Seuil.

Vertovec, Steven. 2007. "Super-Diversity and Its Implications." *Ethnic and Racial Studies* 30 (6): 1024–1054. doi:10.1080/01419870701599465.

What explains diversity-policy adoption? Policy entrepreneurs and advocacy coalitions in two French cities

Michalis Moutselos ⓘ

ABSTRACT
When it comes to public policies that recognize and accommodate ethnic, cultural and religious diversity, cities are active and innovative. However, policy adoption can differ greatly from case to case, with different policy processes leading to different types of instruments across local contexts. This paper focuses on two cases from France, a country usually associated with hostility towards recognizing group-based diversity. In Marseille, there has been a decades-long consensus around group-based multiculturalism. The impetus has come from mayors ("policy entrepreneurs") of both the centre-left and the centre-right. In Grenoble, the uninterrupted dominance of a strong left-wing administration has infused diversity policy with more traditional themes, such as anti-discrimination, universalist participation and civil-society support in the city's stigmatized southern neighbourhoods. The study demonstrates that local-level diversity policy may feature a mix of multicultural, intercultural and universalist elements, and that tracing local policy processes can explain puzzling policy outcomes..

European city administrations are increasingly developing policy instruments and adopting discourses that target the ethnic, cultural and religious diversity – henceforth "diversity" – of their populations (see, among others, Flamant 2017; White 2017; Martínez-Ariño et al. 2019). Locally implemented policies for the recognition, representation and redistribution of resources favouring previously disadvantaged segments of city populations with a minority background (Vertovec 2012) are coupled with normative and discursive openings towards embracing the image of a diverse or inclusive city (Moutselos et al. 2020). On the heels of policy innovation, policy diffusion assumes the form of "diversity labels" and networks of "intercultural cities", "rainbow cities" or "cities of migration" (for an overview focussing mostly on networks sharing experiences with integration policies, see Penninx 2015).

Our knowledge about how the introduction of diversity policies takes place in cities, in other words, how, when and under whose auspices policy change occurs or how city officials consolidate a diversity policy framework is gradually becoming more systematic (see, along with special issue, Caponio, Scholten, and Zapata-Barrero 2019). Which diversity policy instruments do local authorities choose to retain for their cities? What types of urban actors among local politicians, administration and civil society actors are involved in their implementation? In addition, as is the case with most policy innovations, the very actors and processes that lead to initial adoption may privilege certain instruments over others; in other words, "diversity policy" may end up assuming different characteristics in different cities reflecting differential ideological orientations, local path dependencies and access to power of different disadvantaged groups. The present paper aims at applying theories of policy adoption and consolidation in cities to the specific case of diversity policy, two fields that have rarely been studied together. It also attempts to situate the empirical analysis of local diversity policy adoption and consolidation in the broader debates about multiculturalism and interculturalism (see Antonsich 2016; Good 2018).

Empirical investigations of this topic suggest that left-wing and centre-left city councils are more likely to introduce policies that accommodate diversity (de Graauw and Vermeulen 2016; Martínez-Ariño et al. 2019 for France), whether to offer ways to combat discrimination or to represent previously disadvantaged groups. However, this view of left-wing politicians as "policy entrepreneurs" (Mintrom and Norman 2009) for consolidating such policies is empirically nuanced by the willingness of many centre-right mayors to consolidate the image of their city as diversity-friendly. Alternatively, successful progressive mayors who do not see the need to change a winning formula by introducing new policies may opt for inertia or incrementalism. I explore here two such seemingly counter-intuitive cases from France: the city of Marseille, where the centre-right city hall has woven the recognition of ethno-religious groups and a "soft" multiculturalism into the fabric of policy and official discourse; and the city of Grenoble, where one of the historically left-wing municipal councils in the country has not emphasized the recognition and promotion of group-based diversity, but resorted to other policy frameworks (universalism, international solidarity, interculturalism) to deal with local diversity.

The lessons drawn from the two case studies are fourfold: First, French cities can be innovative in dealing with the diversity of their populations (see also Martínez-Ariño 2018). Second, in terms of local policy process, French centre-left mayors are likely to instigate change in this field, but the centre-right can choose to sustain policy innovations initiated by the left.

This explains the puzzling Marseille case. To be sure, a business-friendly view of diversity is more likely to appeal to the centre-right and inform discourse and policy, while social justice for disadvantaged groups may not be equally emphasized. Third, the centre-left in France may introduce policy instruments at the local level, which help, *de facto*, disadvantaged ethnic, religious and cultural groups, but do not necessarily foreground group-based diversity as a principle of policymaking. As the example of Grenoble demonstrates, a strong progressive policy framework – under conditions of an absence of electoral pressures or a crisis – can develop at the expense of group-specific policymaking. Fourth and relatedly, as historical institutionalists have long argued, local actors are more likely to instigate change when they face some kind of crisis; in the case of Marseille, it was a political and social crisis facing the local socialist party in the 1980s, as well as a rise in inter-ethnic and cultural tensions. Grenoble did not face a similar crisis and the local left-wing mayors did not prioritize group-based policies to appease inter-group relations, but incorporated new "diversity actors" (primarily anti-discrimination activists) in a strong, pre-existing network of local associations.

The next section defines the terms of analysis, including a discussion of diversity policy instruments, and explains in some detail the case selection and data, before laying out hypotheses drawn from theories of the policy process. I then test the hypotheses through case studies of the two cities and finally present conclusions about empirical variation in local diversity policies and lessons about how they are introduced and consolidated at the local level.

Research design, data, definitions, and theoretical expectations

There is a well-established scholarly consensus that the French state does not recognize groups as the target of public policy, a domain reserved for individual citizens (Simon and Sala Pala 2010, 94–97). However, developments in the last two decades, such as "positive discrimination" based on territory (Blanc 2010) and the institutionalization of measures for gender equality (Bereni 2015) have provided openings for the recognition and restitution of group-based demands. In addition, French lawmakers have passed ever-more sweeping anti-discrimination legislation, which does not target groups, but prejudices anti-discriminatory actions based on assumed group characteristics (Fassin 2002). With regard to discourse, public officials and private actors in France now use the term diversity (*diversité*) more widely and positively (see Sénac 2012 for a critical overview of developments). These innovations have resulted from initiatives of several disparate actors, rather than the introduction of a new, coherent policy paradigm, but they alter the image of a monolithic "republican" model in French policy-making.

The research design in this paper operates at two levels, the national and the sub-national. As already noted, France is itself a "least-likely" country case for diversity policy (Rohlfing 2012, 84–88), because it has traditionally been associated with policies ignoring group-based differences. Within France, Grenoble and Marseille are, at least at first sight, two "least-likely cases" for observed policy outcomes because the right-wing city hall in Marseille has implemented group-based policy instruments, while the left-wing city hall in Grenoble has not prioritized such policy instruments. As a comparative case study of subnational variation within one country, the paper aims to highlight local-level processes in policymaking, while holding national-level factors constant; as a congruence analysis of two cases with surprising policy outcomes (Blatter and Haverland 2012, 27–29), it seeks to contribute to hypothesis-testing and an improvement of available explanatory frameworks regarding the introduction of diversity policies in cities. The data used in this article stem from resorting to diverse sets documents, such as political memoires, official statements, reports/announcements issued by the city hall and civil society actors in the two cities, municipal council minutes, local and national newspaper reports and secondary literature on local political histories. The author also conducted field research and semi-structured interviews with politicians, urban planners and civil society representatives in Marseille in June-July 2013. In terms of comparability, Marseille and Grenoble both feature large immigrant populations (around 15 per cent foreign-born in the early-2010s, and above the national average),[1] a large percentage of which originated from former French colonies in Africa. There is therefore a "functional need" for introducing new programmes and practices (Dobbin, Kim, and Kalev 2011, 387) based on local demographics. Diversity in Marseille is deemed more visible than in Grenoble, because higher shares of immigrant-origin populations from former French colonies inhabit its city centre and because the port city has historically received large migratory waves (Mitchell 2011). However, it is not clear why this visibility should lead to the explicit endorsement of diversity policies or discursive nods towards "communities" – many similarly "diverse" municipalities in Southern France or in the Paris region have not opted for explicitly pro-diversity policy frameworks.

Public diversity policies, which provide a common thread for this special issue, can be defined as "policy instruments aiming to adjust the public administration and its services to a heterogeneous population and to publicly acknowledge the sociocultural diversity of the population" (Martínez-Ariño et al. 2019, 2). They serve to provide the redistribution of resources, recognition of presence, representation in government and provision of public goods that redresses the handicaps historically weighing down certain groups, for instance ethnic, religious and racial minorities, but also sexual minorities (Eisenberg and Kymlicka 2011; Vertovec 2012). At the level of cities this means, in concrete terms and for the purposes of the analysis here policies

that combine material and discursive elements, such as training and recruitment for the city administration in a way that takes the increasing diversity
of the population into account; formal or informal quota rules for the city
council; city hall funding for associations explicitly promoting diversity; establishing anti-discrimination offices; the public recognition of previously disadvantaged groups in speeches/public statements, festivals and public spaces.

These policy instruments have been selected because they serve the
broader policy functions of administration, service provision, representation
and recognition (see also Martínez-Ariño et al. 2019). They complement
each other, but may be introduced in waves and implemented gradually.
They combine elements of group-based multiculturalism, for instance in
terms of targeted recruitment at the local administration, or recognition in
public spaces, but they also include "intercultural" policy instruments, for
instance in promoting broader diversity training, protecting rights of individuals of diverse backgrounds and providing opportunities for interaction in
public spaces, for instance in festivals and inter-religious forums (see Antonsich 2016). It is, however, important that such policies are explicitly targeting
individuals or groups on the basis of ethnic, religious or otherwise diverse cultural background, so any redistributive policies (for instance through schooling, transportation or housing policy) that have an indirect impact on these
segments of the populations are not included in the analysis here. Furthermore, my focus is on policies that fall under the competences of city administrations and do not simply reflect the implementation of national laws and
directives.

French cities are increasingly interested in such policies. In 2011 a study
conducted in twelve large cities (Marseille and Grenoble were not included)
showed that many French mayors actively engage in some kind of diversity
policy-making, as defined and operationalized above. For instance, they
appoint adjunct mayors in charge of a related portfolio, take actions to
combat discrimination, organize events that inform citizens about diversity
issues, and help religious associations in their handlings with the city administration (although no funding is provided) (Association des Maires de grandes
villes de France 2011). This trend is particularly visible in cities that are historically left-wing or have had a progressive mayor for a long period, such as
Rennes, Lille, Lyon, Montpellier and Nantes (Bereni and Epstein 2015; Martínez-Ariño 2018; Flamant this special issue). Many of them have adopted a
specific strategic choice to present themselves as "diversity-friendly".

Why would French cities innovate in the diversity field? A canonical literature on the policy process offers explanations for the adoption (or lack
thereof) and eventual consolidation of diversity policies. The "multiple
streams" theory of policy change (Kingdon [1984] 1995) introduces the idea
of the "policy entrepreneur" who aligns a problem stream – a specific
interpretation of an existing problem in the public realm –, the policy

stream – concrete policy instruments that offer a solution –, and the politics stream – the political coalition necessary to implement policy change. In the case of diversity policies in French cities, the empirical implication is that progressive activist mayors with disproportionate agenda-setting power act as the "policy entrepreneurs", exploiting windows of opportunity to "surf" on a salient problem and provide their preferred policy solutions (Boscarino 2009). Policy entrepreneurs are also likely to introduce new policy paradigms by turning their cities into nodes of "policy diffusion" from other cities or levels of government (Berry and Berry [2007] 2018). Indeed, French mayors are generally regarded to be powerful compared to their European counterparts, and studies of local policy-making show that they are instrumental in agenda-setting and problem-definition (Borraz 1998; Cadiou 2013). In the cases of Marseille and Grenoble, we should observe activist mayors initiating change in the former, and the absence thereof leading to policy stasis in the latter.

An alternative framework for explaining policy outcomes is the "advocacy coalition" framework (Sabatier and Weible 2007), which emphasizes the shared core beliefs of coalitions of actors, often described as "subsystems". These coalitions are relatively stable over time and the opinions of actors forming them are homogeneous, but they are also rather autonomous from political decision makers. Policymaking is thus fragmented and relies on specialized information these actors possess, while policy change is incremental, requiring shifts in deeply entrenched beliefs or external imposition (Pierce et al. 2017, 16–18). The advocacy coalition framework does not allow as much room for opportunistic behaviour on the part of powerful actors (like mayors in the context of cities) as the multiple streams framework. To the extent that city-level policymaking in France has evolved towards a model of fragmented governance through differentiated policy networks (as argued in Le Galès 2001), the advocacy coalition framework seems fitting for explaining the incremental adoption or even absence of diversity policy instruments, as we see in Grenoble. It can also mean, however, that right-wing mayors refrain from major policy changes against core tenets of an entrenched advocacy coalition.

A third explanatory framework of the policy process focuses more on the pace of change and less on the actors responsible for it. Punctuated equilibrium theory (Baumgartner and Jones 2010) posits that policy adoption happens in short periods of rapid change, after a long period of inertia in which existing institutions and policy actors have exercised policy modifications only incrementally, if at all. When change does happen, it is because pre-existing "policy images" and "policy venues" are challenged under the weight of cumulative "positive feedback" for alternative policy frameworks; at the same time, the attention of main actors turns to the issue for a brief period where rapid change becomes possible. A related idea is that of a *critical juncture* (Capoccia and Kelemen 2007) whereby choices of individual actors in relatively short periods of time have great consequences for the choices available to future actors. Punctuated equilibrium theory can be complementary to the two aforementioned frameworks in explaining policy change (in this case the adoption of diversity policies). Punctuated equilibria or critical junctures, for instance, during a major local crisis, provide openings for policy entrepreneurs and initiate rapid learning for advocacy coalitions.

To summarize the empirical implications for the study of diversity policies in the two puzzling cases of Marseille and Grenoble: actors initiating drastic policy change are likely to be entrepreneurial, progressive mayors (Marseille), while members of an established "advocacy coalition", are likely to avoid major policy shifts and pick policy instruments that conform to established core policy ideas (Grenoble). With regard to the pace of change and adoption of diversity policy instruments, they are likely to accelerate following a "punctuated equilibrium" or "critical juncture", when structural and institutional conditions are in flux, creating an opening for the kind of progressive, pro-diversity mayor who is likely to promote a corresponding pro-diversity policy agenda.

Marseille: city-hall directed multiculturalism

The Southern port city of Marseille is well-known for publicly embracing the diversity of its population and as a historical meeting point of people of various origins (Mitchell 2011; Ambrosini and Boccagni 2015; Downing 2015). In terms of specific policies and discursive openings initiated by the city hall towards the diversity of its population, one can single out the *Marseille Espérance*, a city-hall-led initiative that gathers religious leaders to diffuse tensions in times of local or national crisis, as well as the sculpture monuments associated with it featured in the city's public spaces; a relatively robust presence of council representatives of immigrant origin explicitly courting a "community vote" already since 1989; public city hall support over the years for the building of a Marseille mosque; several discursive nods to the benefits of diversity in Marseille by mayors and local politicians, as well as references to its cosmopolitan past and the city's "communities". In 2013, in an example of many references to local diversity over the years, centre-Right mayor Jean-Claude Gaudin, wrote that "Marseille is the city of diversity. A diversity that is cultural, ethnic, religious. Our co-citizens experience it daily in a spirit of openness and dialogue. It is an opportunity and an advantage for our city".[2]

Urban actors from Marseille publicly and consistently mention its diversity, multiculturalism, welcoming culture and ability to mix populations of different origins as one of the city's relative strengths. It is also notable that the city's local prosecutors regularly inform Marseille's religious leaders of judicial investigations of racist incidents, a portfolio to which French anti-racist and anti-discrimination groups usually enjoy privileged access.[3] Municipal policy-making with specific communities as targets is also reflected in mobilization before elections. If Cesare Mattina has convincingly demonstrated the selection of Armenian and Jewish candidates to represent their groups in Marseille politics over decades (Mattina 2016, 238–246), there is evidence that such practices have been gradually extended to the city's African and Muslim communities. Comorian candidates on the Left and the Right have explicitly campaigned for the Comorian vote, the most recent and perhaps poorest immigrants to arrive in Marseille in the last decades (Baquey 2013). So-called "Muslim candidates" have also been included in electoral lists of both Left and (centre-) Right parties at increasing rates over the last twenty years. Their campaigns have explicitly targeted the needs of the city's Muslims often in relation to the Grand Mosque project, even though the existence of a meaningful Muslim voting bloc remains disputed (Geisser and Kelfaoui 2001; Lorcerie and Geisser 2011, 228–236).

The city of Marseille thus exercises diversity policy using several of the policy instruments mentioned in the introduction: it recognizes the importance of diversity in the city population and allows for the participation and representation of ethnic and religious groups at the municipal council, as well as other policy fora. As we shall see, in some detail later in this section, the city also provides extensive funding for ethnic and religious associations. How did such explicit group-based diversity policy come about? The institutional breakthrough that *Espérance* exemplified, as well as other related policy innovations can be traced back to a crisis in the 1970s and early 1980s that had stigmatized the city nationally as a hotbed of racism. Incidents that contributed to this trend were several murders of North-African workers, the bombing of the Algerian consulate resulting in four dead and several injured, vandalisms against Jewish establishments and cemeteries and the rise of the local Front National (Lorcerie and Geisser 2011, 253–256). In addition to what could be described as a postcolonial crisis, the city was going through a severe economic downturn that saw the clientelist system of the septuagenarian Socialist mayor Gaston Defferre unravel (Peraldi and Samson 2013, 81–91).

In this context, Robert-Paul Vigouroux, a relative outsider in Marseille politics, was able to form a new political alliance that included progressive left-wing and centrist politicians. He was first elected mayor under the banner of the Socialist party succeeding Defferre who died in office in 1986, and then was reelected as an independent candidate in 1989. With regard to managing the ethnic, cultural and religious diversity of the population and besides founding *Marseille Espérance* in 1990, Vigouroux made explicit overtures to the city's religious and immigrant organizations, in an effort to replace Defferre's politics of clientelistic favouritism with elements from the city's civil society. In his book outlining his vision as mayor, Vigouroux explicitly endorsed ethnic community associations for purposes of swift integration of immigrants into the French society and called France a "multicultural society". He concluded that "the role of elected officials is to give them [associations of foreigners] a chance to build bridges with one another" (Vigouroux 1991, 114–116). Vigouroux also specifically addressed ethnic and religious communities *qua* minorities, as opposed to as transient immigrants, transforming them into actors in the local political process. He argued publicly that his electoral lists reflected community-based representation and named a cabinet official as responsible for relations with the Marseille "communities" (Cesari 1994, 72–73).

Vigouroux' activism in institutionalizing group-based policies and a discursive multiculturalism shows that Marseille's present policies originated from a left-wing political coalition, as is commonly thought (Martínez-Ariño et al. 2019). Marseille's early adoption of a multiculturalist policy framework is also explained by combining the punctuated-equilibrium and "multiple-streams" theories of policy change. The severe community-relations and economic crises that overwhelmed the city during the decade leading up to his mayoral term can be described as a classic "problem stream" to which Vigouroux proposed the "policy stream" of community recognition and group-based representation as a solution. Acting as an innovative policy entrepreneur he presented the crisis of clientelism in the city as an opportunity for privileging civil society, in which ethnic communities and their associations played an organic part. His progressive coalition succeeded in aligning the problem and proposed solution with the "politics stream" by directly challenging the candidate supported by the Socialists in 1989 and eventually carrying the municipal elections.

When the centre-Right candidate Jean-Claude Gaudin beat Vigouroux and the Socialist-party candidate in 1995 to become the new mayor, he faced a dilemma between dismantling the multiculturalist framework of his predecessor and continuing it with some revisions that would befit his more conservative coalition. A previous agreement with Front National regional councillors made it plausible that Gaudin would steer city politics towards the right, under pressure from Marseille's ever-strong extreme Right.[4] Perhaps the real puzzle is why Gaudin opted for a more centrist path in his relations with Marseille's communities and retained the policies, discourse and institutions of his predecessor. Indeed, the centre-right mayor endorsed and presided over *Espérance*, placed candidates of immigrant origin on his electoral lists, supported Marseille's Grand Mosque (which was eventually not completed for lack of financing), funded public parades celebrating the city's diversity (such as the parade *Marsilia* in 1999), and adopted the discourse of community coexistence and multiculturalism, as the quote in this section's opening paragraph demonstrates (see also Gastaut 2003; Lorcerie and Geisser 2011, 58).

Gaudin's retention of diversity policies can be explained through the prism of the advocacy coalition framework. Not facing a crisis similar to the one that brought Vigouroux to power, Gaudin operated with the pre-existing, established actors/policy networks in this field he inherited from his predecessor (in this case, Marseille's religious and ethnic community leaders). Acting within this policy framework, Gaudin opted for incremental changes, rather than a complete overhaul in what can be described as an example of "paradigmatic pragmatism" (Schiller 2015): he cultivated personal relations with the representatives or the regional council of Muslim faith (CRCM) and provided its offices at Marseille's city centre, partly in order to combat the extreme fragmentation among the city's Muslims. Gaudin's city hall also continued to distribute funds for ethnic and cultural associations in many of Marseille's neighbourhoods, leading to a sort of community-based clientelism (Moore 2001). One can argue that Gaudin added new policy framings of diversity and new actors to pre-existing policy networks, which suited his coalition better, but did not alter the core tenets of the pro-diversity advocacy coalition formed during the Vigouroux years. Besides moderate Catholic leaders that supported the initiatives of religious dialogue and funding implicitly targeting religious groups, the local centre-Right in Gaudin's coalition courted pro-business networks that sought to benefit from the image of a multicultural metropolis. As a result, large projects aiming at revitalizing the city, such as the reconstruction of a neighbourhood near the port and the candidacy for the European capital of culture, and tourist campaigns aimed at wealthy international visitors made specific references to the dynamism stemming from the city's diversity and multiculturalism.[5]

This kind of policy, which combines preferential treatment for ethno-religious groups and a commercial use of the diversity discourse is not without critics. In a masterful treatment of urban clientelism in Marseille, Mattina (2016, 238–290) has argued that the city hall practices a very uneven distribution of symbolic and material resources among these recognized communities. On one side there are winners: Armenians, Jews and the French repatriated from Algeria, who receive recognition, political support and subsidies; and on the other side there are clear losers, namely the Maghrebi and Comorian communities. In addition, an implicit group-based attribution of social housing leads to spatial segregation in the city. In 2013 the adjunct mayor in charge of municipal policies against exclusion blamed "clientelist policies inherited from past administrations" for the geographic concentration of populations of non-European immigrant origin in Marseille's 13th, 14th, 15th and 16th *arrondissements*.[6] Mattina, his critique of the distributive outcomes of such policies notwithstanding, confirms that municipal practices with regard to funding ethnic and religious associations lead to a further "hardening" of ethnic groups in Marseille (2017, 283–288, see also Césari 1993, 90–92).

In addition, Marseille mayors explicitly use group-based "diversity" policy and in particular *Espérance* for social control, that is, to avoid conflicts (often of a violent nature) between members of the city's communities, for instance in the wake of the 2005 Paris attacks. Thus diversity policy is in this case considered as preventative and contributing to peace, reflecting the more extreme circumstances in which the policy framework was first adopted by Robert Vigouroux. At the same time, and in comparison to other French cities, the city of Marseille does not have consolidated policies that combat individual instances of racism and discrimination through training of city officials, administrators of the *politique de la ville*, educators and municipal police on related issues.[7] Anti-discrimination measures are, of course, one important dimension of diversity policies, if perhaps the most conventional and least innovative, with their emphasis on individual cases, they are less suited for a group-based policy framework, such as the one practiced in Marseille. The pro-diversity policy framework is very different in the case of Grenoble.

Grenoble: a progressive city with a conservative approach to diversity

Grenoble, a prosperous city at the foot of the French Alps, is well-known in France as a bastion of progressive politics and prides itself in a long-standing democratic socialist tradition, starting in the 1960s with iconic mayor Hubert Dubedout (Frappat and Dubedout 2016). The progressive coalition of Grenoble has historically combined the clout of economically outward middle-class professionals, non-Communist trade unions and "new left" ecologists, in what is known as the "Grenoble model" or "myth" (Bruneteau 1998). The city's emphasis on high-technology innovation and its dynamism can be contrasted with Marseille's long-term struggles with economic stagnation. Consequently, the city has not faced a crisis of economic or inter-ethnic tensions similar to Marseille.

Interestingly, the city's narrative of success does not encompass ethnic, religious or cultural diversity, the recognition of communities or group-based policymaking, as it does in Marseille. As I show below, Grenoble's urban actors have been very cautious to mention ethnic or cultural mixing as a source of the city's dynamism and focus instead on its innovation-driven economic prosperity, geographic location, and strong network of local associations. No specific initiative like the *Marseilles Espérance* has emerged as the focal point of community relations in the city. Diversity, when it appears in official discourse, is typically described as a synonym for the international outlook of the city's companies and universities, in a standard reiteration of the business case for diversity that focuses on skills and creative lifestyle (Florida 2005; Page 2007).

Mayoral speeches and programmatic statements from Grenoble's recent past have similarly lacked discursive nods to diversity, indicating that successive progressive mayors have not acted as policy entrepreneurs in this new field. For instance, Eric Piolle, the mayor elected in 2014 under the banner of a Left-Green coalition that seems peculiar to Grenoble's progressive politics, devoted no words to specific ethnic or religious communities of the city, the diversity of its population and instruments to recognize or represent it in his 120 programmatic positions. The programme was otherwise full of innovative ideas about local democracy, environmental sustainability and the duties of councillors vis-à-vis their citizens.[8] Piolle's predecessor wrote an entire book about his legacy as a twenty-year-long Socialist mayor of Grenoble; the book is marked by a similar absence of any references to diversity or ethnic-religious communities (Destot 2015). This absence is all the more striking, if, as already noted in the introduction, one considers the relatively high numbers of immigrants in the city that are comparable to Marseille (16 per cent in 2013, with about half of them of North- and Sub-Saharan African origin).

Along with the absence of discursive or symbolic overtures towards the diversity of the population, and in contrast with Marseille, Grenoble's political factions also do not mobilize the "community vote". To be sure, many councillors of African origin have been elected to the city council over the years, but there is no evidence of explicit mobilization or publicly stated representation of specific ethnic or religious communities. The public biographies of present and former councillors with non-European immigrant background paint the picture of a progressive city council with a high emphasis on classic left-wing themes, like social and international solidarity. Some examples that stand out are: Salima Djidel (progressive activist), Sonia Yassia (responsible for the realization of small-size projects in the Villeneuve neighbourhood), Sadok Bouzaiene (former political exile from Tunisia) and the former council in charge of fighting discrimination, Linda El-Haddad (director of Grenoble's SOS-Racisme branch).[9] Still, in their biographies and other public interventions these immigrant-origin councillors do not claim to represent a specific ethnic/religious group, unlike their Marseille counterparts.

The silence surrounding multiculturalism in Grenoble can also be observed in a recent special issue of the municipal magazine, entitled "Grenoble: place of welcome" (terre d'accueil). In the text, an initial emphasis on "internationalization since the great industrial migrations" quickly shifts to the present international orientation of the city for foreign students and researchers.[10] The North-African populations of the city are celebrated exclusively in connection with earlier generations who arrived in the 1960s to build the venues of the Winter Olympic Games. Tellingly, in a 2008 speech named "Solidarity in a multicultural society" in Grenoble, former Minister of Culture Catherine Tasca recognized the importance of past immigration from Italy and the Maghreb for the city, but tied local practices of intercultural exchange to more conventional neighbourhood policies (for instance in the neighbourhood of Villeneuve) and the cultural offerings at the *Maison de la Culture*.[11]

Tasca's comments are symptomatic of a general pattern: diversity policy in Grenoble is inflected through established, progressive policy frameworks that emphasize non-discrimination, solidarity and, to a lesser extent intercultural exchange. Gradual introduction of diversity policy instruments rests on an entrenched advocacy coalition that consists, as a first part, of members of the local administration involved in policy fields presumed of direct importance to immigrants and their descendants (for instance, cultural or housing policy). If Marseille officials and civil society actors openly consider problems and solutions in their city as inter-communal, their counterparts in Grenoble are concerned about the social segregation in their city, exacerbated by features of its urbanistic characteristics. The Southern suburbs, including the aforementioned Villeuneuve neighbourhood, suffer from socio-spatial inequality and a sense of lack of security. They are targets of city-level and national *"politique de la ville"* and combine high unemployment rates, a large share of persons of immigrant origin (in some of them surpassing 30 per cent) and a large percentage of social housing units. Therefore, Grenoble should not be considered an interethnic heaven. In many ways, the city has not escaped the nation-wide pattern of tensions in its *banlieues*: in 2005, 2010 and 2019 riots erupted between the police and local youth following perceived police brutalities.

There is, in addition to established *politique de la ville* actors, a second part of Grenoble's established advocacy coalition that pushes for gradual change in the local diversity policy framework: anti-racism or anti-discrimination associations. Their centrality among the city's urban actors and strong ties with the city hall would make it misleading to characterize Grenoble as neglectful of diversity issues. In particular, policy instruments with regard to anti-discrimination are abundant. Grenoble's adjunct mayor of Equality of Rights is in charge of overseeing actions and policies against racism in the city, while the administration has, over the years, harmonized its approach against discrimination with other regional and national state actors, such as the *Défenseur des Droits*.[12] By way of comparison, Marseille only instituted an adjunct mayor responsible for anti-discrimination in 2014, following a well-publicized campaign by the Representative Council of Black Associations (CRAN).[13] Grenoble has also always been at the forefront of progressive causes with regard to asylum-seekers, refugees and undocumented immigrants. Many associations advocating the rights of such groups are funded by the city hall and house in the House of Associations (*Maison des Associations*). Grenoble has additionally strived to integrate its immigrant population, especially those without formal rights, into municipal governance structures. In the spirit of civic universalism and intercultural exchange, it encouraged, already since 2000, the participation of foreign residents in neighbourhood councils, coordinated pro-immigrant associations in the follow-up of the 2015 asylum crisis and created a mentorship programme for the city's irregular migrants.[14] Otherwise, the city hall provides brochures and other public documents in a number of languages and has funded, according to the municipal magazine, as many as 110 African organizations for activities "that resonated with current events".[15]

Summarizing, one can argue that Grenoble's municipal council followed a strategy that emphasized anti-discrimination measures and the support of associations dedicated to the issue of racism, discrimination, universalist "equality of treatment". The municipal councillor responsible for the "fight against discrimination and for Human Rights", Linda El Haddad, constituted a municipal plan in 2010, with the 3-pronged goal of training municipal employees, providing help to Grenoble citizens that were victims of discrimination and funding the relevant associations.[16] In this sense, Grenoble is a good example of the process of institutionalizing and prioritizing anti-discrimination policies at the city level and across various municipal policy fields (employment, housing, schooling, culture) as described by Debenedetti (2018, 141–172). It is no coincidence that in 2015 the city applied to obtain a "Diversity Label", in an effort to gain outside recognition of its initiatives in the field of anti-discrimination.

Through the prism of these established policy frameworks (*politique de la ville*, anti-discrimination policies) that incorporate aspects of the city's diversity, but do not challenge core tenets of longstanding advocacy coalitions, the Grenoble case is no longer puzzling. In the absence of any major crisis, the city has continued to do what it is famous for – namely progressivism through strong neighbourhood-level associations, but with no elevated privileged role for ethnic or religious community representatives. Take for instance the central role assigned by the city hall to the Consultative Council of Foreign Residents of Grenoble (CCREG) and the Observatory of Discriminations and Intercultural Areas (ODTI). These associations are mentioned by Grenoble urban actors as key representatives of the interests of immigrant populations and their names appear regularly in coordinating initiatives of the city hall.[17] Their founding can be traced back to the rich associational milieu of the city, and they have enjoyed full support of the city hall. Their expansion of duties happened gradually and in the follow up of external crises (such as the recent refugee crisis) to which the city responded with a typical call for solidarity. Their character fits better with a policy framework that emphasizes universal rights to participation (CCREG) and intercultural understanding (ODTI), as principles of living in local diversity, but avoids group-based advocacy.

When Grenoble did experience an internal crisis, which could have been construed as a "problem stream" of inter-communal relations, the Grenoble mayors, the possible instigators of entrepreneurial innovation, turned, again, to established policy frameworks and networks to offer solutions. In July 2010 the suburb of Villeneuve was affected by three days of violent rioting, following the death of a local youth who had been chased by the police. The event assumed national importance because of a speech by the then President Nicolas Sarkozy (heretofore cited as the divisive "Grenoble speech") who tied the riots to failures of immigration and integration. The response of the then Socialist mayor Destot avoided a security-based approach or any mention of group-based local grievances, but was otherwise typical of well-established policy solutions of the French Socialist party nationally and locally. His team devised a 3-year plan for Villeneuve promising more local jobs, more money for neighbourhood associations, a plan for urban renovation and more policing. The plan included no policy considerations for mending local community relations or local perceptions of discriminatory state institutions, such as the police.[18] The city hall document actually reflected the positions and policy frames of local associations from the Villeneuve associational milieu, the latter having officially demanded more funding for their existing neighbourhood activities ("education", "dialogue with the youth", "living together") in a "white book" towards the mayor.[19]

Discussion and conclusions

The comparison between municipal policymaking in Marseille and Grenoble with regard to ethnic, religious and cultural diversity reveals two different approaches in how these types of policies are introduced and consolidated. Marseille's multiculturalism features an entrepreneurial mayor, Robert-Paul Vigouroux, who introduced principles of community/group-based policymaking in a moment of crisis; and a second mayor, Jean-Claude Gaudin, who inherited this policy framework and adapted it to the needs of his electoral coalition. Thus, despite the persistence of inequalities among ethno-religious groups, diversity recognition and representation in Marseille can be described as more group-based, top-down, explicit in terms of symbolic recognition, and, geared towards inter-communal peace. Ethnic and religious associations are major interlocutors with policymakers and members of the city council act as community representatives. During the initial phase of policy adoption (the Vigouroux period) the Marseille case fits better the punctuated equilibrium and multiple streams framework; during the later phase of policy consolidation under Gaudin the advocacy coalition framework better explains policy continuity and the less radical innovations introduced to the city's community-based multiculturalism.

Grenoble, on the other hand, has, for a long time, featured progressive mayors, such as Michel Destot and Éric Piolle, who inherited a robust, uninterrupted city tradition of policymaking based on a neighbourhood-level, progressive civil society. Innovations in the field of ethnic, cultural and religious diversity have been incremental and introduced as additions to the pre-existing associational milieu of the city. Local associations and experienced local policymakers in the fields of the *politique de la ville* and anti-discrimination policy are the major actors in local networks of policy-making. In the meantime, the lack of any crisis in inter-communal relations has prevented radical shifts, such as the introduction of group-based policy or discursive multiculturalism. The kind of incremental change within established left-wing policy networks in Grenoble fits better the advocacy coalition framework. This incrementalism has not prevented the city from positioning itself at the vanguard of pro-refugee and anti-racism or anti-discrimination struggles and from adopting less group-specific diversity policy instruments, such as diversity training.

The article has broader implications for the study of the policy process in the field of diversity policy in cities. It shows that diversity policy instruments can look very different depending on whether group-based demands and representation are recognized as the basis of public discourse and public policy (as is the case in Marseille). Alternatively, municipal policy may be based on broader principles of solidarity and anti-discrimination; in which case intermediation with the city hall and representation of diversity may materialize through more established channels among the city administration or through a progressive associational milieu (as is the case in Grenoble). Differing diversity policies in the two cities demonstrate empirically how multicultural and intercultural policies work at the local level (Good 2018; Zapata-Barrero and Cantle 2019). Grenoble's approach can be thought of as a combination of traditional civic universalism and interculturalism, because the city does not target specific groups, but provides spaces, resources and opportunities for the protection against discrimination and for the expression of intercultural understanding at the neighbourhood level. Marseille, on the other hand, has adopted more of an openly multicultural approach, even if some of its initiatives can be considered intercultural (for instance, the city parades, and the interaction among religious leaders in the context of Marseille *Espérance*). As already noted, the two cities do not constitute "ideal types": anti-discrimination measures are more developed in Grenoble, while Marseille's centre-right ruling coalition often uses local multiculturalism pragmatically, to promote an image of a globally open city (see Schiller 2015, 1126 for a similar analysis). In any case, it is fascinating that such empirical variation is found in a country like France, with its supposedly monolithic approach to citizenship-based public policy. The article also argues that local policy frameworks are "sticky", as has long been argued by scholars studying national-level policy frameworks. A centre-right mayor, such as Jean-Claude Gaudin, found it more convenient to continue rather than dismantle the apparatus in the field of diversity, created by his predecessor. Similarly, Grenoble mayors are constrained to consult and cooperate with powerful established actors in the city administration and civil society, and the policy outcomes reflect these constraints.

Notes

1. "Etrangers et immigrés en 2012, Commune de Marseille". Accessed May 15, 2019, https://www.insee.fr/fr/statistiques/2130578?geo=COM-13055. "Etrangers et immigrés à Grenoble" Accessed February 2, 2019, https://www.ades-grenoble.org/wordpress/2017/01/13/etrangers-et-immigres-a-grenoble/
2. Programme of the third Regional Biennale on "History, Memory, Immigration, Territories" (2015), Introduction by mayor Jean-Claude Gaudin. Available at: https://www.scribd.com/document/279389387/3e-biennale-Histoire-Memoire-des-Immigrations-et-Territoires-en-PACA
3. Commission Nationale Consultative des Droits de l'Homme (2014), *La Lutte contre le Racisme, l'Antisémitisme et la Xénophobie*: 368.
4. Le Monde, "À Marseilles, l'Ogre Gaudin", September 28, 2013.
5. Indeed Gaudin launched the official candidacy of Marseille as the European capital of culture for 2013 by representing it as a "mosaic city, that is, for centuries, a symbol of exchanges among civilizations, through the diversity of communities that constitute it and the cultural currents that nourish it". See Ville de Marseille (2006).
6. "Lutte contre le Racisme: pourquoi Marseille est mal noté". Metronews, December 4, 2013.
7. Baromètre contre le Racisme. Classement des Villes de France en matière de lutte contre le Racisme. Accessed February 2, 2019. http://www.le-cran.fr/document-cran-associations-noires-de-france/71-barometre-des-villes-contre-le-racisme.pdf.
8. "Grenoble, Une ville pour tous". Accessed January 25, 2019, http://unevillepourtous.fr/wp-content/blogs.dir/839/files/2014/02/ProjetGrenobleUneVillePourTous.pdf
9. Biographies for Djidel, Yassia and Bouzaiene found at http://unevillepourtous.fr/elus, accessed May 16, 2019; biography for Linda El-Haddad found at http://www.poteapote.com/Portrait/Linda-El-Haddad, accessed May 16, 2019.
10. GRE-MAG, Le Magazine de la Ville de Grenoble, 2016 (12), 17.
11. "La solidarité dans la société multiculturelle", speech by Catherine Tasca, 1st National Convention, *Inventer à Gauche*.
12. See Emmanuel Carroz, "Grenoble lutte contre toutes les discriminations". comments at municipal council, 21 March 2016.
13. Baromètre contre le Racisme. Ibid.
14. Ibid., 18.
15. GRE-MAG, Le Magazine de la Ville de Grenoble, 2016 (8), 42.
16. Plan Municipal de Prévention et de Lutte contre les Discriminations: Billan et Perspectives accessed May 15, 2019, https://www.grenoble-ensemble.fr/tribunes-et-analyses/plan-municipal-de-prevention-et-de-lutte-contre-les-discrimination-bilan-et-perspectives/.
17. For the history and functions of CCREG, see "Conseil Consultatif des Résidents Etrangers Grenoblois", accessed February 2, 2019. For the current role of ODTI in the refugee crisis, see "Aide aux réfugiés: la plateforme de coordination est

en place" in "Grenoble, Terre d'Accueil", Gre.mag, Accessed February 3, 2019, at http://www.gre-mag.fr/actualites/aide-aux-refugies-la-plateforme-de-coordination-est-en-place/

18. Municipal council minutes, City of Grenoble, April, 18, 2011. See also *Le Point*, July 7, 2011. "Un an après les émeutes de Grenoble" accessed March 6, 2019 at https://www.lepoint.fr/societe/un-an-apres-les-emeutes-de-grenoble-20-07-2011-1354677_23.php

19. Collectif Inter Associations de la Villeneuve, January 11, 2011. "Le Livre Blanc".

Disclosure statement

No potential conflict of interest was reported by the author(s).

ORCID

Michalis Moutselos 🆔 http://orcid.org/0000-0002-8454-1124

References

Ambrosini, Maurizio, and Paolo Boccagni. 2015. "Urban Multiculturalism Beyond the 'Backlash': New Discourses and Different Practices in Immigrant Policies Across European Cities." *Journal of Intercultural Studies* 36 (1): 35–53.

Antonsich, Marco. 2016. "Interculturalism Versus Multiculturalism – The Cantle-Modood Debate" *Ethnicities* 16 (3): 470–493.

Association des maires de grandes villes de France. 2011. Étude politique de la ville: la diversité dans les grandes villes, un enjeu majeur pour les élus. Online publication 16 November. http://franceurbaine.org/espace-presse/communiques-de-presse/etude-politique-de-la-ville-la-diversite-dans-les-grandes-villes.

Baquey, Cécile. 2013. "Municipales à Marseille: quelle représentation pour les Mahorais et les Comoriens?" *France Info, Outre-mer la Première*. December 6.

Baumgartner, Frank R., and Bryan D. Jones. 2010. *Agendas and Instability in American Politics*. Chicago: University of Chicago Press.

Bereni, Laure. 2015. *La bataille de la parité. Mobilisations pour la féminisation du pouvoir.* Paris: Economica.

Bereni, Laure, and Renaud Epstein. 2015. "Instrumenter la lutte contre les discriminations: le «label diversité» dans les collectivites territoriales." Diss. CNRS-Centre Maurice Halbwachs; Université de Nantes-Droit et Changement Social.

Berry, Frances Stokes, and William D. Berry. (2007) 2018. "Innovation and Diffusion Models in Policy Research." In *Theories of the Policy Process*, edited by Christopher M. Weible and Paul A. Sabatier, 263–308. New York, NY: Routledge.

Blanc, Maurice. 2010. "The Impact of Social Mix Policies in France." *Housing Studies* 25 (2): 257–272.

Blatter, Joachim, and Markus Haverland. 2012. *Designing Case Studies: Explanatory Approaches in Small-N Research*. Basingstoke: Palgrave Macmillan.

Borraz, Olivier. 1998. *Gouverner une ville: Besançon, 1959–1989*. Rennes: Presses Universitaires de Rennes.

Boscarino, Jessica E. 2009. "Surfing for Problems: Advocacy Group Strategy in US Forestry Policy." *Policy Studies Journal* 37 (3): 415–434.

Bruneteau, Bernard. 1998. "Le 'mythe de Grenoble' des années 1960 et 1970. Un usage politique de la modernité." *Vingtieme siecle. Revue d'histoire* 58 (2): 111–126.

Cadiou, Stéphane. 2013. "Jeux et enjeux de connaissances. L'expertise au service de la gouvernance municipale." In *La gouvernance territoriale. Pratiques, discours et théories*, edited by Simoulin Vincent, and Pasquier Romain, 197–221. Paris: LGDJ.

Capoccia, Giovanni, and R. Daniel Kelemen. 2007. "The Study of Critical Junctures: Theory, Narrative, and Counterfactuals in Historical Institutionalism." *World Politics* 59 (3): 341–369.

Caponio, Tiziana, Peter Scholten, and Ricard Zapata-Barrero, eds. 2019. *The Routledge Handbook of the Governance of Migration and Diversity in Cities*. New York, NY: Routledge.

Césari, Jocelyne. 1993. "Les Leaders Associatifs Issus de L'immigration Maghrébine: Intermédiaires ou Clientèle." *Horizons Maghrébins – Le Droit à la Mémoire* 20 (1): 80–95.

Cesari, Jocelyne. 1994. "Marseille face à ses communautés." *Esprit* 202 (6): 66–77.

de Graauw, Els, and Floris Vermeulen. 2016. "Cities and the Politics of Immigrant Integration: A Comparison of Berlin, Amsterdam, New York City, and San Francisco." *Journal of Ethnic and Migration Studies* 42 (6): 989–1012.

Debenedetti, Marie-Christine Cerrato. 2018. *La lutte contre les discriminations ethno-raciales en France: de l'annonce à l'esquive (1998–2016)*. Rennes: Presses universitaires de Rennes.

Destot, Michel. 2015. *Une Passion for Grenoble*. Paris: Editions de l'Aube.

Dobbin, Frank, Soohan Kim, and Alexandra Kalev. 2011. "You Can't Always Get What You Need: Organizational Determinants of Diversity Programs." *American Sociological Review* 76 (3): 386–411.

Downing, Joseph. 2015. "Understanding the (Re)Definition of Nationhood in French Cities: A Case of Multiple States and Multiple Republics." *Studies in Ethnicity and Nationalism* 15 (2): 336–351.

Eisenberg, Avigail, and Will Kymlicka. 2011. "Bringing Institutions Back In How Public Institutions Assess Lolentity." In *Identity Politics in the Public Realm: Bringing Institutions Back In*, edited by Avigail Eisenberg and Will Kymlicka, 1–30. Vancouver: UBC Press.

Fassin, Didier. 2002. "L'intervention Française de la Discrimination." *Revue française de science politique* 52 (4): 403–423.

Flamant, Anouk. 2017. "L'incomplète construction des politiques municipales de lutte contre les discriminations raciales. Enquête dans les villes de Lyon, Nantes et Strasbourg (2001–2012)." *Revue Internationale de Politique Comparée* 24 (3): 257–292.

Florida, Richard. 2005. *Cities and the Creative Class*. New York: Routledge.

Frappat, Pierre, and Hubert Dubedout. 2016. *Hubert Dubedout, une pensée en action: écrits et discours*. Grenoble: Presses Universitaires de Grenoble.

Gastaut, Yvan. 2003. "Marseille cosmopolite après les décolonisations: un enjeu identitaire." *Cahiers de la Méditerranée* 67: 269–285.

Geisser, Vincent, and Schérazade Kelfaoui. 2001. "Marseille 2001, la communauté réinventée par les politiques." *Migrations société* 13 (77): 55–77.

Good, Kristin R. 2018. "Municipal Immigration Policymaking in Canadian Cities: The State of the Art 1." In *The Routledge Handbook of the Governance of Migration and Diversity in Cities*, edited by Tiziana Caponio, Peter Scholten, and Ricard Zapata-Barrero, 216–228. New York: Routledge.

Kingdon, John W. (1984) 1995. *Agendas, Alternatives, and Public Policies*. Boston: Little, Brown.

Le Galès, Patrick. 2001. "Urban Governance and Policy Networks: On the Urban Political Boundedness of Policy Networks. A French Case Study." *Public Administration* 79 (1): 167–184.

Lorcerie, Francoise, and Vincent Geisser. 2011. *Muslims in Marseille*. New York: Open Society Foundations.

Martínez-Ariño, Julia. 2018. "Conceptualising the Role of Cities in the Governance of Religious Diversity in Europe." *Current Sociology* 66 (5): 810–827.

Martínez-Ariño, J., M. Moutselos, K. Schönwälder, C. Jacobs, M. Schiller, and A. Tandé. 2019. "Why Do Some Cities Adopt More Diversity Policies Than Others? A Study in France and Germany." *Comparative European Politics* 17 (5): 651–672.

Mattina, Cesare. 2016. *Clientélismes urbains: gouvernement et hégémonie politique à Marseille*. Paris: Presses de Sciences Po.

Mintrom, Michael, and Phillipa Norman. 2009. "Policy Entrepreneurship and Policy Change." *Policy Studies Journal* 37 (4): 649–667.

Mitchell, Katharyne. 2011. "Marseille's Not for Burning: Comparative Networks of Integration and Exclusion in Two French Cities." *Annals of the Association of American Geographers* 101 (2): 404–423.

Moore, Damian. 2001. "Marseille: Institutional Links with Ethnic Minorities and the French Republican Model." In *Multicultural Policies and Modes of Citizenship in European Cities*, edited by Alisdair Rogers, and Jean Tillie, 123–141. Aldershot: Ashgate.

Moutselos, Michalis, Christian Jacobs, Julia Martínez-Ariño, Maria Schiller, Karen Schönwälder, and Alexandre Tandé. 2020. "Economy or Justice? How Urban Actors Respond to Diversity." *Urban Affairs Review* 56 (1): 228–253.

Page, Scott E. 2007. *The Difference: How the Power of Diversity Creates Better Groups, Firms, Schools, and Societies*. Princeton: Princeton University Press.

Penninx, Rinus. 2015. "European Cities in Search of Knowledge for Their Integration Policies." In *Integrating Immigrants in Europe*, edited by Peter Scholten, Han Entzinger, Rinus Penninx, and Stijn Verbeek, 99–115. Cham: Springer.

Peraldi, Michel, and Michel Samson. 2013. *Gouverner Marseille: enquête sur les mondes politiques marseillais*. Paris: La découverte.

Pierce, Jonathan J., Holly L. Peterson, Michael D. Jones, Samantha P. Garrard, and Theresa Vu. 2017. "There and Back Again: A Tale of the Advocacy Coalition Framework." *Policy Studies Journal* 45 (S1): S13–S46.

Rohlfing, Ingo. 2012. *Case Studies and Causal Inference: An Integrative Framework*. Basingstoke: Palgrave Macmillan.

Sabatier, Paul A., and Christopher M. Weible. 2007. "The Advocacy Coalition Framework." *Theories of the Policy Process*, edited by Paul A. Sabatier, 189–220. Boulder, CO: Westview.

Schiller, Maria. 2015. "Paradigmatic Pragmatism and the Politics of Diversity." *Ethnic and Racial Studies* 38 (7): 1120–1136.

Sénac, Réjane. 2012. *L'invention française de la diversité*. Paris: Presses Universitaires de France.

Simon, Patrick, and Valérie Sala Pala. 2010. "'We Are Not All Multiculturalist Yet': France Swings Between Hard Integration and Soft Antidiscrimination." In *The Multiculturalist Backlash. European Discourses, Policies and Practices*, edited by Steven Vertovec, und Susanne Wessendorf, 92–111. London: Routledge.

Vertovec, Steven. 2012. "'Diversity' and the Social Imaginary." *European Journal of Sociology/Archives Européennes de Sociologie* 53 (3): 287–312.

Vigouroux, Robert. 1991. *Un parmi les autres*. Paris: Albin Michel.

Ville de Marseille. 2006. "Lancement official de la Candidature de Marseille-Provence, Capitale Européenne de la Culture 2013." *Dossier de Presse*, December 14.

White, Bob W., ed. 2017. *Intercultural Cities: Policy and Practice for a New Era*. London: Springer.

Zapata-Barrero, Ricard, and Ted Cantle. 2018. "City Governance of Migration and Diversity: Interculturalism as a City Policy Paradigm." In *The Routledge Handbook of the Governance of Migration and Diversity in Cities*, edited by Tiziana Caponio, Peter Scholten, and Ricard Zapata-Barrero, 193–203. New York: Routledge.

Externalization or imitation: the 2015–16 asylum-seeker immigration as a catalyst for local structural change

Miriam Schader

ABSTRACT
When in 2015–2016, several hundred thousand new asylum-seekers arrived in Germany, this put local administrations to a test. In contrast to scholars who identified a "crisis of the administration" or a situation of "state failure", this article argues that the events in some cases served as a motor for administrative change. Drawing on the sociology of organizations, the paper shows that this period is better understood as a time of fundamental uncertainty rather than a crisis of the administration, and that the local state proved capable of dealing with uncertainty. In line with theories of organizations and based on qualitative interview data collected in three German cities, the paper identifies two ideal-typical strategies for reducing uncertainty – externalization or change through imitation. The text demonstrates how two of the three municipalities moved towards change.

In 2015, the already stretched Common European Asylum System (CEAS) and several national asylum systems in Europe were close to collapse. Although increasing numbers of refugees[1] had been reaching European states since 2012, the European Union had not been able to find solutions for the most pressing problems of the CEAS. When numbers peaked in 2015 – in order to remove pressure from the system and to avoid a humanitarian emergency – the German Federal Government decided not to reject a large number of people, who came to Germany via other EU states – despite the option to send them back in accordance with EU legislation. Instead, it decided to process their asylum applications in Germany by applying the sovereignty clause foreseen in the EU Dublin Regulation. As a result, several hundred thousand people entered Germany within a few months.

According to many media sources, as well as scholarly, accounts, the period following this decision was a "migration" or "refugee crisis", which led to a crisis of the administration. Some academic authors even speak of a situation of "state collapse" or "state failure" (e.g. Hesse 2015; Hahlen and Kühn 2016). In contrast, this article argues that the state was generally well equipped to deal with this situation.[2] Based on empirical studies in selected cities, this contribution will show that, in some cases, the events were even a motor for administrative change and instigated a – if belated – local adaptation to migration-induced diversity.

As local administrations are decisive for the reception and inclusion of newcomers, the much-cited "crisis of the administration" should have manifested itself primarily there. It is thus essential to broaden our understanding of how *local* administrations adapted to the rapid refugee immigration.

This is relevant, as the reception and inclusion of refugees is a specific, but nonetheless empirically and theoretically interesting case for analyzing change and stability of local welfare administration. By studying the pressure on local administrations in 2015–16, we can learn more about the perceived "crisis" and the functioning of local administrations as well as local structural change. Furthermore, the reception of asylum-seekers and their inclusion into the welfare system can be considered a small, but in many ways indicative part of social policy. It is in many ways typical for how the welfare state generally treats those depending on benefits (cf. Schader forthcoming).

Literature on local migration policies – defined here as local instruments and measures designed to govern migration and migration-induced diversity (Schammann 2018, 68) – has grown over the last decade (e.g. among many others: Caponio and Borkert 2010; Glick Schiller and Çaglar 2010; Jørgensen 2012; Filomeno 2017; Baumgärtel and Oomen 2019; Caponio, Scholten, and Zapata-Barrero 2019; Kühn and Münch 2019; Martínez-Ariño et al. 2019; Schiller 2019; Moutselos et al. 2020).[3] Since the early 2010s, research on refugee immigration to Europe has greatly increased, too, with special attention to integration (Kleist 2018). Especially the local reception and inclusion have received much scholarly attention (e.g. Doomernik and Glorius 2016; Dick and Schraven 2017; Bygnes 2019). There is also a growing literature on local administrations and officials in the realm of asylum and refugee reception (e.g. Ellermann 2006; Eule 2014; Dahlvik 2017).

What is still partly understudied and under-theorised, however, is the perception of the 2015/16 immigration movement by local officials and its local repercussions, and, significantly, its longer-term consequences. The present study contributes to filling this gap. It presents original data on three German municipalities and the ways they dealt with the new immigration. Drawing on Apelt's and Senge's work on organizations and uncertainty

(2015), the paper argues that the period in 2015–16 should more appropriately be described as a time of fundamental uncertainty, and not as a "crisis of the administration" or "state failure". I thus emphasize the ability of the local state to adapt to the challenges. Based on qualitative interview data, I identify two types of organizational strategies of uncertainty reduction – externalization and change through imitation. The article thus adds to our understanding of local migration policies and organizational change.

Research design and data

The analysis is based on a comparison of two medium-size cities (NorthernCity, SouthernCity) and one smaller city (SmallNorthernCity) in the regional state of Lower Saxony. In order to counter the "extreme case bias" evidenced in much research on local migration policies (Schammann et al. forthcoming), three "ordinary" cities were selected. They are "ordinary" insofar as they are neither particularly large nor small, and, significantly, at the time of case selection, they neither stood for radically open or radically closed policies regarding migrant reception and inclusion. In addition, there are also important differences between the cities, which make a triangular comparison particularly useful.

By focusing on three municipalities in one regional state[4], it is furthermore possible to keep the legal and political context "constant". This is important because the federal states largely determine the leeway municipalities have in accommodating refugees. The regional states are in charge of implementing federal law, and local administrations are part of the regional state. Regional ordinances may specify details of the implementation and thus instruct the local authorities (Schader 2019, 383–386). Although the municipalities have some discretion and also have to deal with legal and planning uncertainties, it is therefore important to study cases within one regional state and thus within the same institutional framework.

In all three city councils, the Social Democrats (SPD) are strongest, followed by the Christian Democrats (CDU) and the Green Party; all mayors (*Oberbürgermeister*) belong to the SPD. SmallNorthernCity has the highest number of representatives of the extreme right *Alternative für Deutschland* (AfD) in its city council.[5] NorthernCity and SouthernCity are university cities with more than 165,000 and 130,000 inhabitants respectively, while the former industrial city SmallNorthernCity only has around 80,000 inhabitants. All three municipalities have their own Foreigners' Authorities, *Ausländerbehörde*, concerned with legal status, deportation, and similar issues.[6] The proportion of people with a migration history is significantly lower in NorthernCity than in the other two cities. While in NorthernCity, the share of the population with a "migration background"[7] is estimated at 16 per cent (as of 2010), shares are higher in SouthernCity (24–27 per cent in 2018) and in SmallNorthernCity

(28 per cent 2010). NorthernCity is also the wealthier city. Here, the disposable income per household is above the regional average, while it is below in both SmallNorthernCity and SouthernCity. In smaller SmallNorthernCity, GDP per capita is also significantly lower than in the other two municipalities, and the unemployment rate is higher (Jacobs and Bolz n.d.).

The data was collected in the form of interviews with members of the three municipal administrations (from low to high-ranking officials) and volunteers over a period of three years (January 2017 to January 2020).[8] These captured – in retrospect – the experiences during the peak of refugee immigration as well as changes in the administrative structures during and after this phase. Additionally, the analysis draws on a corpus of primary documents, issued by the municipalities (including their concepts for integration, reports on refugee reception etc., local statistics), media reports in local newspapers as well as information gathered at visits to relevant locations (including accommodation centres) between 2015 and 2020. The analysis of the interview data and the corpus of documents was based on qualitative content analysis.

Analytical framework

The CEAS, including the Dublin Regulation, forms a European legal framework, in which federal and regional state asylum policies and laws are integrated. After registration at the German border, asylum-seekers are usually assigned to a regional "first-reception centre". From there, they are distributed to municipalities in the respective regional state. Between summer 2015 and spring 2016, a large number of asylum-seekers were additionally allocated directly to municipalities by the regional states within the framework of administrative assistance (*Amtshilfe*), because first-reception facilities had no more capacities. In addition to rising allocation quota, municipalities thus had to provide places for asylum-seekers who should have been accommodated in regional reception centres. They therefore needed to react flexibly and quickly to the situation. Often, they had to deal with new arrivals of refugees daily with only short notice and had to provide accommodation and initial care, clothing, translation and further support virtually overnight. Local administrations as organizations were therefore confronted with a rapidly changing environment during this period.

In order to define theoretically more precisely the uncertainties municipalities had to process, it is helpful to draw on concepts borrowed from the sociology of organizations. Apelt and Senge (2015, referring to Dequech 1999) distinguish between risk, incertitude and fundamental uncertainty. *Risk* means a relatively low degree of uncertainty: the relevant stakeholders are aware of the probabilities of environmental conditions to occur, which depend on their decisions. It is unknown which condition will occur. *Incertitude* refers to a situation in which possible future conditions arising from a decision are known, but due to a lack of information or cognitive skills it is unknown how likely their occurrence is. *Fundamental uncertainty* arises from the reflexivity of social interactions. Here, neither all possible conditions are known, nor can probabilities be attributed (Apelt and Senge 2015).

Risk and incertitude thus denote situations, in which potential future developments are foreseeable. If an actor in situation A opts for action B, outcome C, D or perhaps E will occur. In a situation of *risk*, it is also known how likely C, D or E will occur. Under conditions of *incertitude*, these probabilities are unknown. *Fundamental uncertainty* describes a situation, in which, due to complex social interactions, it is neither clear what changes can occur in an organization's environment, nor with what probability something will happen. However, while such a situation is characterized by a lack of knowledge – what outcomes are possible? How probable is it that environmental state Y occurs if I choose action X? – it also creates space for creativity (Dequech 1999). Finally, but relevantly, even under conditions of fundamental uncertainty, organizations still have to produce reliable outcomes (Apelt and Senge 2015, 3).

If we now apply this model to the reception of asylum-seekers in Germany, we can argue that risk and incertitude are the daily business of officials in this realm, whereas fundamental uncertainty rarely occurs. Risk is, for instance, inherent to the German system of regional and local asylum-seeker allocation. Due to the quota system, officials usually know that a maximum number of x new asylum-seekers will be sent to their municipalities within a certain period. They do not know the actual composition of the new arrivals nor their precise needs, but based on statistics and earlier experiences, they can calculate probabilities. Most likely, more men than women will arrive, more accompanied than unaccompanied minors etc. Thus, it is possible to estimate the need for accommodation, translation, health services, places in schools ... – based on known probabilities.

Incertitude is, for example, observable when the federal or state governments introduce new measures or rules and municipalities can foresee the intended outcomes, but do not know if the new measures or rules are effective. When the federal government introduced the "80-cents-job" programme for asylum-seekers (FIM)[9], for instance, municipalities knew that a certain number of places would be available in their regional state, but they did not know how efficient the measure would be or whether it would work at all. Thus, municipalities at the time created "80-cents-jobs" without knowing how likely these would be filled.

Fundamental uncertainty, in contrast, is less likely to occur on a regular basis as previous experiences, statistics and regulations usually make either potential future developments or probabilities or both (more or less) foreseeable. If the quota system for the local allocation of newly arrived refugees collapses, however, or laws and regulations at the state, federal or European

Table 1. Risk, incertitude and fundamental uncertainty in local refugee reception.

Risk	Potential future developments are foreseeable, probabilities are known	General characteristic of asylum-seeker reception; arises for instance when quota are known but the exact composition of the respective number of asylum-seekers is unknown
Incertitude	Potential future developments are foreseeable, probabilities are unknown	More substantial form of uncertainty that arises, for example, when new measures or regulations are introduced at the state or federal level and municipalities do know the potential effects but not, how likely they will materialize
Fundamental uncertainty	Potential future developments are not foreseeable and probabilities are unknown	Exceptional situation; when legislation, regulations, statistics etc. do not provide enough knowledge about potential developments and the likelihood of their occurrence

levels do not seem to apply any longer, neither future developments nor probabilities are known (Table 1).

Municipalities as organizations have different options for dealing with situations of risk, incertitude or fundamental uncertainty. In the case of risk, it is most rational for them to decide according to the probabilities they know. Based on statistics, experience and the availability of accommodation, for instance, municipalities may provide a certain number of places in accommodation centres or private housing. In situations of incertitude, decisions depend on either local policy- and decision-making or on routines within the administration (cf. Eule 2014). They may also turn to higher levels of policy-making, e.g. in order to obtain a regional ordinance taking responsibility off them or clarifying the situation (Head of Department, NorthernCity).

Situations of fundamental uncertainty resemble those of incertitude insofar as members of the administration rely on political decisions or have to come up with their own solutions. At the same time, periods of fundamental uncertainty open up space for more creative forms of adaptation, due to their more radical and substantial character (cf. Dequech 1999). It is thus reasonable to expect that municipalities, while under pressure, could use the period of rapid refugee immigration for organizational change and adaptation or rely on strategies of externalization in order to reduce the uncertainty they face.

This is in line not only with Apelt's and Senge's conceptualization, but, despite different theoretical premises, also with new institutionalist approaches to organizational behaviour under conditions of uncertainty. From this point of view, the most likely forms of adaptation to a situation of fundamental uncertainty that can be expected are change through imitation – or in new institutionalist terms: mimetic isomorphism (DiMaggio and Powell 1983, 151) – and externalization. While it is possible that municipalities as organizations develop entirely new structures and measures in order to reduce uncertainty and to prevent future situations of fundamental uncertainty, it is more likely that they draw on a model or several models. Just like in a situation of incertitude, they may as well choose to shift responsibility off them by relying on other actors for reducing uncertainty.

Despite the proclaimed local turn in migration research, the theorization of local migration policies is less developed than theories for the national level or for the multi-level governance of migration (cf. Scholten and Penninx 2016; Scholten 2019). It is all the more useful to draw on existing theories and concepts. In their work on active and passive local migration policy-making, Schammann and his colleagues propose a valuable synopsis of different explanatory approaches (Schammann et al. forthcoming). While very broad, it is also helpful for making sense of the different local responses to the period of rapid refugee immigration. Schammann et al. (forthcoming) distinguish between the *institutional framework*, mainly made up of the legal and political setting, *structural conditions*, especially a municipality's demography, rurality / urbanity and financial situation, *framing / political culture* which refers to different frames of migration, diversity and (demographic) change, and *agency / key actors* including individual and collective stakeholders in order to identify factors that explain a municipality's active or passive stance on migration.

For the present analysis, it is important to note that the legal and political setting is mainly defined by policies and legislation at the EU, federal and regional state levels. Since all three municipalities are located in Lower Saxony, the *institutional framework* is the same. As outlined above, the *structural conditions* differ to a degree, with SouthernCity and NorthernCity being structurally more alike than SmallNorthernCity.

"My civil servant's heart was bleeding": experiencing risk, incertitude and fundamental uncertainty in local refugee reception

In accordance with the quota for the distribution of asylum-seekers in Germany, Lower Saxony received over 9 per cent in 2015 (as in the years before and after). Between summer 2015 and spring 2016, SouthernCity, NorthernCity and SmallNorthernCity received several hundred asylum-seekers. The respective allocation quota were repeatedly adjusted to the situation, as were the numbers of people to be admitted additionally within the framework of administrative assistance. At peak times, all three cities accommodated around one hundred newly arrived refugees each week (Northern-City 2016; Head of Unit 1, SouthernCity). At the end of 2016, around 1400 asylum-seekers lived in SouthernCity. In SmallNorthernCity the highest number was around 1200 and in NorthernCity around 2000 (NorthernCity 2016; SouthernCity 2016; Head of Office, SmallNorthernCity).

From the point of view of the local administrations, this period represented an immense challenge. It was characterized above all by the higher numbers and the rapidity of new arrivals and the lack of political and organizational preparation. Although the number of asylum applications in Germany had already risen before summer 2015, the federal and regional governments had failed to ensure sufficient reception capacities in cooperation with the municipalities.

Not only did many people come to local refugee centres without registration or without having filed their asylum application, the municipalities also had no advance information about numbers, characteristics and needs of the new arrivals. At times, they relied on the information transmitted by the bus drivers, who counted their passengers. Moreover, after the 2015 decision, it was not clear how many people would altogether be allowed to enter the country and over what period of time. For the municipalities this increased not only the incertitude immensely as probabilities were no longer known. The fact that the Dublin regulation was applied very differently than before – i.e. by making use of the sovereignty clause and not sending people back – created a situation of uncertainty where future events were not foreseeable:

This becomes particularly clear in a quotation from a head of department from SmallNorthernCity, in which he describes how unorganized and for the municipalities hardly plannable the distribution of the new immigrants took place. Due to the short-term nature of the admissions, the municipalities constantly had to improvise. A second quotation, from SouthernCity, further illustrates the unpredictability of the future as perceived by officials responsible for refugee reception.

> The fact that all this was done very, very disorderly by the federal government at that time is a completely different story. So my civil servant's heart was bleeding. I admit that quite openly. So I had huge problems at that time with the way it was done, people were just sent here according to the motto: Now you get off the bus and from now, you can do whatever you want. I still don't think that's right, but that's another story. (Head of Office, SmallNorthernCity)

> The [quota; MS] was 1200 at the time. The quota says nothing. The quota is a number that is given at a particular time, in other words, it was then mid-December 2015, when this huge quota came. And then, there is no end. A quota starts on a day, but they do not tell you, when it ends. The timeframe is not fixed. (Head of Unit, SouthernCity)

While all interview partners describe situations of increased risk and incertitude, the general perception of the situation was one of uncertainty marked by unpredictable effects of political events and decisions. For all three local administrations, the period 2015/16, before the main migration routes were closed, can in Apelt's and Senge's terms be described as a phase of fundamental uncertainty. Knowledge about possible environmental conditions – Who will come when? Who will have which needs? What decisions, regulations and funding by state and federal governments can be expected? Etc. – and about the respective probabilities was missing.

Three main factors can be identified as leading to this fundamental uncertainty: (1) time and numbers (i.e. the fact that higher – and partly unknown – numbers of individuals seeking protection arrived in a short period of time), (2) the contingency of future developments (will political leaders negotiate a closure of important migration routes? will the role of municipalities in the multi-level system of refugee reception remain the same?) and (3), closely related to (2), a high number of important changes in German legislation within a short period of time.[10]

These created an exceptional situation as all responsible officials note. In their eyes, however, this cannot be characterized as a situation of failure of the state or the administration. Although all three municipalities emphasize that they had reached their limits and criticized legislative decisions at higher levels, emphasis on their ability to cope with the situation is equally prevalent. The following excerpts from interviews with responsible officials underline this:

> We have been able to do it, so far. We have been able to do it, but that is// if this is a priority in the country for a certain period, then it is a true statement: "Wir schaffen das" [we can do it]. [...] We have been able to do it and above all, the emphasis is, the municipalities were the ones who have done it, weren't they? [...] we did the work. (Head of Department, SouthernCity)

> But crisis, I believe, in my view, this is not the right term. Last week [...] we had the opportunity to introduce our work to our apprentices. And I reflected on past events and said that it was an incredibly exciting time, because we were lucky that, if you were still sitting in the office at ten in the evening or on Saturdays, then you were not sitting there alone, because you saw that in the office to the left and right the lights were still on. And that was a time that also brought people together and created a sense of community. [...] Something like that gets to you, one could not keep up for a long time this way, this pace. But [...] it was also an incredibly positive experience, because you had the chance to perform. And because you just perceived that everyone really contributed and no one evaded responsibility. (Head of Unit, NorthernCity)

In various interviews, the term "crisis" was used to describe the time when many refugees arrived in the municipalities virtually overnight, when information gaps were large and the workload was high. Contrary to what is often argued, however, it is not the collapse of structures that is evident at the local level, but the functioning and increased cohesion of different organizational units and individual officials – albeit under conditions of increased uncertainty and strain.

Reducing uncertainty and envisaging structural change

As outlined above, organizations – including municipalities – have different options for dealing with increased uncertainty. In the short-term all three focussed cities relied on emergency measures combined with strong support by civil society actors, mainly volunteers. A quote from SouthernCity illustrates, how officials opted for routines created for – different – exceptional situations in order to reduce uncertainty quickly:

> […] And we therefore chose a work organisation that corresponds to our plans for disaster relief. So please do not understand me as if I was saying the arrival of refugees was a disaster. But we had to try in some way to accommodate people in dignity. (Head of Unit, SouthernCity)

The cooperation of different organizational units outside their line activities and across hierarchies and portfolios were central to this form of dealing with fundamental uncertainty. With some small exceptions, the forms of cooperation in all three municipalities were similar. The three municipalities differ, however, in the degree to which they emphasize emergency measures. While officials and bureaucrats in SouthernCity focus particularly strongly on the exceptional character of the situation, their colleagues from NorthernCity and SmallNorthernCity more often refer to existing and newly created structures that facilitated dealing with the fundamental uncertainty of the time. Furthermore, the two northern municipalities undertook additional steps towards longer-term adaptation already in 2015, while SouthernCity did not.

As expected, two types of medium- and long-term uncertainty reduction can be identified: externalization and organizational change through imitation. While SouthernCity can be described as an almost ideal-typical case of externalization, NorthernCity clearly belongs to the second category. Small-NorthernCity followed a mixed strategy of both externalization and imitation (Table 2).

SouthernCity's externalization strategy goes hand in hand with a quick return to the status quo ante and is evident at two levels: a reliance on higher levels of decision-making and a delegation of refugee reception to other municipalities and the regional state. When the numbers of newly arrived asylum-seekers had fallen from spring 2016 onwards, SouthernCity quickly returned to the habitual work organization. Neither were new organizational structures created nor did the municipality aim at an anticipatory adaption to potential future migration. Strikingly, the structure and tasks of the "Integration Office" (Büro für Integration) remained unchanged – although the Office is only a small staff unit, consisting of one fifty-percent position (Interview with Head of Office, SouthernCity). In contrast to the perception of the situation in the two northern municipalities, in the eyes of responsible SouthernCity officials, the events of 2015–16 had not disclosed deficits that required more substantial change. Rather, the city relied on federal and state policies to ease the situation:

> […] if this had gone on like this now, yes, if there had not been any deal with some [countries; the author] in Southeast Europe and further, and if the neighbouring countries […] had continued to let everyone cross the borders, yes, then

Table 2. Types of uncertainty reduction.

	Type 1: Externalization	Type 2: Organizational change through imitation
Focus	- Immediate challenges and short-term "disaster relief" measures - Limited capacities	- Immediate challenges and short-term measures - Limited capacities, but "impressive" capabilities, flexibility and solidarity - Previous successes in dealing with diversity
Uncertainty reduction	*Externalization*: → delegation of refugee reception to other municipalities or break in allocation → relying on policies and legislation at higher levels → no new structures or significant changes	*Change*: → new agencies and structures imitating model municipalities
Cases	SouthernCity, [SmallNorthernCity]	NorthernCity, SmallNorthernCity

the point would have come when we would not have been able to deal with this any longer [...]. (Head of Department, SouthernCity)

Furthermore, SouthernCity refused to meet the reception quota set by Lower Saxony in 2015/16 and insisted instead on having to accept only as many people as the city, in their view, had places available (Head of Unit). Although the situation in many municipalities in Lower Saxony was comparable – their housing markets had already been tense before 2015 and the accommo-dation of newcomers was challenging – SouthernCity thus refused to accept responsibility for some of the people assigned to the city and expected them to be accommodated elsewhere.

Responses in SmallNorthernCity and NorthernCity were different. Both fol-lowed the examples of pioneering municipalities and created new structures to facilitate a long-term adaptation to migration movements. In these two cases, we therefore observe change through imitation – in more institutional-ist terms: isomorphism – as the central strategy of uncertainty reduction.

Important references like Cologne, Freiburg or Wuppertal were models that were available in this situation, because they had already undertaken substan-tial restructuring in the realm of refugee-reception, migration and diversity. Significantly, Freiburg had used the rapid arrival of refugees for particularly comprehensive changes that had been envisaged before and could then be implemented quickly. Their newly founded Office for Migration and Inte-gration unites various tasks in this area. Most remarkably, it integrates, as sub-ordinate part, the Foreigners' Authorities, which in most municipalities is part of the Department for Order and Code enforcement. According to the Head of Office, "integration" thus has become the central goal of an agency charged also with deportation, legal status and similar matters[11] (Head of Office, Freiburg).

NorthernCity and SmallNorthernCity did not go as far, but took inspiration from the reforms in Freiburg and other municipalities (Head of Office, Head of Unit, NorthernCity; Head of Unit, SmallNorthernCity). A new Office for Immigration and Integration was founded in NorthernCity and in SmallNorthern-City the new unit Child Subsistence Allowances, Immigration and Integration was introduced.

Both cities started in 2015 to adapt their structures not only to the short-term situation marked by fundamental uncertainty, but also to its longer-term consequences. Under the impression of the events, a "small office" (Head of Unit, NorthernCity) for Central Refugee Management was founded in NorthernCity in 2016. This in turn resulted in 2017 in the establishment of the larger Office for Immigration and Integration that unites two new units – for Refugee Management and for Integration. In this newly created office, in addition to the Head of Office and the two Heads of Unit, nineteen employees are responsible for different areas of Refugee Management and sixteen for Integration (Head of Office, Head of Unit, Head of Unit, Northern-City). In relation to the size of the city, this is a considerable investment. The unit Refugee Management involves various tasks previously assigned to different units and, in some cases, to different departments (Head of Unit, NorthernCity). Likewise, the Integration Unit includes tasks and employees previously based in different units and departments (Head of Unit, Northern-City). Importantly, the head of this unit is at the same time the city's Integration Officer, which strengthens the latter position, because the Integration Officer thus is not only responsible for conceptual and committee work, but can also shape decisively the way in which migration-related diversity is dealt with in practice.

In smaller and less prosperous SmallNorthernCity, a restructuring in the area of migration and refugee reception had already been planned before 2015, but had been postponed due to major financial problems at the municipal hospital (Head of Department, SmallNorthernCity). However, Small-NorthernCity, too, did not only focus on short-term emergency solutions. 150 Integration Guides – volunteers, who accompany new migrants during their first months (or years) of settling in the city – received new contracts from 2015 onwards, thus strengthening existing support structures in light of the events (Head of Department, SmallNorthernCity). In addition, a Coordination Office for Refugees and Intercultural Affairs was founded, made up of two social workers for refugees, who closely cooperated with the existing Coordination Office for Migration and Participation and which was further expanded in 2016 (Coordinator for Migration and Participation, SmallNorthernCity).

Following the example of NorthernCity (Head of Unit, SmallNorthernCity), administrative structures in SmallNorthernCity were further adapted in 2018: related tasks and structures were merged in the new unit Child

Subsistence Allowances, Immigration and Integration. The new structures and first experiences in NorthernCity had explicitly served as a model; the unit is, however, considerably smaller than in the neighbouring city. Like in Northern-City, the existing staff unit Coordination Office for Refugees and Intercultural Affairs became part of the new unit and various tasks and offices were also centralized spatially in order to promote cooperation and accessibility. Close cooperation with civil society actors is specific for the new structures in SmallNorthernCity (Head of Unit, Head of VolunteerSercive, SmallNorthern-City). In SmallNorthernCity like in NorthernCity, the new unit aims not only at dealing with the consequences of the situation of 2015/16, but more broadly with a diversifying society.

SmallNorthernCity's strategy of imitation and change went along, however, with a strategy of (limited) externalization. From spring 2017, the municipality obtained a break in the allocation of new asylum-seekers from first-reception centres; in addition, persons granted international protection elsewhere after November 2017 were banned from moving there (*Zuzugsstopp*) (Coordinator for Migration and Participation; Head of Department, SmallNorthernCity). Unlike SouthernCity, SmallNorthernCity did not refuse to accept asylum-seekers during the height of the refugee immigration movement, but later requested the regional government's support. For SmallNorthernCity, these measures were part of an enduring quarrel with neighbouring municipalities and aimed at pushing those to greater efforts in social housing and social inclusion (Head of Department, Coordinator for Migration and Participation, SmallNorthernCity). Furthermore, the government of Lower Saxony had created incentives for municipalities to apply for a ban, as this was linked to financial support by the regional state: SmallNorthernCity received two million euros for 2017, and similar amounts for the following two years (Head of Department, Head of Unit, SmallNorthernCity) for integration measures.

" ... and then, the refugees ruined all our efforts": framing immigration and uncertainty reduction

Nevertheless, in SmallNorthernCity like in NorthernCity, the framing of the situation and their capacities of dealing with it differed from those in South-ernCity. While the SmallNorthernCity administration in particular emphasized that the fundamental uncertainty experienced by municipalities was due to poor planning and organization and political mistakes at higher levels, they also stressed their experience in including new migrants in local society suc-cessfully. Decades ago, they had begun to adapt their local policies and struc-tures – especially regarding housing, urban planning and social work – to a continuously diversifying local population. This goes along with pride in the achievements of the administration and civil society, in the existing structures as well as their adaptability. According to members of the administration, the population deals with new immigration "in a laid-back manner", Small-NorthernCity has "very good social work", sufficient social housing and a very good infrastructure (Coordinator for Migration and Participation, Small-NorthernCity). Furthermore, officials and bureaucrats in SmallNorthernCity stressed the importance of the municipality's working-class heritage and strong culture of social justice and welfare (Head of Office; Head of Unit, Small-NorthernCity). Accordingly, "super" was also the central attribute with which officials and bureaucrats in SmallNorthernCity characterized their handling of the situation in 2015–16 and their city, where "everyone would like to live" (Coordinator for Migration and Participation, SmallNorthernCity).

In NorthernCity – a city with fewer experiences in dealing with migration-related diversity – significantly, the head of the new Office for Immigration and Integration as well as the heads of its two units stressed the capacities and the potential of the new structures and the comparative advantage they had due to the restructuring. As described above, they, too, described the period of fundamental uncertainty in 2015 and 2016 as challenging, but put even more emphasis on the opportunities it had created (Head of Office, Heads of Unit, NorthernCity). They expressed pride in the instruments and measures the new office offered for better social and urban planning in the realm of refugee and migrant reception and participation – including improved and encompassing statistics and control, social work, training –, for improved cooperation within the administration, for a more sophisticated and inclusive concept of "integration" (Head of Office, Heads of Unit, North-ernCity) as well as in their adaptation to potential future developments: "NorthernCity will be prepared" (Head of Unit, NorthernCity). Furthermore, NorthernCity became part of the European network "Arrival Cities", founded in 2015 "against a backcloth [sic] of rising discrimination and prejudice against immigrants" and in order to bring together cities who "had to tackle the new and old challenges to ensure the migrants' integration" (Arri-valCities n.d.). In 2018, it became a member of the "Safe Harbour" movement of cities and towns willing to accept additional migrants rescued in the Med-iterranean Sea (Seebrücke n.d.). The city thus positioned itself proactively as an actor in translocal networks demonstrating its – at least discursive[12] – openness.

In SouthernCity, a "Safe Harbour" city since 2019 (Seebrücke n.d.), in con-trast, the framing is less clear-cut. SouthernCity, too, is described as an open city, characterized by its academic tradition and by its liberal stance on immigration and legal status – especially in comparison with neighbouring towns. Simultaneously, the same officials use racist stereotypes when refer-ring to refugees and other migrants, while others highlighted the fact that residents in an upper-class / upper middle-class neighbourhood including the head of a university of applied sciences located there had argued most outspokenly, and in racist terms, against the opening of a new accommo-dation centre there (Head of Office; Head of Unit; Head of Department; SouthernCity).

Most significantly, the rapid immigration of refugees in 2015/16 was per-ceived as hampering urban development and progressive change. One head of department feared that the regional state might not cover the muni-cipality's medium- and long-term expenditures for social benefits that were likely to arise from the reception of several hundred refugees (Head of Depart-ment, SouthernCity), while one head of office saw the potential reunion of refugees with their families as a major problem, because it would increase the number of newcomers by the factor of seven or eight (Head of Office, SouthernCity).

Although not all responsible officials saw the reception of the newcomers as a necessary, but inconvenient duty, the general framing of the situation was one of an immense challenge that had not opened up new opportunities. In a public event on the municipality's efforts in climate protection, a member of the unit responsible for the event went as far as to say in her opening pres-entation: "[…] und dann haben uns die Flüchtlinge alles kaputt gemacht" – "and then, the refugees ruined all our efforts[13]". While this event took place in December 2019, thus after the height of the rapid refugee immigration, it reflects well a general perception of the situation in retrospect.

Discussion and conclusion

The period of rapid refugee immigration created a situation perceived as a challenge in all three municipalities. As has been shown, this time was charac-terized by a major lack of information regarding the likelihood of future events and the consequences of municipal actors' decisions. According to Apelt and Senge's (2015) typology, it was thus marked not only by incertitude, but also by fundamental uncertainty. The administration did not collapse, however, but proved capable of dealing with migration-related uncertainty.

In the short term, all three cities relied on "emergency" measures that allowed them to structure responsibilities and cooperation in a different way than usual. While SouthernCity soon after returned to the status quo ante, the other two cities opted for structural change, imitating pioneering municipalities that had already implemented similar transformations. In line with theories of the sociology of organizations, we thus observe two types of uncertainty reduction: externalization and organizational change through imitation.

SouthernCity opted for a strategy of externalization by delegating its responsibilities partly to third-party actors. It also chose to rely on others when it comes to preventing a recurrence of the situation. In contrast, Small-NorthernCity and NorthernCity did not – or to a limited degree – pass their responsibilities on to others. They both created new structures following the example of Freiburg and other municipalities and thus chose a strategy of organizational change.

While it is beyond the scope of this study to draw conclusions about causality in a strict sense, it is nevertheless possible to identify differences that played an important role for the variance observed. Significantly, officials and bureaucrats in SouthernCity focused on the challenging character of the period of fundamental uncertainty and stressed the limited capacities of the municipality. Their counterparts in SmallNorthernCity and NorthernCity could build on previous experiences, were better prepared and had already envisaged smaller changes. While they described the time as equally challenging, they also strongly underlined the capabilities of their administrations. The framing of the situation and of the municipalities' capabilities and capacities thus diverges most clearly, highlighting similarities between NorthernCity and SmallNorthernCity – which, in structural terms, are rather different.

Following Schammann et al. (forthcoming), these differences in the framing of the situation – as well as of migration, diversity and social policy more generally – can be considered relevant factors for shaping the way municipalities deal with migration and diversity. Officials in SmallNorthernCity and NorthernCity framed the situation as opening up new opportunities. They perceived their municipal structures as – more or less – a match to the situation and as adaptable enough for encompassing change. Unlike their SouthernCity counterparts, they did not emphasize the longer-term uncertainty the rapid immigration of refugees induced, but the strategies they favoured for reducing it. Especially officials in SmallNorthernCity also expressed their pride in the working-class and migration heritage of their city that made them adopt a "welfare" approach to immigration, including refugee reception.

Further qualitative studies within administrations will provide additional insights contributing to a specification of the role of framing in local refugee reception, migration policies and structural change.

Notes

1. The term "refugee" as it is used here includes asylum-seekers, recognized refugees, and other persons seeking international protection – with or without a specific legal status. It is thus not restricted to persons granted international protection in accordance with the Geneva Convention.
2. At the same time, this did not exclude important forms of exclusion experienced by asylum-seekers and refugees (cf. a special issue co-edited by the author as well as Schader forthcoming).
3. For a current state of the art, see also Schammann et al. forthcoming.
4. With almost eight million inhabitants, Lower Saxony is Germany's fourth largest state.

5. SmallNorthernCity: seven of 44, NorthernCity: two of 50, SouthernCity: zero of 46.
6. NorthernCity and SmallNorthernCity are independent cities (*kreisfreie Städte*) and do not belong to a larger administrative district (*Landkreis*); SouthernCity is specific in that it belongs to a district (*kreisangehörige Stadt*), but in many aspects is independent of it and, importantly, does not depend on decisions made in or cooperation with the district.
7. According to the German Statistical Office, persons have a "migration background" if they or at least one parent were not born as German citizens (Statistisches Bundesamt 2013, 26).
8. The central topic of the interviews was the perception of the rapid asylum-seeker immigration in 2015–16 and the consequences drawn locally in the years directly after the Chancellor's claim that Germany would manage the challenges. In the focussed cities, some fifteen interviews were conducted. For the period of 2016–17, additional data was collected in SouthernCity in a large pilot project coordinated by the author. This project's focus were asylum-seeker reception and the needs and aspirations of asylum-seekers The data consists of interviews with officials, social workers and refugees, participant observation in shelters, focus group discussions with refugees and a large body of clippings from local two newspapers.
9. Launched in 2016 and funded by the federal government, the FIM programme aims at including asylum-seekers quickly into the labour market, while supporting their learning German. It allows state and welfare organizations and companies running shelters for asylum-seekers etc. to employ asylum-seekers for 80 cents / hour (https://www.bmas.de/DE/Themen/Arbeitsmarkt/Infos-fuer-Asylsuchende/arbeitsmarktprogramm-fluechtlingsintegrationsmassnahmen.html).
10. Rohmann and Hruschka (forthcoming) identify over 30 changes in the respective legislation, partly contradictory, between 2015 and 2019.
11. Charged also with deportation, legal status etc.
12. At the time of writing, the Federal Ministry of the Interior was blocking the direct allocation of migrants to one of the "Safe Harbour" cities.
13. In reducing the emissions of municipality-owned buildings.

Disclosure statement

No potential conflict of interest was reported by the author(s).

References

Apelt, Maja, and Konstanze Senge. 2015. *Organisation und Unsicherheit*. Wiesbaden: Springer Fachmedien Wiesbaden.
ArrivalCities Network. n.d. https://urbact.eu/arrival-cities.
Baumgärtel, Moritz, and Barbara Oomen. 2019. "Pulling Human Rights Back in? Local Authorities, International Law and the Reception of Undocumented Migrants." *The Journal of Legal Pluralism and Unofficial Law* 51 (2): 172–191.
Bygnes, Susanne. 2019. "A Collective Sigh of Relief: Local Reactions to the Establishment of New Asylum Centers in Norway." *Acta Sociologica*. Advance online publication.

Caponio, Tiziana, and Maren Borkert, eds. 2010. *The Local Dimension of Migration Policymaking*. Amsterdam: Amsterdam University Press.

Caponio, Tiziana, Peter Scholten, and Ricard Zapata-Barrero, eds. 2019. *The Routledge Handbook of the Governance of Migration and Diversity in Cities*. Abington: Routledge.

Dahlvik, Julia. 2017. "Asylum as Construction Work: Theorizing Administrative Practices." *Migration Studies* 5 (3): 369–388.

Dequech, David. 1999. "Expectations and Confidence Under Uncertainty." *Journal of Post Keynesian Economics* 21 (3): 415–430.

Dick, Eva, and Benjamin Schraven. 2017. "Urban Governance of Forced Displacement: Premises, Requirements and Challenges in the Light of New Humanitarian Trends." *Raumplanung* 193 (5): 23–29.

DiMaggio, Paul, and Walter W. Powell. 1983. "The Iron Cage Revisited: Institutional Isomorphism and Collective Rationality in Organizational Fields." *American Sociological Review* 48 (2): 147–160.

Doomernik, Jeroen, and Birgit Glorius. 2016. "Refugee Migration and Local Demarcations: New Insight into European Localities." *Journal of Refugee Studies* 29 (4): 429–439.

Ellermann, Antje. 2006. "Street-level Democracy: How Immigration Bureaucrats Manage Public Opposition." *West European Politics* 29 (2): 293–309.

Eule, Tobias. 2014. *Inside Immigration Law: Migration Management and Policy Application in Germany*. Research in Migration and Ethnic Relations Series. London: Routledge.

Filomeno, Felipe Amin. 2017. *Theories of Local Immigration Policy*. Cham: Springer International Publishing.

Glick Schiller, Nina, and Ayse Çaglar. 2010. *Locating Migration: Rescaling Cities and Migrants*. Ithaca: Cornell University Press.

Hahlen, Johann, and Hannes Kühn. 2016. "Die Flüchtlingskrise als Verwaltungskrise – Beobachtungen zur Agilität des deutschen Verwaltungssystems." *Verwaltung und Management* 22 (3): 157–167.

Hesse, Joachim Jens. 2015. "Staatsversagen? Bankrotterklärung Europas? Anmerkungen zur Flüchtlingskrise." *Zeitschrift für Staats- und Europawissenschaften* 13 (3): 336–355.

Jacobs, Andreas, and Meike Bolz, n.d. "Verfügbares Einkommen der privaten Haushalte in Niedersachsen 2012." https://www.statistik.niedersachsen.de/download/95862.

Jørgensen, Martin Bak. 2012. "The Diverging Logics of Integration Policy Making at National and City Level." *International Migration Review* 46 (1): 244–278.

Kleist, J. Olaf. 2018. "Flucht- und Flüchtlingsforschung in Deutschland: Akteure, Themen und Strukturen, with a contribution of Lars Wirkus." Flucht: Forschung und Transfer. State-of-Research Papier 01. Osnabrück: (IMIS) / (BICC).

Kühn, Manfred, and Sybille Münch. 2019. "Zuwanderungspolitik – ein neues kommunales Aufgabenfeld?" *disP - The Planning Review* 55 (3): 22–30.

Martínez-Ariño, Julia, Michalis Moutselos, Karen Schönwälder, Christian Jacobs, Maria Schiller, and Alexandre Tandé. 2019. "Why Do Some Cities Adopt More Diversity Policies Than Others? A Study in France and Germany." *Comparative European Politics* 17 (5): 651–672.

Moutselos, Michalis, Christian Jacobs, Julia Martínez-Ariño, Maria Schiller, Karen Schönwälder, and Alexandre Tandé. 2020. "Economy or Justice? How Urban Actors Respond to Diversity." *Urban Affairs Review* 56 (1): 228–253.

Rohmann, Tim, and Constantin Hruschka. forthcoming. "Excluded by enhanced migration management?"

Schader, Miriam. 2019. "Total spontan? 'Krisen' bearbeitung in der lokalen Aufnahme Geflüchteter." In *Migration, Refugees and Asylum. Concepts, Actors, Practices Since the Second World War in Global Perspective*, edited by Agnes von Bresselau, 381–396. Göttingen: Vandenhoeck & Ruprecht.

Schader, Miriam. forthcoming. "Refugees as "Disciplinary Individuals"? Exclusion and Inclusion in Local Asylum-seeker and Refugee Reception and the German Welfare System."

Schammann, Hannes. 2018. "Migrationspolitik." In *Soziale Arbeit in der Migrationsgesellschaft: Grundlagen – Konzepte – Handlungsfelder*, edited by Beate Blank, Süleyman Gögercin, Karin E. Sauer, and Barbara Schramkowski, 67–85. Wiesbaden: Springer Fachmedien Wiesbaden.

Schammann, Hannes, Danielle Gluns, Christiane Heimann, Sandra Müller, Tobias Wittchen, Christin Younso, and Franziska Ziegler. forthcoming. "Ambitious Activity above a Pattern of Passivity: Re-Dimensioning the 'Local Turn' in Migration Policy-Making."

Schiller, Maria. 2019. "The Local Governance of Immigrant Integration in Europe: The State of the Art and a Conceptual Model for Future Research." In *The Routledge Handbook to the Governance of Migration and Diversity in Cities*, edited by Tiziana Caponio, Peter Scholten, and Ricard Zapata-Barrero, 204–215. Abingdon: Routledge.

Scholten, Peter. 2019. "Two Worlds Apart? Multilevel Governance and the Gap between National and Local Integration Policies." In *The Routledge Handbook to the Governance of Migration and Diversity in Cities*, edited by Tiziana Caponio, Peter Scholten, and Ricard Zapata-Barrero, 157–167. Abingdon: Routledge.

Scholten, Peter, and Rinus Penninx. 2016. "The Multilevel Governance of Migration and Integration." In *Integration Processes and Policies in Europe*, IMISCOE Research Series, edited by Blanca Garcés-Mascareñas and Rinus Penninx, 91–108. Cham: Springer International Publishing.

Seebrücke. n.d. https://seebruecke.org/startseite/sichere-haefen-in-deutschland/.

Statistisches Bundesamt: Zensus 2011: Ausgewählte Ergebnisse, Wiesbaden. 2013.

A relational approach to local immigrant policy-making: collaboration with immigrant advocacy bodies in French and German cities

Maria Schiller ⓘ, Julia Martínez-Ariño ⓘ and Mireia Bolíbar ⓘ

ABSTRACT
The role of immigrant advocacy bodies in collaborative policy–making in cities is so far insufficiently researched. This article investigates the ties between relevant urban actors and immigrant advocacy bodies in cities in two Western European countries. We draw on an original survey in forty French and German cities as well as fieldwork in one French and one German city to analyze whether urban actors from a variety of policy sectors and domains of society cooperate with immigrant councils and immigrant associations, and which factors explain such collaboration. Counter to the existing literature on the role of intermediaries between municipalities and immigrant populations, we find a widespread existence of ties with immigrant advocacy bodies. However, such ties are not mainstreamed. Instead, collaboration is most present among actors in charge of immigrant affairs, and when actors meet in policy fora that allow interaction between urban actors and immigrant advocacy bodies.

Introduction

Representation of immigrant interests has existed for many decades in European cities, but often immigrant advocacy bodies were not recognized as partners by urban administrative, political, economic and civil society actors (Però and Solomos 2010; Schrover and Vermeulen 2005; Thränhardt 2013). In the meantime, top-down policy-making has been complemented by collaborative forms of policy-making, also referred to as a trend towards governance (Klijn 2008). New networks of stakeholders have been created and new practices of collaborative policy-making have emerged in cities (Aar-saether, Nyseth, and Bjorna 2011; Ansell and Gash 2008; Barnes, Newman, and Sullivan 2006). These can foster the participation of immigrant advocacy bodies and the inclusion of immigrant perspectives in policy-making. Has the distance between urban actors and immigrant advocacy bodies decreased as a result of these developments? Are urban actors considering immigrant advocacy bodies as important collaborators in policy-making today?

Some research has investigated the ties of collaboration between a variety of urban actors and immigrant advocacy bodies in the context of policy-making (Caponio 2005; Pilati 2012; Triviño-Salazar 2018). Research has shown, also for Germany (Halm 2015; Thränhardt 2013) and France (Downing 2015, 2016), that such ties are fragile and often dependent upon public funding, which implies the risk of co-optation. Yet there is still much to be done to fully capture the patterns of collaboration between urban actors and immigrant advocacy bodies in light of a trend of collaborative governance. We assume that in a context where networks and collaboration are emphasized as key means of policy-making, ties with immigrant advocacy bodies are ascribed more importance, and that those ties allow to gather important information, generate agreement, and legitimize policies within a diverse polity.

In this article, we analyze the ties between relevant urban actors and immigrant advocacy bodies in processes of policy-making in big French and German cities. The main questions guiding the research are whether and to what extent urban actors collaborate with immigrant councils and immigrant associations, which factors enhance such collaboration, and why.

We draw here on data yielded from a survey with a range of urban actors in 40 large cities in Germany and France, sampled based on their population size, complemented by insights from qualitative case studies in one French and one German city. The focus of the article is to aggregate findings from 40 large cities in both countries but not to perform a country comparison, because more systematic comparison of cities and urban governance of migration and diversity is needed (Martinez–Ariño 2018), of which actor collaboration is an important element.

The article is structured as follows. We first briefly review the relevant literature on the presence of immigrants and of ties between state and non-state actors in policy-making. We then present the data and methods of our study in German and French cities. The next section discusses our findings, divided into three parts: (a) the descriptive results concerning collaborations with immigrant advocacy bodies; (b) the regression analysis to elucidate factors that increase the likelihood of such collaborations; and (c) an interpretation of the mechanisms underlying such effects based on qualitative fieldwork in two cities. We conclude elaborating on the contributions of our study and suggesting avenues for future research.

Local immigrant political participation and governance networks

Immigrant political participation has been a matter of academic interest for some time. This has been approached in different ways, focusing on the representation of immigrants in parties and parliaments (Garbaye 2005; Schönwälder, Sinanoglu, and Volkert 2013), on immigrant organizations and collective forms of mobilization (Però and Solomos 2010), and on fora of deliberation created by governments to involve immigrants and their organizations in decision-making (Bausch 2011; Cerrato Debenedetti 2010; Takle 2015). Scholarship has focused on whether immigrant organizations can represent immigrant populations vis-à-vis policy-makers and whether their existence contributes to the integration of immigrants (Schrover and Vermeulen 2005). However, there is much less research on how different urban actors reach out to immigrants and their organizations.

An established strand within that literature argued that immigrant organizations compensate for lack of political opportunities and increase opportunities for participation in formal and informal politics (Eggert and Pilati 2014; Fennema and Tillie 2004). Other research has analyzed the direct interrelations between municipal actors and immigrant populations in policymaking (De Graauw and Bloemraad 2017; Ireland 2016; Nguyen Long 2015; Nicholls and Uitermark 2016; Però 2007; Uitermark 2012; Uitermark and Duyvendak 2008) stressing the role of intermediaries, such as large welfare organizations and political parties, implying that immigrant advocacy bodies themselves are rarely direct partners of the local administration (Caponio 2005; Pilati 2012; Triviño-Salazar 2018) and when they are, the relationship is fragile (Downing 2016). Counter to such findings and because of a trend of collaborative governance, we expect to find direct links and interactions between urban actors and immigrant advocacy bodies.

Looking towards institutionalized governance structures, some literature has posited that an integration policy field has emerged in cities, where a defined set of bureaucratic actors (often in interaction with collective immigrant actors) are concerned with deliberating, advocating and selecting different courses of action in immigrant policy-making (Bousetta 1997, 221). Inversely, another strand of the literature posits that an integration policy field has dissolved and actors from different policy sectors, such as education, housing and employment, take responsibility for integration. Authors refer to this as mainstreaming (Scholten and van Breugel 2018). Following the first line of argumentation, we expect that collaboration happens primarily within an integration policy field, i.e. that there is close collaboration between those urban actors with the mandate of working on immigrant incorporation and immigrant councils and immigrant associations. A different, more extensive, pattern of collaboration would exist if actors outside of the integration policy field, e.g. actors working on education or urban planning, as well as economic actors and other civil society actors, also collaborated with immigrant advocacy bodies in the city. Furthermore, we assume that collaboration is not only determined by the character of the policy field, but also by the ways in which actors more generally conduct local politics.

Political scientists commonly claim that interrelationships of state and nonstate actors with the goal of promoting a certain service or policy, denoted as a trend of governance, have become more important (Jessop 1995; Klijn 2008). Governance is also considered as increasingly present in the design and implementation of public policies in cities (Aarsaether, Nyseth, and Bjorna 2011; Nyseth and Ringholm 2008), including French (Pinson 2010) and German cities (Bogumil and Holtkamp 2004; Sack 2012). Against this background, building networks is a crucial precondition for participation in politics (Campbell 2013; Mcclurg 2003; Teorell 2003). In the qualitative analysis of this article, we focus particularly on collaborative governance, which "brings public and private stakeholders together in collective forums with public agencies to engage in consensus-oriented decision making" (Ansell and Gash 2008, 543). More specifically, we offer empirical insights into the modus operandi of fora of collaboration and their effects on the establishment of ties between urban actors.

Proposing a relational approach to urban immigrant policy-making that systematically generates and analyzes empirical data on actors' relationships, we focus on the ties of collaboration between important urban actors and immigrant advocacy bodies in German and French cities. The former include political, administrative, economic and civil society actors,[1] whereas the latter include immigrant councils and immigrant associations.[2] While immigrant councils are more common in German cities, they also exist in French cities. Other actors may draw on immigrant advocacy bodies when they want to have the interests of immigrants considered in policy-making. Our aim is to find out whether urban actors consider these bodies as collaboration partners in urban policy-making, which factors increase the likelihood of such collaboration, and why.

In their comparative study of Berlin, Amsterdam, New York City and San Francisco, De Graauw and Vermeulen (2016) consider the interaction of three local factors as determining the implementation of local immigrant integration policies, namely the existence of left-leaning governments, a high proportion of immigrants in the city electorate and decision-making structures, and the existence of a civil society that represents the interests of immigrants in local policy-making. Drawing on this literature, we expect that the likelihood of establishing an intense collaboration with an immigrant advocacy body will be higher in bigger cities where the share of immigrants is generally higher, in cities with a higher share of foreign-born inhabitants, and in cities leaning towards the left side of the political spectrum. We also expect that the likelihood of building collaborations with immigrant advocacy bodies will be higher for actors involved in local policy fora, where regular contact takes place.

Research design, data and methods

Research design and data

We use an explanatory sequential mixed methods design (Creswell 2013), where ethnographic fieldwork is used to interpret the findings from a survey. Both sets of data stem from the Cities and the challenge of diversity project[3] conducted at the Max Planck Institute for the Study of Religious and Ethnic Diversity.[4] A survey, conducted between April and July 2015 in German cities and from September 2015 to March 2016 in French cities, targeted relevant urban actors in 20 large cities in Germany and 20 large cities in France.[5] Table A1 in the appendix shows the cities included and their main characteristics. In this article, we do not compare the two countries. Instead, we are interested in a systematic comparison of the existence of collaboration among urban actors across big European cities. Including cities from these two countries allows us to consider general trends in similar, yet contrasting Western European contexts, as these two countries have both a long tradition of immigration but different approaches to immigrant policy making.

The survey asked urban composite actors (Scharpf 1997, 114) about their collaborations with other actors in relation to local policy-making. We posed the question:

> Politics in cities is nowadays often conducted in networks. If you think about the last twelve months, with whom, and how intensively, have you collaborated in the context of your professional work or working for your organization? We refer here to collaborations in the context of politics in your city.

The survey question listed types of urban actors, including local political parties, different departments of the local administration, trade unions, economic actors, and actors representing minority interests (migrant organizations, youth organizations and disabled organizations, among others) (see appendix 1).

Our research examines ties of a range of urban actors with local immigrant councils and immigrant associations as most likely collaboration partners for other urban actors when they seek to involve the perspectives of immigrants in policy-making. Immigrant councils are consultation bodies created by city councils and composed of immigrant representatives and, in some cities, members of the city council and the administration. They exist in large German and, to a lesser extent in French cities, where they are less consolidated. They advise local policy-makers and administrations and channel information to immigrant communities (Bausch 2011; Flamant 2016). There is an ongoing debate about how independent such councils are from local administrations or whether they co-opt immigrants (Schiller 2018). Yet, we ascertain that these bodies provide an important platform for immigrants to have a say in local policy-making, as third-country nationals do not enjoy local voting rights in France and Germany. Immigrant associations – usually composed mostly of foreign-born members – are another important platform for immigrants to organize and have their interests represented, and they can be found in all large cities. Immigrant associations in Germany have been supported and strengthened over the years through public funding, but also by being recognized as experts and cooperation partners (Halm 2015). In France, the creation of organizations based on ethnicity has been and still is difficult, because they may be deemed communitarianist and anti-universalist (Montague 2013). However, municipalities subsidize a wide variety of associations, including those formed by immigrants.

The Cities and the challenge of diversity survey targetted actors likely to intervene in policymaking on the integration of immigrants and other minorities.[6] The response rate of the survey (see distribution of respondents in Table 1) is 45 per cent for German cities ($n = 445$) and 21 per cent for French cities ($n = 249$).[7] The wide scope of urban actor selection is, to the best of our knowledge, the first of its kind (see Baglioni and Giugni 2014 for a similar selection procedure).

Analysis

The analysis of the survey data on collaborations was performed in two stages that correspond to the first two result sections of this article. First, we pooled the data collected across the cities to show descriptive results on the ties of collaboration with immigrant advocacy bodies. We aim to identify the *types of actors* that are more closely connected with immigrant advocacy bodies, and to analyze whether ties of intense collaboration happen within an integration policy field or whether immigrant integration is addressed in a variety of policy sectors, which could be the result of mainstreaming immigrant integration. Second, a multilevel logistic regression analysis was performed that inquired about the factors that increase the likelihood of non-immigrant urban actors collaborating intensively with immigrant advocacy bodies. The dependent variable is defined as "intense collaboration with an immigrant advocacy body". The independent variables are (1) type of composite actor, (2) participation in a local policy forum, (3) characteristics of the cities and (4) country.

By "type of composite actors", we distinguish urban actors positioned in different policy sectors and state or non-state actors. This typology helps us analyze a possible correlation between type of actor who responded to the survey and this actor's likelihood of building ties with immigrant advocacy bodies. The survey also asked respondents about "participation in a local

Table 1. Type of actors included in the sample (with valid responses in the question on ties of collaboration).

	Count	Valid %
Business actor (associations for the promotion of the local economy)	55	8,3
Trade unions (individual trade unions and the German confederation DGB "Deutscher Gewerkschaftsbund")	38	5,8
Welfare organizations	68	10,3
Political actors (leaders of local political parties' and council factions not holding a governing position in the administration, i.e. councillor or mayor)	116	17,6
Immigrant advocacy bodies (immigrant umbrella associations, representatives of local immigrant and diversity councils and anti-racist organizations)	64	9,7
Other diversity actors (local councils for the youth, the elderly and the disabled)	38	5,8
Public administration actors	(277)	(42,0)
• Territorial / Urban planning (actors of the administration related to urban planning and housing, transportation, infrastructure, and "politique de la ville"[a] in France)	27	4,1
• Economic development (local agencies for economic development, public agencies for work and public job centres)	37	5,6
• Integration (actors of the administration responsible for immigration, equality of opportunities and anti-discrimination)	26	3,9
• Strategic management (mayors and deputies)	102	15,5
• Social/Educational (actors of the administration related to cultural and social affairs, education, sports, health and youth)	55	8,3
• Ecological (actors of the administration related to the local Agenda 21)	14	2,1
• Organizational (actors of the administration related to human resources and citizen affairs)	16	2,4
Other	4	0,6
Total	660	100,0

[a]In France, these include administrative actors working for the *politique de la ville*.

policy forum" within the previous year, and we categorized their answers into types of policy fora, namely policy fora focused on migration and diversity issues or policy fora focused on other issues.[8] We assume that such fora are spaces of repeated and routinized interactions that can generate interorganizational ties (Levine 2013) and may facilitate collaboration with immigrant advocacy bodies in the short, medium and long term. Regarding the characteristics of the cities, we investigated the influence of (a) population size, (b) the percentage of foreign-born inhabitants, and (c) the predominant political orientation (percentage of left-wing voters in the last local election).

The multilevel model takes into account the hierarchical nature of nested data (see Snijders and Bosker 1999). In our case, it takes into consideration that composite actors of the same city might not be independent of each other, but share an urban setting that might explain their behaviour towards collaborating with immigrant advocacy bodies. By using multi-level regressions, we can assess the effects of actor variables controlling for their belonging to a particular city and city-related factors. As commonly accepted in these types of studies, the models generated in the multilevel regression analysis and presented in the second empirical section include the independent variables as fixed effects and city variance as a random effect. They have been fitted using a maximum likelihood approach (Laplace approximation) using the glmer function (from lme4 package) in R statistical software.

The analysis of the qualitative data was carried out inductively from 2015 to 2016, following a Grounded Theory methodology that starts from the data to build concepts and theory instead of using pre-conceived theoretical concepts to analyse the data (Strauss and Corbin 1990). Mannheim and Rennes were chosen because these cities had experimented in the previous years with new forms of involvement of immigrant residents, installing new fora for interaction between the municipality and immigrant residents. Participant observations in fora meetings (three in Rennes, two in Mannheim) are complemented by interviews with local officials (two in Rennes, two in Mannheim) and an analysis of publications and websites pertaining to these fora. For this article, we used the codes that capture the links between actors and activities that sought to foster collaboration within these fora. Through this, we analyze how the functioning of urban policy fora may enhance the formation of ties of collaboration.

Empirical results

The two initial questions we sought to answer with our quantitative analysis are whether and to what extent urban actors collaborate with immigrant advocacy bodies, and which factors enhance that collaboration.

Who collaborates with immigrant advocacy bodies?

This section presents descriptive results on the extent to which a range of composite urban actors build intense ties with immigrant advocacy bodies. As Table 2 shows, such collaborations are strongly circumscribed within a field of actors that focuses on immigrant issues: the branches of the administration concerned with immigrants' integration as well as immigrant advocacy bodies themselves establish more intense collaborations with immigrant advocacy actors. This stands in contrast to private and state economic actors, such as business actors and administrative actors working on economic development and labour market issues, who develop fewer intense ties with immigrant advocacy bodies. Other branches of the municipal administration related to its internal organization (i.e. human resources and citizens affairs) and to urban planning, as well as political actors and trade unions also establish fewer collaborations with immigrant advocacy bodies than administrative units responsible for integration.

The findings show that ties are mostly built among actors within a local integration policy field. Less intense collaboration is found for local public agencies working on economic and urban planning policy. One possible interpretation is that economic and urban planning departments do not

Table 2. Existence and intensity of collaboration with immigrant advocacy bodies ($n = 660$).

	Intensity of Collaboration			
	No collaboration	Occasional and rare collaboration	Intense collaboration	Total
City unit responsible for integration	**0,0%** **−2,0**	**19,2%** **−4,0**	**80,8%** **5,7**	100,0%
Immigrant advocacy bodies	**0,0%** **−3,2**	**25,0%** **−5,5**	**75,0%** **8,2**	100,0%
Other diversity actors	5,3% −1,4	57,9% ,1	36,8% ,9	100,0%
Social/Educational (admin)	5,5% −1,6	60,0% ,4	34,5% ,7	100,0%
Welfare Organizations	10,3% −,5	57,4% ,0	32,4% ,4	100,0%
Strategic management (admin)	6,9% −1,8	64,7% 1,6	28,4% −,5	100,0%
Ecological (admin)	7,1% −,6	71,4% 1,1	21,4% −,7	100,0%
Political actors	13,8% ,5	**66,4%** **2,2**	19,8% **−2,7**	100,0%
Trade Unions	**23,7%** **2,2**	60,5% ,4	15,8% **−2,0**	100,0%
Economic development (admin)	5,4% −1,3	81,1% 3,0	**13,5%** **−2,3**	100,0%
Urban planning (admin)	11,1% −,2	77,8% 2,2	**11,1%** **−2,2**	100,0%
Business actors	**50,9%** **9,1**	**40,0%** **−2,7**	**9,1%** **−3,6**	100,0%
Organizational (admin)	18,8% ,8	75,0% 1,4	**6,3%** **−2,1**	100,0%
Total	12,3%	57,3%	30,3%	100,0%

Note: Percentages and adjusted residuals (significant cells with adjusted residuals greater than ±1.96 are in bold).
Cramer's $V = 0{,}401$, $p < 0{,}000$.

consider it necessary to have intensive links with immigrant advocacy bodies, and that they consider immigrant issues or claims as primarily dealt with by integration officials. This finding challenges the assumption of a widespread mainstreaming of responsibilities for immigrant integration.

Which factors enhance this collaboration?

We now turn to analyzing the factors that enhance intense collaborations of non-immigrant actors with immigrant advocacy advocacy bodies.

Following the null model with no independent variables, several sets of models were generated, including both independent models with the four types of independent variables (actor type, actor's participation in local fora, city characteristics and country) separately and a full model that combines all variables.[9]

The results shown in Table 3 confirm previous results regarding the distance between public and private economic actors and immigrant advocacy

Table 3. Regression coefficients and standard errors (between brackets) of binary multilevel regression models predicting intense collaborations of nonimmigrant actors with an immigrant advocacy body by actor type (m1), actor's participation in local policy for a (m2), city characteristics (m3), country (m4) and full model with all variables at the same time (m5).

	Null model	m1	m2	m3	m4	m5 (Full model)
Random effects						
City variance	0,039	0	0	0	0	0
Fixed effects						
Intercept	-1,108(0,11)***	-0,738(0,26)**	-1,969(0,17)***	-1,164(0,10)***	-0,872(0,11)***	-1,495(0,33)***
Actor status						
Type of actor: Trade Union		-0,997(0,51)+				-0,949(0,54)+
Type of actor: Business actor		-1,604(0,54)**				-1,200(0,56)*
Type of actor: Political actor		-0,660(0,35)+				-0,648(0,38)+
Type of actor: Other diversity actors		0,158(0,42)				0,006(0,46)
Type of actor: Strategic management (admin)		-0,213(0,34)				-0,160(0,37)
Type of actor: Social/educational (admin)		0,071(0,38)				0,045(0,41)
Type of actor: Integration (admin)		2,173(0,56)***				1,834(0,59)**
Type of actor: Urban planning (admin)		-1,342(0,66)*				-1,010(0,69)
Type of actor: Ecological (admin)		-0,562(0,70)				-0,193(0,72)
Type of actor: Economic development (admin)		-1,119(0,55)*				-1,186(0,57)*
Type of actor: Organizational (admin)		-1,970(1,06)+				-1,804(1,09)+
Actor's participation in local policy fora						
Participation in migration-related fora			1,494(0,20)***			1,260(0,22)***
Participation in other general fora			0,573(0,20)**			0,505(0,22)*
City characteristics						
City Size – number of inhabitants				-0,065(0,10)		-0,050(0,12)
Proportion of foreign-born inhabitants				0,211(0,10)*		0,080(0,13)
Proportion of left-wing votes				0,270(0,12)*		0,151(0,14)
Country						
France (vs. Germany)					-0,704(0,21)**	-0,211(0,30)
AIC	680,8	636,2	612,3	667,2	671,5	585,9
BIC	689,6	693,4	629,9	689,1	684,6	669,1
ICC	1,2	0	0	0	0	0

Signif. codes: "***" 0,001 "**" 0,01 "*" 0,05 "+" 0,1.

bodies, as well as the circumscription of collaboration ties mostly within the immigrant policy field. They also indicate that the participation in local policy fora increases the likelihood that a composite actor has an intense collaboration with an immigrant advocacy body. Results show that participation in both what we called "migration-related fora" and participation in fora concerned with other issues or policy sectors, such as social affairs and urban development, increases the likelihood to collaborate intensively with immigrant advocacy bodies. This suggests that such fora in general foster the creation of ties of collaboration between local actors and immigrant advocacy bodies. However, participation in migration-related fora has the highest impact on the existence of such links, suggesting that dedicated fora in the integration policy field are relevant spheres for creating collaboration between urban actors and immigrant advocacy bodies.

The third model presents the effects of city-level variables. It shows that, despite the small relevance of the city level in itself – indicated by the low intraclass correlation coefficient (ICC),[10] the share of foreign-born people and the political orientation of the electorate are factors at the city level that enhance the propensity of non-immigrant actors to collaborate with immigrant advocacy bodies. The fourth model indicates that composite actors in German cities are more likely to build intense collaborations with immigrant advocacy bodies than in French cities. However, in the full model only the type of composite actor and the participation of actors in local policy fora present significant effects, which means that variation in the existence of intense collaboration with immigrant advocacy bodies is not explained by respondents' embeddedness in different cities and countries, all other factors being equal, but by the type of actor and particularly by the participation of actors in local policy fora.

Understanding the mechanisms that enhance ties of collaboration: qualitative findings

One of the most interesting findings of our quantitative analysis is that participating in policy fora increases the likelihood that an urban actor intensively collaborates with immigrant advocacy bodies. But how do urban actors actually foster collaboration in such fora? Is it simply presence in the meetings that promotes the establishment of ties (Levine 2013) or are there other mechanisms at play? In this last section we provide an exploratory interpretation based on fieldwork in the "Rennes au Pluriel" and Mannheim "Bündnis für Vielfalt" policy fora.

"Rennes au Pluriel" (*Rennes in Plural*) is a municipal consultative body set up by the municipality of Rennes in December 2015 as part of a broader city plan to reinforce local democracy (*La Fabrique Citoyenne*). It is formed by 60 individual citizens and representatives of civil-society associations selected through a public call for candidatures. Its official objectives are: (1) to encourage citizens to express themselves on issues of the promotion of equality and the fight against racism and discrimination; (2) to be a space of reflection, monitoring and exchange of experiences and points of view; and (3) to co-construct and monitor the public policy against discriminations. One of its main tasks is to organize the two-week "Rennes au Pluriel" festival.

In the German city of Mannheim, the "Alliance for Diversity" (*Bündnis für Vielfalt*) is an instrument to foster collaboration between different urban actors working on different dimensions of diversity, such as gender, migration, sexual orientation, age and disability. Instigated by a funding programme of the German Ministry for Families, the Elderly, Women and Youth and co-funded by the City of Mannheim, it exists since 2016. Its main activities entail networking meetings to allow participants to build up new ties of collaboration with other actors, a funding scheme for projects where actors work together across different dimensions of diversity, the organization of a one week festival ("einander.Aktionstage"), where these different projects are showcased to the whole city, and the prevention of conflicts between different population groups by signing and ratifying the "Mannheim declaration for living together in diversity".[11]

By observing the activities and interactions in the two fora and drawing on interviews with officials who coordinate them, we identified four collaboration-supporting mechanisms: Participation fora are sites where municipal administrations actively try to foster *a shared perspective and sense of belonging* that cross-cuts specific identifications of its members (Barnes, Newman, and Sullivan 2006). Commonalities between members can increase levels of trust, and, ultimately, lead to new and sustained ties of collaboration (Klijn, Edelenbos, and Steijn 2010). In our case studies, the two fora promoted a perspective on diversity that considers several dimensions of difference as interconnected (such as gender, sexual identity, immigrant background, etc.) and cooperation across different actor-types. In the case of "Rennes au Pluriel", for example, the responsible city councilor presented the diversity of the committee members as a source of wealth, in a context where everyone should find his or her own sense and place. If such a goal is met, we argue, it is more likely that actors interact with each other and trust each other more, and potentially establish new collaborations.

Furthermore, collaborative policy fora may also work towards *creating a shared vocabulary and culture* that allow communication and understanding between members and ultimately facilitate collaboration. Two of the first meetings of "Rennes au Pluriel" were aimed at ensuring that all its members "had a common culture in mind" about discrimination and diversity (interview with the committee's coordinator). This was done through trainings offered to the members by external experts. Similarly, the "Mannheim declaration for living together in diversity" was meant as "a way to reach agreement ("Verständigung"), a Mannheim language, on how things are happening here. And this process of reaching an agreement, bringing groups into exchange with each other, stood at the outset of the 'Alliance for Diversity'" (Interview with a city official).

Fora provide a space to develop *projects and means of action with each other* that steer the action of their members in a common direction (Barnes, Newman, and Sullivan 2006). In the case of Mannheim, shared projects were fostered by making funding for projects conditional on the cooperation of actors across different dimensions of diversity. One of the resulting projects was a collaboration between the city's DITIB mosque with the city's shelter for battered women. Together, they initiated a women's group within the mosque that provides consultation to women suffering domestic violence. The project fit the goals of the Alliance, as it cross-cuts the dimensions of religion and gender and thereby "cooperation partners open up to diversity and strengthen their competences in dealing with diversity" (Interview with a city official). "Rennes au Pluriel" set as its main objective for its first working period (2015-2017) the revision and monitoring of the "Municipal plan of the fight against discrimination". Members were also asked to participate in the evaluation of projects submitted to the participatory budjet of the city. By taking part in these activities, committee members were expected to develop a sense of co-responsibility, expected to eventually lead to collaborations beyond the time frame and tasks of the forum.

Participatory policy fora are also a means to *foster capacities and skills* (Geissel 2009; Michels and De Graaf 2010; Murray, Tshabangu, and Erlank 2010), and hence serve as what has been captured as "schools of democracy" in the literature (Takle 2014). In the case of "Rennes au Pluriel", the coordinator invited an expert on discrimination in France, who provided participants with basic knowledge on the French legal framework on discrimination. This was meant to train them in recognizing discrimination, and to transfer this knowledge to their respective associations. In Mannheim, the Alliance sought to foster recognition among its members of each other's worth. They did so by enlisting members of the forum as selection committee for project funding. According to the coordinator of the Alliance, the learning effect was that committee members after some time moved away from supporting projects that would solely benefit their own community to supporting projects that cross-cut different communities. Professionalization through the fostering of capacities and skills can make different actors operate on eye-level and thereby facilitate collaboration. Identifying these four mechanisms of creating a shared perspective and sense of belonging, a shared vocabulary and culture, shared goals and projects, and capacities and skills helps us understand the conducive effect of participation in fora for collaboration between participating actors.

Conclusion

In this article, we have contributed to an evolving field of research on local immigrant policy-making and immigrant political participation by focusing on relations of collaboration between municipal actors and immigrant advocacy bodies. By combining a large survey as well as in-depth fieldwork, we systematically study relations in urban immigrant policy-making and gain valuable insights into the ties that a range of urban actors build with immigrant advocacy bodies. Our findings show that a variety of actors in French and German cities reach out and intensively collaborate with immigrant councils and associations representing immigrants' rights. This finding reflects larger trends towards increased recognition of immigrant advocacy bodies as well as towards more collaborative forms of policy-making.

Yet, not all types of urban actors have strong linkages with these bodies. Actors from policy sectors such as economic development and urban and territorial planning to date collaborate to a lesser extent with immigrant advocacy bodies than administrative actors responsible for immigrant integration, though some collaboration exists. The likelihood of an intensive collaboration with immigrant advocacy bodies depends on the type of actor that collaborates, as our regression analysis shows. Being a city unit responsible for integration increases the likelihood of establishing intense collaboration with an immigrant advocacy body. Most intense collaborations with immigrant advocacy bodies remain within the circle of "usual suspects" of actors engaged in immigrant policy-making, confirming our expectation that an integration policy field is a relevant context for collaboration. Possibly, this is due to the lack of mainstreaming and a perceived lack of responsibility for policy issues relating to immigrant integration by actors outside of the integration policy field, such as economic actors or urban planners. At the same time, we altogether find that collaboration with immigrant advocacy bodies has become, to varying degrees, a common element of policy-making in German and French cities. Immigrant advocacy bodies are no longer considered mere recipients of subsidies and support, but have acquired the status of collaboration partners for state and non-state actors.

Furthermore, the regression analysis has shown that it is not only the type of actor that matters. An actor's participation in a local policy forum also increases the likelihood of establishing intense collaboration with an immigrant advocacy body. Non-immigrant actors in cities with a larger share of immigrants and leaning towards the left side of the political spectrum build more intense collaborations with immigrant advocacy bodies because they participate more in local policy bodies, particularly in migration-related fora.

This indicates that institutional arrangements at the city and country level matter for the establishment of collaborations.

Based on qualitative findings we outline why such collaborative fora can serve as motors for the build-up of ties of collaboration with immigrant advocacy bodies. These fora are not simply spaces that create repeated interaction. Municipal administrations also seek to change the quality of the contact by generating a shared perspective and sense of belonging, a common culture and language, and shared projects. Moreover, by training their members and professionalizing them, they seek to build up capacities and skills necessary to facilitate cooperation, and which certify immigrant advocacy bodies as respectable partners for other urban actors.

All four mechanisms combined, we argue, are likely to increase mutual knowledge and trust (Klijn, Edelenbos, and Steijn 2010). They foster the creation of "communities of practice" (Adler 2008), defined as likeminded groups of practitioners who are informally as well as contextually bound by a shared interest in learning and applying a common practice (Adler and Pouliot 2011; Wenger 1998). More research is needed to determine whether relations between urban actors in the immigrant policy-field and collaboration that stems from interactions in policy-fora change the design and implementation of policies. We have shown that the collaboration necessary for joint policy-making exists.

Notes

1. In our survey we targeted composite actors ("komplexe Akteure"). Following a terminology suggested by Scharpf (1997, 114), the term "composite actors" covers corporate (korporative) actors that have some degree of formal organization and collective actors, that is, looser umbrella structures or social movements. Criteria for the selection of actors were that they were (1) involved in local politics and (2) likely to intervene in diversity-relevant fields. We excluded organizations that may have local offices but mainly formulate claims at the national level (e.g. some environmental or human rights associations). We also excluded organizations that may inform local policy decision-making, but are organized on the regional or national level. We only included actors with a minimum level of organization, i.e. when they had an office and identifiable representatives. We thus do not capture shorter-term forms of social mobilization. We also aimed to only include types of actors that could be identified across the different cities at least within the same country. We accepted that we may thus not include possibly relevant actors in specific cities (see also Moutselos et al 2017).
2. We use the term "immigrant council" to refer to all kinds of councils set up locally to address immigrant affairs in local policy-making. They are institutionalized in different ways across cities and names differ (e.g. "immigrant council", "foreigners council" or "local representation of foreigner's interests"). As targets of the survey analyzed here, we focused on organisations that frame themselves as "immigrant associations" and/or whose main aim is to

advance the interests and rights of immigrants, which may exclude some initiatives by immigrants (such as sports or recreational associations) and the so-called "second generation". Only the first part of the quantitative analysis uses responses of such immigrant organizations (namely local immigrant associations' umbrella organizations in German cities, foreigner councils (Conseils des Résidents Étrangers in France,) and city-level branches of organisations like the Ligue Internationale Contre le Racisme et l'Antisémitisme (LICRA), Mouvement contre le racisme et pour l'amitié (MRAP), Association Solidarité avec Tous les Immigrés (ASTI), Comité inter mouvements auprés des évacués (La Cimade), Ligue des Droits de l'Homme, or SOS Racisme). Besides, key results presented in this article draw on survey answers on how other actors collaborate with immigrant associations and councils (see appendix).

3. For more information see (Moutselos et al 2017, p.10).
4. Team members are: Christian Jacobs, Christine Lang, Julia Martínez Ariño, Michalis Moutselos, Maria Schiller, Karen Schönwälder, Alexandre Tandé, Lisa Szepan.
5. For more information on the sample of cities see (Moutselos et al 2017, p.10).
6. We excluded individuals who act without an institutional base and less established initiatives. For a detailed description of the sampling procedure see Moutselos et al Technical report, p.10ff.
7. Of which 423 in Germany and 237 in France completed the network question of the questionnaire. Thus, in this article $n = 660$. Data of two cities were excluded from the multilevel analysis due to low response rates at the individual city level (therefore $n = 590$).
8. By migration-related fora we mean local policy fora in which issues related to immigration and cultural diversity are discussed.
9. All possible combinations off independent variables were tested, showing similar results than the full model. It's only worth mentioning that the inclusion of the variable concerning participation in local policy fora is what makes the country variable turn into a non-significant predictor.
10. This measure expresses the proportion of the variability in the outcome attributable to the units at the aggregated level (Field 2009) –the cities, in our case. Following Snijders and Bosker (1999, 224), the intraclass correlation coefficients (ICC) have been computed using the formula: $\rho_1 = \sigma^2/(\sigma^2 + 3.29)$, where $3.29 = \pi^2/3$. In other words, in this study it shows that overall there is almost no variation in establishing intense collaborations with immigrant advocacy bodies explained by differences between cities, but almost exclusively by differences within cities.
11. In Mannheim, there had been several incidents in the past where conflicts from the Middle East had spilled over to conflicts between immigrant groups in the city. City politicians and officials accorded high importance to such declarations as a means to prevent such conflicts from happening and to have tools to bring actors to the table and remind them of their responsibility for protecting a peaceful coexistence in the city.

Acknowledgement

We would like to thank Karen Schönwälder, Michalis Moutselos, Christine Lang, Christian Jacobs, and Alexandre Tandé for their comments on a previous version of this paper.

Disclosure statement

No potential conflict of interest was reported by the author(s).

Funding

This research was funded by the Max Planck Institute for the Study of Religious and Ethnic Diversity (Germany). In addition, Mireia Bolíbar holds a Juan de la Cierva Incorporación fellowship (Ref: IJCI-2017-33999), funded by the Agencia Estatal de Investigació (AEI) of the Spanish Ministry of Science, Innovation and Universities.

ORCID

Maria Schiller ⓘ http://orcid.org/0000-0002-4453-1642
Julia Martínez-Ariño ⓘ http://orcid.org/0000-0002-8893-0899
Mireia Bolíbar ⓘ http://orcid.org/0000-0001-9525-0907

References

Aarsaether, Nils, Torril Nyseth, and Hilde Bjorna. 2011. "Two Networks, One City: Democracy and Governance Networks in Urban Transformation." *European Urban and Regional Studies* 18 (3): 306–320.

Adler, E. 2008. "The Spread of Security Communities: Communities of Practice, Self-Restraint, and NATO's Post—Cold War Transformation." *European Journal of International Relations* 14 (2): 195–230. doi:10.1177/1354066108089241.

Adler, E., and V. Pouliot, V. 2011. "International Practices." *International Theory* 3 (1): 1–36. doi:10.1017/S175297191000031X.

Ansell, Chris, and Alison Gash. 2008. "Collaborative Governance in Theory and Practice." *Journal of Public Administration Research and Theory* 18 (4): 543–571.

Baglioni, Simone, and Marco Giugni, eds. 2014. *Civil Society Organizations, Unemployment, and Precarity in Europe*. Wiesbaden: Springer.

Barnes, Marian, Janet Newman, and Helen Sullivan. 2006. "Discursive Arenas: Deliberation and the Constitution of Identity in Public Participation at a Local Level." *Social Movement Studies* 5 (3): 193–207.

Bausch, Christiane. 2011. "'Ich komm besser ran an die Menschen als ein Deutscher' - Deskriptive Repräsentation am Beispiel von Ausländer- und Integrations(bei)räten." In *Krise und Reform politischer Repräsentation*, edited by Markus Linden, and Winfried Thaa, 257–278. Nomos Verlag: Baden-Baden.

Bogumil, Jörg, and Lars Holtkamp. 2004. "Local Governance und gesellschaftliche Integration." In *Governance und gesellschaftliche Integration*, edited by Stefan Lange, and Uwe Schimank, 147–166. Wiesbaden: Springer.

Bousetta, Hasan. 1997. "Citizenship and Political Participation in France and the Netherlands: Some Comparative Reflections on Two Local Cases." *New Community* 23 (2): 215–231.

Campbell, David E. 2013. "Social Networks and Political Participation." *Annual Review of Political Science* 16: 33–48.

Caponio, Tiziana. 2005. "Policy Networks and Immigrants' Associations in Italy: The Cases of Milan, Bologna and Naples." *Journal of Ethnic and Migration Studies* 31 (5): 931–950.

Cerrato Debenedetti, M. C. 2010. "L'invention locale des discriminations ethnoraciales: La carrière en accordéon d'un problème public." *Migrations Société* 131 (5): 153–170.

Creswell, John W. 2013. *Research Design: Qualitative, Quantitative and Mixed Methods Approaches*. Thousand Oaks: Sage.

De Graauw, Els, and Irene Bloemraad. 2017. "Working Together: Building Successful Policy and Program Partnerships for Immigrant Integration." *Journal on Migration and Human Security* 5 (1): 105–123.

De Graauw, Els, and Floris Vermeulen. 2016. "Cities and the Politics of Immigrant Integration: A Comparison of Berlin, Amsterdam, New York City, and San Francisco." *Journal of Ethnic and Migration Studies* 42 (6): 989–1012.

Downing, Joseph. 2015. "European Influence on Diversity Policy Frames: Paradoxical Outcomes of Lyon's Membership of the Intercultural Cities Programme." *Ethnic and Racial Studies* 38 (9): 1557–1572.

Downing, Joseph. 2016. "Influences on State–Society Relations in France: Analysing Voluntary Associations and Multicultural Dynamism, co-Option and Retrenchment in Paris, Lyon and Marseille." *Ethnicities* 16 (3): 452–469.

Eggert, Nina, and Katia Pilati. 2014. "Networks and Political Engagement of Migrant Organisations in Five European Cities." *European Journal of Political Research* 53 (4): 858–875.

Fennema, Meindert, and Jean Tillie. 2004. "Do Immigrant Policies Matter? Ethnic Civic Communities and Immigrant Policies in Amsterdam, Liege and Zurich." In *Citizenship in European Cities*, edited by Rinus Penninx, Karen Kraal, Marco Martiniello, and Steven Vertovec, 85–106. Aldershot: Ashgate.

Field, Andy. 2009. *Discovering Statistics using SPSS*. London: SAGE Publications.

Flamant, Anouk. 2016. "Donner la parole aux étrangers? De la creation d'une participation politique à l'usage ethnicisé de la catégorie d'"étranger" par las municipalités." *Participations* 14 (1): 237–264.

Garbaye, Romain. 2005. *Getting into Local Power: The Politics of Ethnic Minorities in British and French Cities*. Oxford: Blackwell Publishing.

Geissel, Brigitte. 2009. "Participatory Governance: Hope or Danger for Democracy? A Case Study of Local Agenda 21." *Local Government Studies* 35 (4): 401–414.

Halm, Dirk. 2015. "Potenzial von Migrantenorganisationen als integrationspolitische Akteure." *IMIS Beiträge*, Heft 4.

Ireland, Patrick. 2016. "Tales of the Cities: Local-Level Approaches to Migrant Integration in Europe, the U.S, and Canada." In *Handbook on Migration and Social Policy*, edited by Gary P. Freeman, and Nikola Mirilovic, 377–398. Cheltenham: Edward Elgar.

Jessop, Bob. 1995. "The Regulation Approach, Governance and Post-Fordism: Alternative Perspectives on Economic and Political Change?" *Economy and Society* 24 (3): 307–333.

Klijn, Erik-Hans. 2008. "Governance and Governance Networks in Europe: An Assessment of Ten Years of Research on the Theme." *Public Management Review* 10 (4): 505–525.

Klijn, Erik-Hans, Jurian Edelenbos, and Bram Steijn. 2010. "Trust in Governance Networks: Its Impacts on Outcomes." *Administration & Society* 42 (2): 193–221.

Levine, Jeremy R. 2013. "Organizational Parochialism: 'Placing' Interorganizational Network Ties." *City & Community* 12 (4): 309–334.

Martinez-Ariño, J., C. Jacobs, M. Moutselos, K. Schoenwaelder, M. Schiller, and A. Tande. 2018. "Why Do Some Cities Adopt More Diversity Policies Than Others? A study in France and Germany." *Comparative European Politics*: 1–22. doi:10.1057/s41295-018-0119-0.

Mcclurg, Scott D. 2003. "Social Networks and Political Participation. The Role of Social Interaction in Explaining Political Participation." *Political Research Quarterly* 56: 448–464.

Michels, Ank, and Laurens De Graaf. 2010. "Examining Citizen Participation: Local Participatory Policy Making and Democracy." *Local Government Studies* 36 (4): 477–491.

Montague, Dena. 2013. "Communitarianism, Discourse and Political Opportunity in Republican France." *French Cultural Studies* 24 (2): 219–230.

Moutselos, M., C. Jacobs, J. Martínez-Ariño, J., M. Schiller, M., K. Schönwälder & A. Tandé (2017). Cities and the Challenge of Diversity (CityDiv): The Survey, Technical Report. MMG Working Paper, (17–09).

Murray, Jessica, Busani Tshabangu, and Natasha Erlank. 2010. "Enhancing Participatory Governance and Fostering Active Citizenship: An Overview of Local International Best Practices." *Politikon* 37 (1): 45–66.

Nguyen Long, Le Anh. 2015. "Institutions, Information Exchange, and Migrant Social Networks in Rome." *Ethnic and Racial Studies* 38 (15): 2722–2737.

Nicholls, Walter, and Justus Uitermark. 2016. *Cities and Social Movements: Immigrant Rights Activism in the US, France, and the Netherlands, 1970-2015*. Chicheser: Wiley.

Nyseth, Torill, and Toril Ringholm. 2008. "Municipal Response to Local Diversity: Flexibility in Community Governance." *Local Government Studies* 34 (4): 471–487.

Però, Davide. 2007. "Migrants and the Politics of Governance: The Case of Barcelona." *Social Anthropology* 15 (3): 271–286.

Però, Davide, and John Solomos. 2010. "Introduction: Migrant Politics and Mobilization: Exclusion, Engagements, Incorporation." *Ethnic and Racial Studies* 33 (1): 1–18.

Pilati, Katia. 2012. "Network Resources and the Political Engagement of Migrant Organisations in Milan." *Journal of Ethnic and Migration Studies* 38 (4): 671–688.

Pinson, Gilles. 2010. "The Governance of French Towns. From the Centreperiphery Scheme to Urban Regimes." *Análise Sociale* 45 (197): 717–737.

Sack, Detlef. 2012. "Urbane Governance." In *Handbuch Stadtsoziologie*, edited by Frank Eckardt, 311–335. Wiesbaden: Springer.

Scharpf, Fritz W. 1997. *Games Real Actors Play: Actor-Centered Institutionalism in Policy Research*. Boulder: Westview Press.

Schiller, Maria. 2018. "The Local Governance of Migration-Based Diversity in Europe: The State of the Art and a Conceptual Model for Future Research." In *Routledge Handbook on the Governance of Migration and Diversity in Cities*, edited by Ricardo Zapata-Barrero, Tiziana Caponio, and Peter Scholten, 204–215. Abingdon: Routledge.

Scholten, Peter, and Ilona van Breugel. 2018. *Mainstreaming Integration Governance: New Trends in Migrant Integration Policies in Europe*. Cham: Palgrave Macmillan.

Schönwälder, Karen, Cihan Sinanoglu, and Daniel Volkert. 2013. "The New Immigrant Elite in German Local Politics." *European Political Science* 12 (4): 479–489.

Schrover, Martin, and Floris Vermeulen. 2005. "Immigrant Organisations." *Journal of Ethnic and Migration Studies* 31 (5): 823–832.

Snijders, Tom A. B., and Roel J. Bosker. 1999. *Multilevel Analysis: An Introduction to Basic and Advanced Multilevel Modeling*. London: SAGE Publications.

Strauss, A., and J. Corbin. 1990. *Basics of Qualitative Research: Grounded Theory Procedures and Techniques*. Beverly Hills, CA: Sage.

Takle, Marianne. 2014. "Immigrant Organisations as Schools of Bureaucracy." *Ethnicities* 15 (1): 99–111.

Takle, Marianne. 2015. "Institutional Design and Political Representation: the Council of Immigrant Organisations in Oslo." *Journal of International Migration and Integration* 16 (4): 1195–1211.

Teorell, Jan. 2003. "Linking Social Capital to Political Participation: Voluntary Associations and Networks of Recruitment in Sweden." *Scandinavian Political Studies* 26 (1): 49–66.

Thränhardt, Dietrich. 2013. "Migrantenorganisationen. Engagement, Transnationalität und Integration." In *Migrantenorganisationen: Engagement, Transnationalität und Integration*, edited by Günther Schultze, and Dietrich Thränhardt, 5–20. Bonn: Friedrich Ebert Stiftung.

Triviño-Salazar, Juan Carlos. 2018. "The Politics of Immigration Locally: Alliances between Political Parties and Immigrant Organizations." *Ethnic and Racial Studies* 41 (9): 1728–1746.

Uitermark, Justus. 2012. *Dynamics of Power in Dutch Integration Politics: From Accommodation to Confrontation*. Amsterdam: University of Amsterdam Press.

Uitermark, Justus, and Jan W. Duyvendak. 2008. "Citizen Participation in a Mediated Age: Neighbourhood Governance in the Netherlands." *International Journal of Urban and Regional Research* 32 (1): 114–134.

Wenger, E. 1998. *Communities of Practice. Learning, Meaning and Identity*. New York: Cambridge University Press.

Appendix 1. Survey question on collaboration with other urban actors

Local politics today often take place through networks. Thinking about the last twelve months, with whom and how intensively have you collaborated in the context of your work or that of your organization? We refer here to the collaborations linked to local politics in your city.

	Intensive Collaboration	Occasional Collaboration	Rare collaboration	No collaboration
With a representative of the city responsible for integration	☐	☐	☐	☐
With a representative of the city responsible for urban planning (and "politique de la ville" in FR version)	☐	☐	☐	☐
With the (office of the) mayor	☐	☐	☐	☐
With the representative of …				
… political factions/parties.	☐	☐	☐	☐
… labour unions	☐	☐	☐	☐
… the local agency for economic development.	☐	☐	☐	☐
… the public agency for work	☐	☐	☐	☐
… a job centre ("Maison de l"emploi' in FR version)	☐	☐	☐	☐
… **welfare** organizations	☐	☐	☐	☐
… associations for the promotion of the local economy (e.g. chamber of commerce)	☐	☐	☐	☐
… the local immigrant council (in FR also conseil de la citoyenneté / conseil de la diversité)	☐	☐	☐	☐
… an immigrant association	☐	☐	☐	☐
… a youth association	☐	☐	☐	☐
… an association of the disabled	☐	☐	☐	☐
… an association of the elderly	☐	☐	☐	☐

Table A1. List of the sampled cities and their characteristics regarding population size, percentage of foreign-born inhabitants, percentage of leftwing voters in the last local elections and percentage of surveyed actors participating in local policy fora.

	Population size	Foreign-Born 2012 (%)	Left-wing power (%)
München	1353186	27,4	49,9
Köln	1007119	22,2	55,2
Frankfurt am Main	679664	30,8	49,2
Stuttgart	606588	26,7	44,8
Düsseldorf	588735	24	55,0
Dortmund	580444	22,1	59,6
Essen	574635	16,4	52,4
Dresden	523058	7,9	46,7
Leipzig	522883	10,5	57,8
Hannover	522686	25	61,0
Nürnberg	505664	28,5	56,4
Duisburg	489559	19,5	45,8
Bochum	374737	19,1	58,0
Wuppertal	349721	23,5	50,9
Bonn	324899	22,4	47,3
Bielefeld	323270	22,9	53,6
Mannheim	313174	27,3	50,7
Karlsruhe	294761	23,4	45,4
Münster	279803	14,8	53,2
Wiesbaden	275976	23,8	48,9
Lyon	1321495	17,3	52,8
Lille	1119832	10,7	59,3
Marseille	1045805	20,2	39,4
Bordeaux	730116	12,6	34,8
Toulouse	725052	16,3	49,2
Nantes	602853	7,9	60,8
Nice	520990	23,6	25,5
Strasbourg	473495	18,8	52,7
Montpellier	434189	18,5	67,7
Toulon	425609	16,1	18,6
Rennes	408428	7,8	58,1
Grenoble	405156	18,5	69,0
Saint-Étienne	374922	13,3	43,3
Angers	267119	7,7	48,1
Dijon	245685	11,9	58,2
Nîmes	239919	17,8	37,2
Reims	209421	10,7	49,4
Le Havre	173142	9,5	43,9
Villeurbanne	146282	20	57,8
Le Mans	143599	9,4	56,7

Cultural policies mixing commonality and difference? The case of public libraries in French cities

Alexandre Tandé

ABSTRACT

Libraries are a core element of local cultural policies. In a country historically marked by national integration policies aiming at cultural homogeneity, what is the relationship of local public libraries to the socio-cultural diversity of populations? The results of qualitative studies conducted in three major cities (Bordeaux, Rennes and Nantes) display a growing awareness of more diverse users and adaptations to their demands. Librarians, at the same time, do not give up the universalist ideals central to the history of their institutions and their current activities. Despite differences between cities, the case of public libraries illustrates the possibility to combine universalism and diversity in the policies implemented in France, here in the cultural field. My study demonstrates how local institutions can use their room for manoevre and combine elements of the republican ideal and adjustments to a diverse social reality.

Introduction

New migration dynamics, but also the affirmation of long marginalized social characteristics (gender, sexual orientation, disability), contribute to diversifying lifestyles and identities within populations of large European cities. At the same time, inverse dynamics contribute to a cultural integration of urban populations. The widespread inclusion of states, cities and their populations in the global capitalist economy results in the dissemination of cultural goods (music, cinema, video games) and standardized consumption patterns (food, leisure, information and communication). At the national and local levels, political and administrative institutions contribute to an integration and harmonization of cultural references and practices (Alba and Duyvendak 2019). Finally, the contemporary urban context can further a third kind of dynamic, that of hybridization (or creolization): this occurs when populations with different cultural identities and practices meet and create new cultural references that may exceed traditional belongings and community cleavages (Cohen 2007; Martiniello 2014).

These dynamics of reconfiguration constitute a major challenge for the public authorities of big European cities, and one of their levers to respond to them is cultural policies. The creation and renewal of infrastructures, such as museums, theaters, libraries, as well as the multiplication of public events, corresponds to cultural motivations in the primary sense of the term, that is preserving, disseminating and supporting the creation of cultural properties. This human, material and financial investment also reflects the desire of cities to assert themselves as social, economic and political spaces: in accordance with the creative city theory, culture is now meant to attract tourists, residents with significant academic capital and investors, in order to optimize the economic development of cities in their regional, national and international environments (Florida 2002). Cultural policies are thus gaining importance as part of growth strategies (Navarro and Clark 2012). But beyond that, urban cultural policies are also, in the terms of Navarro and Clark (2012, 638) part of the "educational city" that promotes "equalitarian access" to various goods and thus to practiced citizenship. Cultural policies are used to address a wide range of urban issues, ranging "from neighborhood revitalization and community engagement to job creation, talent attraction, and achieving 'world city' status." Cultural policies may aim at "fostering local representation, building connections among diverse citizens, and enhancing the abilities of underrepresented groups to influence neighborhood change" (Grodach and Silver 2012, 3). Scholarly attention to the cultural policies of cities is also justified given the importance of the resources invested in this domain: local authorities are now the primary financial contributor to these policies in France (before the national state, all ministries combined), and the total amount of city expenditures (about 6 billion Euros a year) far exceeds that of regional authorities (Delvainquière and Tugores 2017).

Urban cultural policies can be classified according to their relationship to the sociocultural diversity of local populations. First, they may aim to contribute to the construction of a common culture, which can imply the rediscovery or the invention of a local history. Second, they may aim to reflect and encourage cultural diversity within the population by encouraging, for instance, the artistic expression of groups with a different cultural identity. And third, they may aim to reconcile homogeneity and cultural diversity, aiming for the invention of new cultural references and identities specific to the cities where they are created.

One might think that France is not affected by these dynamics. The cultural policies developed since the 1950s were initially national policies, impelled by the central state and pursuing the goals of the assimilation and cultural homogeneity of the French population. After the Second World War and the collapse of the colonial empire, one core purpose of the Ministry of Cultural

Affairs promoted by President De Gaulle was to support the gathering of the French nation around an ideal of artistic excellence (Dubois 1999). The interest of this policy in cultural diversity concerned works of art from all over the world and those produced in France by foreign and immigrant artists, but never the ways of life of the immigrant populations (Escafré Dublet 2014), even in the early 1980s when ruling socialists made "the right to cultural difference" a priority for the ministry (Martin 2015). Yet, research on local cultural policies has produced a more complex picture. To meet the expectations of composite urban populations, cities often diversify their cultural policies, developing an offer for educated middle classes and another for the working class, and sometimes targets specifically immigrant population. These types of offer may be compartmentalized or, in contrast, embedded in the agenda of establishments and cultural events (Négrier 2006). Analyses of the cultural component of the national policy for neighbourhood development (*politique de la ville*) have also shown that the diversity of the local population is an issue for local authorities to which they respond differently: they may seek to dissolve this in a homogeneous whole, or preserve it (Chaudoir and de Maillard 2004).

How do big French cities react to the reconfiguration of their populations? Do their cultural policies aim to shape the local population, and if so in what ways? And in particular, how do they position themselves regarding the alternative of commonality and difference? In principle, local authorities can alternately promote the homogeneity or the heterogeneity of the population, or take a third approach that aims to create commonality among the local population while also recognizing and valuing its cultural diversity. This article is based on the hypothesis that, contrary to national cultural policy that is linked to the "French integration model", a way to conceive common belonging through the ignorance of ethnicity issues (Bertossi 2007), cultural policies of big French cities display a more open relationship to cultural diversity. Beyond the apparent uniformity of this universalist and colourblind model, studies have shown variations in the action of public authorities (Bertossi 2012), especially at the local level (Downing 2015). I explore this hypothesis through the study of a particular type of cultural institution: local public libraries. This is particularly suitable because cultural diversity, has long been incorporated into French cultural policies (Glasze and Meyer 2009: 194-195) and this policy field may therefore be particularly open to diversity. At the same time, language – a core theme of libraries – is in France strongly linked with national identity. How do these seemingly contradictory impulses play out? As noted in a recent article "the intercultural opening of public libraries is an extremely common instrument", adopted in more than three quarters of the biggest French and German cities (Martínez-Ariño et al. 2018, 8). It is all the more surprising how little attention has so far been devoted to the relationship between public libraries and cultural diversity in

France, except in student work and the professional literature of librarians. My research therefore aims to fill this gap.

This text is structured as follows: In the next section, I will explain the particular importance of public libraries in the policies of large French cities, and the significant changes in their relationship with the public that occurred in recent years. I will also indicate what theoretical tools allow me to think of public intervention in "public reading and libraries". I will then outline the methodological framework of my research, case selection and data. In the fourth section, I will examine how three networks of local public libraries, in Bordeaux, Rennes and Nantes, are positioned vis-à-vis the diversity of the local population. I will, in particular, investigate their understanding of their tasks and challenges, ways in which they adapt their services, and whether and how they aim to embrace local cultural diversity. After a fifth section putting these observations into context, the conclusion will summarize the main results and the contribution of this article to the literature.

Public libraries as Swiss knives of local cultural policies

The traditional function of public libraries in France is to preserve and to allow the population access to literature, information and scientific knowledge (Carbone 2012). As an integral part of the development of local cultural policies since the late 1970s, libraries have gradually been associated with the use of culture for economic development. These institutions, their funds and their staff are thus invited to transform the "intrinsic values of culture (memory, creativity, critical knowledge, ritual, elitism, beauty, diversity and others)" into "social, human and symbolic capitals" (Arnaud 2011, 109). For cities, using culture strategically is part of attempts to position themselves in a competitive environment. The renovation and, increasingly, the construction of libraries is an important part of such strategies, and often buildings of high architectural quality symbolize both economic and political success, as well as the attachment to knowledge and art. The financial, material and human resources that local governments spend on libraries have increased since the early 1990s; France has more than 16,000 libraries – including neighborhood branches and reading places in small towns – making libraries the country's leading cultural network, ahead of music schools and cinemas (Robert 2015).

This presence of libraries in urban space is not only aimed at positioning cities vis-à-vis external actors, but also directly targets local populations. New functions are highlighted, such as developing links between residents, integration and participation of different and disadvantaged social groups, and contributing to a sense of belonging to the city (Servet 2009). Over the past twenty years, this expansion of library missions has resulted in an evolution of the activities and services offered to users. Libraries now make available books, magazines and, increasingly, digital resources. The latest and most far-reaching innovation is the wide variety of workshops on their premises, ranging from street art to theater, children's story time, yoga and video game competitions. In addition to leisure activities, users can participate in debates, take language courses and get professional training. Increasingly, cultural institutions are designed as open spaces (or "third places" as conceived by Ray Oldenburgvs 1989), allowing a wide range of activities (most of the time for free) and open to the local population as well as visitors. Third places are described as open spaces, distinct from both the home and the workplace, that allow different people to meet and build relationships. Transforming libraries into third places open to a multitude of uses and valuing popular as well as "high" cultures provokes as much enthusiasm as opposition (Jacquet 2015; Starke 2015). This way of conceiving the role of libraries, common in North America and parts of Europe, conflicts with traditional visions and professional practices in France.

The relationship to the socio-cultural diversity of local populations is equally contested. Among librarians, attention to this theme is increasing, as reflected in student librarians' theses and working groups within the Association of Librarians of France. This national association encouraged libraries to endorse a Charter stating that "collections, resources and contents available in or from libraries are a reflection of the plurality and diversity of society" (2015). But some works also emphasize the persistence of an integrationist approach, hostile to the recognition of distinct communities among users and reluctant to adapt the offers.

This study investigates whether French conceptions of national culture and homogeneity, on the one hand, and recognition of cultural diversity can be reconciled in local political practice. I hypothesize that – under pressure from both traditional Republicanism and changing local realities – practitioners may find ways to reconcile the aims to reproduce a common urban culture and, at the same time, integrate and value the cultural diversity of the local population.

Adopting a political sociology perspective, I define "public reading" policies (*politiques de lecture publique*) as collective and institutionalized actions, determined and implemented by a plurality of public actors (local political leaders, network and site managers, librarians) in partnership with private actors (mainly users and associations). Library policies may be conceptualized as fields: actors mobilize around particular issues, their relations are marked by solidarity and conflict, and as specific social spaces, such policies have some autonomy but also boundaries (Dubois 2015). Three main actor groups will generally be present. The political one is that of deputy mayors in charge of culture (or of public reading) and their direct collaborators. After the city council has passed the annual budget, deputy mayors determine the general orientations of policy and monitor its implementation. Second, the library networks (central management with an administrative team) build a common agenda (themes, major events), provide administrative follow-up and coordinate the actions of the various neighborhood libraries. The third group are the neighborhood branches that welcome the public. Placed under the responsibility of a director, these branches implement the orientations decided by the headquarters. In the absence of a national law regulating the direction and functioning of libraries, local politicians generally have decisive influence on the activities of these institutions in their city: an official hierarchy applies, from the political decision to the daily action of librarians (Lahary 2015). However, control is rarely perfect, and when their expertise (or other strategic resources) allow them to do so, executive actors are likely to discuss, accept or refuse instructions from elected officials. They can also propose actions that are then endorsed by elected officials. Each public reading and library policy is a configuration of interacting actors: the dynamics specific to each of these configurations and the results of their aggregation will produce particular results.

Methodological approach and profile of cities

Urban cultural policies are investigated by way of three case studies in Bordeaux, Rennes and Nantes. These cities have declared their openness to diversity, a claim, in some ways, confirmed by previous scholarship (Bereni and Epstein 2015). Qualitative fieldwork was conducted between May 2016 and June 2017. About thirty semi-structured interviews with interlocutors involved in the local politics of public reading and libraries were conducted. I sought to meet actors invested in three domains of local politics (political actors, network and local-site managers). I also interviewed actors not directly involved in the public reading policy, but knowledgeable about local political issues, in particular the functioning of the administration and the strategic importance of culture. Interviews focussed on (1) history, orientations and functioning of the local public reading policy; (2) scope and limitations of the third place approach in the activity of the network and local libraries; (3) relationship of the city's libraries to the socio-cultural diversity of the population (perception, adaptation, enhancement). Second, this study is based on document analysis (specifically public statements and strategic documents). Preliminary information was gained through participant observation in the exploratory phase of the research.

All three featured cities are prosperous and political, administrative and economic centres of their regions. Prefecture of the department of Gironde and capital of the New Aquitaine region, Bordeaux concentrates many administrative jobs. The dynamism of its economy is based on trade, finance, services and advanced industries. Prefecture of the department of Ille-et-Vilaine and the Brittany region, Rennes concentrates administrative and university functions. The city claims a status as an intellectual and cultural centre with the slogan: "Vivre en intelligence". Since the 1980s, the weakness of industry has been offset by an innovative technology sector. A working-class city until the mid-1980s, Nantes is today a city of managers and inter-mediate professions. Prefecture of the department of Loire-Atlantique, the city has attracted large service companies since the 1990s, which are seduced by the proximity of Paris by TGV and low-cost land.

Bordeaux (239,157 inhabitants), Rennes (215,366 inhabitants) and Nantes (283,000 inhabitants) are smaller big cities in comparison with Paris, Lyon or Marseille. The importance and attractiveness of these cities is more ade-quately captured by reference to their urban areas with 700–800,000 inhabi-tants. In all three cities, the proportion of inhabitants with an immigrant background is rather low compared to other major French cities: Rennes (9.7%) is followed by Bordeaux (7.6%) and Nantes (4%).[1] If the presence of immigrants is old in Bordeaux, it is more recent in Rennes and especially in Nantes. In all three cities, however, immigrant shares have been rising in recent years.

In Bordeaux, Rennes and Nantes, culture is one of the main budget items of the municipality. From the 1990s, Bordeaux has developed a network of cul-tural establishments (opera, theaters) and a training system (conservatory, school of fine arts, university courses) that contribute to the current reputation of its policy in France and abroad. Thus, the city centre was labelled a UNESCO World Heritage Site. In Rennes, local elites invested in the cultural field as early as the 1950s. The aim was to "make Rennes an international metropolis, based on culture" (Vion and Le Galès 1998, 8), and to foster social cohesion in a rapidly expanding city. Culture became the driving force behind the develop-ment of Nantes in the 1990s. Local elites sought to reshape the image of the city, given the collapse of its industry and the closure of shipyards. The mul-tiplication of cultural establishments and events have since made Nantes a cultural centre of international standing.

The cultural policies of Bordeaux, Rennes and Nantes all include a network of libraries. These three networks respond to a number of objectives: urban development, cultural service of proximity and relay of the local cultural policy, training, employment assistance and social cohesion. The use of culture for prestige purposes appears clearly in the central libraries of Bor-deaux (Bibliothèque Mériadeck) and Rennes (Library of Champs-Libres), less so in the case of Nantes where the central building (Bibliothèque Jacques Demy), opened in 1985, is today old-fashioned. The Bordeaux network com-prises a central library and ten neighborhood libraries, endowed with impor-tant resources and a prestigious heritage fund. Placed under a common direction, the libraries of Rennes are organized into two distinct networks: the metropolitan library (Rennes and the surrounding communes) on the one hand, and the city network on the other (eleven neighborhood branches, one travelling library). The Nantes network includes a central library, four neighborhood branches and several associative libraries whose size and supply are smaller.

Finally, these three cities have in common a certain openness to cultural diversity, which is expressed both by a specific policy and by taking this theme into account in the cultural policy of the city. Defined by its mayor as the city of the "identité heureuse" (*happy identity*), Bordeaux has an observatory of equality and organizes an annual "*Quinzaine* of equality, diversity and citizenship", under the aegis of the Equality and Citizenship Deputy Mayor. Cultural and equality policies can be combined: the History Museum of the city offers a permanent exhibition on the involvement of Bordeaux in the slave economy, and organizes an annual cycle of exhibitions, concerts and screenings to "celebrate one of the communities of the city" (Bordeaux, museum director). From the 1980s, Rennes encouraged migrant people to form associations, and then supported the creation of the intercultural festival *Convergences* (2000, renamed *Rennes au Pluriel* in 2014). The development of mechanisms to fight against discrimination was accompanied by a desire to "take into account and promote cultural diversity in all its forms, focussing on going beyond the segmentation of audiences and populations" (Rennes Métropole 2013). In its public communication, Nantes presents itself as a cosmopolitan and hospitable city, close to the ocean and open to cultural contributions from other parts of the world. The municipality supported research on the town's slavery past, concretized by a permanent exhibition on the banks of the Loire river (Masson et al. 2013). Nantes has also co-financed the multicultural festival *Tissé Métisse* since 1993. During interviews conducted in all three cities, however, representatives of associations voiced criticism, regretting the cumbersome administrative procedures, the timidity of the elected officials and the tendency to value international cultural diversity more than local cultural diversity.

Checking all boxes? Libraries and their relationship with the public

Perceived and targeted audiences

In interviews, Bordeaux librarians first mentioned the heterogeneity of the public in socio-economic terms. They were cautious about cultural and national origins, saying they did not want to reduce users to exclusive membership. The arrival of foreign populations in Bordeaux, however, is considered as a real challenge, although not a novel one: "We think of migrants arriving today from the Middle East, but we have always had migrants, with international geopolitics: Ethiopia, South Sudan, Caucasus, Chechnya ... All this is not new." (interview Bordeaux, director) But the intensification of migration flows in recent years has increased librarians' attention to diversity. Further-more, the function of libraries is rethought. Libraries are regularly presented as places of mixing: "In this library located in a *politique de la ville* district, we have newcomers, many intermediate professions, some more well-off populations. And all these publics mingle." (interview Bordeaux, political actor) Reflection on the socio-cultural diversity of the public finds a limit in the low knowledge of the librarians. Information comes mainly from their exchanges with users and partners (administration, associations) involved for example in the reception of newcomers and refugees. Efforts are being made, however, to improve information about the public who frequent libraries (or do not). In 2016, a survey was conducted to explain the non-use of libraries. Interviewers were required to speak other languages than French in order to reach non-French speaking populations.

The libraries of Rennes see the migrant public with reference to their legal status in France. Sites close to the prefecture and shelters note a more sys-tematic use of their premises by immigrants, partly explained by free access to computers. Staff question the role they should play vis-à-vis users who have "no other activity than to wait for their situation to evolve" (interview Rennes, Direction 2) and spend a lot of time in libraries. Yet, this growing attention to diversity is not accompanied by a better knowledge of it. The registration forms provide limited information (socio-professional category, place of residence), and do not capture those who frequent the buildings without registering or borrowing. In the absence of a survey to determine user profiles, the management recognizes not knowing if the "diversity" of the users is representative or not of the population of the city as a whole. Knowledge of the social and cultural diversity of the public is thus mainly informal, based on impressions of staff, interactions with the public and the demand for specific advice and literature (e.g. in a foreign language, for learn-ing French). Associations are the other main source of information for librarians.

In Nantes, the socio-cultural diversity of the public is today an issue for the management and staff of the library network. But this is a recent trend, and not a policy built in years. Libraries in Nantes are just beginning to become interested in the cultural diversity of their publics (and non-publics). While Nantes was one of the two French cities to obtain the national Diversity Label (Bereni and Epstein 2015), librarians do not associate the term diversity with their action, and instead link it to the field of human resources. Focussed on its own actions, the network is also little associated with festivals and exhi-bitions celebrating cultural diversity conducted by the city. On the whole, librarians have limited knowledge of their audience. This is due in part to the limited information collected during subscriptions: it relates to the place of residence, gender, age and financial resources (to determine whether someone has a right to free access). In the past, the network conducted surveys of its public, but these have not been renewed for ten years. Knowledge is mainly obtained through informal exchanges with users, and through partnerships with various external actors, such as officials in the National Education service and social assistance, and members of associations dealing with the reception of migrants or non-French speaking people.

Implementing measures for users

Libraries in Bordeaux do not generally target users based on their nationality. However, the importance of resources to learn French, present throughout the network, suggests that traditional integration efforts are supported. Moreover, there is no policy of putting together collections specifically dedicated to minority communities as common in North-American and other European countries (Zielinska 2001). Some actions aimed at all publics remote from libraries directly affect people of foreign origin: help with administrative procedures, training in digital tools, writing workshops. In order to improve communication with non-French-speaking audiences and appear more welcoming, the network adapts signage in buildings (using pictograms) and prepares a multilingual information booklet (English, Spanish, Portuguese, Arabic, Russian, certain African languages). Foreign language books and newspapers are available in the central library and several neighborhood sites. Selected with teachers working with newly arrived students, they are mainly aimed at a young audience. The management wants to develop this collection to reach non-French speaking adults: "It is necessary that people can come and flourish in the library, with access to documents that are in their language, and also to learn French (…) It is good to learn French but you also need to read things in your own language. (…) So we develop our collections so that these two objectives are achieved." (interview Bordeaux, Director)

In Rennes, responding specifically to the needs of a diverse audience is not a goal stated by the management: it officially sticks to a breakdown of the public by age groups and the catch-all category of "people distant to cultural offers" (Rennes 2014). However, a strategy is implemented to ensure that French-language learning resources are available in the whole network. Librarians are also becoming increasingly aware of the need to adapt their communication in order to reach non-Francophone users. In the city centre, staff are encouraged to improve their English, especially to better accommodate tourists. In immigration areas, some documents are translated, but often on the initiative of other institutions. The library network does not have a real strategy in this domain. A collection of works in foreign languages exists, but it is relatively small and unevenly distributed: the central institutions are little (or not) endowed, unlike the libraries of the working-class neighborhoods and the travelling library. In these cases, the collection (English, German, Spanish, Turkish, Arabic) has often been compiled in partnerships with associations who then relay information to their audiences. The use of these books encourages, in turn, the librarians to buy new ones.

Adapting the offer of libraries in Nantes to the socio-cultural diversity of the public is not on the agenda of the network, and the special needs that some users might have, have not been the subject of particular attention. The network has a fund in foreign languages, but it has been built up over the years without any real strategy. A contrast thus appears with the majority of the collections, constituted "in a rather intellectual way" with reference to an "ideal library" (interview Nantes, Director 1). The management ignores the content of the collection of foreign language books, and to find out more, I was directed to those in charge of neighborhood libraries. On the other hand, French-language learning materials are systematically present and purchased in coordination with the administration and associations accompanying non-French-speaking migrants. The network management wishes to improve its communication and the reception of non-French speaking publics: "Equal access to the public service [implies] to be able to understand and read the instructions, in any case the conditions of access to the service." This required better "taking into account languages, differences, and making available translated materials." (interview Nantes, Director 2) While waiting for a strategy change at the network level, neighborhood libraries communicate pragmatically with non-Francophone adults through their children and associative intermediaries. Librarians oscillate between reasonable accommodation, respect for the religious calendar (Ramadan) when organizing moments of conviviality, and sensitivities, for example when foreigners learning French complain about nudity scenes in a movie shown at the library. Some librarians refuse to comply with what they perceive as "censorship" (interview Nantes, Branch manager 1).

Showcasing the city and its population(s)

For the libraries of Bordeaux, representing and reflecting the diversity of the population is an identified and adopted mission: "If diversity is part of the identity of the territory, it must be found in the library, through collections, books that deal with the history of the territory and books written by immigrant authors (…) The library must represent this diversity that constitutes the identity of its territory. It must also do so through its activities" (interview Bordeaux, Director 1). The Central Library hosted an exhibition on the treatment of migration in comic books, in partnership with the National Museum of Immigration History. In the different districts of Bordeaux, libraries implement actions with associations and users. In the Saint-Michel district, a historic immigration district, the library lends a space to an association supporting women with a migration background. Life stories, recipes and other stories have been collected and published: the books are now in the library catalog. In the neighborhood of Bacalan, the library works with Roma communities (outdoor activities, help with professional integration, exhibitions on migration routes). And yet, diversity is not the only concern of libraries: "It is a subject that we address as much as others. The difficulty for libraries is that, unlike a museum, we are supposed to cover all fields of knowledge (…) Here, the key word is: balance" (interview Bordeaux, Director 1).

Regularly associated with events celebrating international cultural diversity, the libraries of Rennes showcase artists and cultural practices from other countries. This is less the case for populations of foreign origin settled in the city, even if certain initiatives are supported. A local library has hosted an exhibition devoted to costumes and festive menus: "For the vernissage, inhabitants who had brought documents explained how weddings took place in Brittany in the 1950s, what is a Kabyle wedding or [how to prepare] a typical Vietnamese dish." (interview Rennes, branch manager 1) On the other hand, the objective of promoting diversity, as stated in the Cultural Project of the Metropolis (Rennes Métropole 2013) is not reflected in the activities of the central library. The library has integrated the Encyclopedia of Migrants, a collection of testimonials and scientific articles on the theme of migration, into its collections – an associative project born in the district of Rennes Blosne. But about the *Rennes au Pluriel* Festival, which the Metropolitan Library does not associate with, a director says: "It is not sufficiently along our political, artistic and cultural line" (interview Rennes, Director 2). Even librarians of the municipal network point to the lack of a real diversity promotion strategy as one of the possible causes of low attendance in their institutions (interview Rennes, branch managers 1 and 2).

Highlighting the diversity of Nantes' populations through collections, exhibitions and cultural events has never been a focus for the Nantes library network. When the city or one of its cultural institutions implements such actions, the network usually stays away. Even in neighborhood libraries where a large part of the public is of immigrant origin, few initiatives go in this direction. Very recently, a series of meetings and an exhibition devoted to migration to the Nantes region (The Encyclopedia of Migrants) was the first major action on this theme for the network. This cycle of events and the exhibition are therefore an innovation. The network management would like to go further: "Through the life stories of migrants and the reflections on the migratory experience, diversity is [highlighted]. In addition, we have the project to develop training action at the scale of the Nantes agglomeration with all libraries, in order to address the theme of migration and the reception of migrant audiences" (interview Nantes, Director 2). To date, it is difficult to know if this experience will lead to a greater investment in this theme, or if it will remain an isolated event.

Integration or diversity? The dynamics of local policy fields

Of the three cities, Bordeaux is the city where attention to diversity is the greatest, whether for public knowledge, actions carried out at the neighborhood or agglomeration scale, or in terms of projects aimed at better meeting the needs of the public and the expectations of a diverse audience. Libraries in Bordeaux consider French populations with a migration background as targets of their action, seeking a balance between integration and the preservation of cultures of origin. The case of Bordeaux shows that cohesion and common identity can be combined with diversity in a public policy conducted in France. We find an interculturalist approach, halfway between Republican integration and multiculturalism: "On some points, we try to convey republican values. [With] foreign users who have a [problematic] relationship with the female sex, we are uncompromising. (...) But on the other hand, on all that is cultural, we are really in diversity. There are a lot of actions to promote the different cultures [present in] neighborhoods" (interview Bordeaux, Director).

This combination occurs in a context where the views of political actors, network managers and neighborhood librarians tend to converge. When the Mayor publicly values the "peaceful relations between inhabitants [of the city], regardless of their origins, sexual orientation or their religions", he points to both the "historical temperance" of the territory and the "proactive policy" intended to achieve a common sense of belonging (*"vivre ensemble"*) (Bordeaux 2016b). The cultural policy as a whole is also part of this perspective, for instance by affirming its contribution to "the promotion of cultures" in collaboration with anti-discrimination and local integration policies (Bordeaux 2016a). A similar dynamic can be seen at the level of the library network, where diversity is presented as a principle of action, and its respect as a goal to be achieved: "The diversity of audiences will be more fully taken into account, for example linguistic diversity or diversity of abilities (disability situations)" (Bordeaux 2016). In neighborhood branches, teams of librarians have also been involved in diversity issues for years, often in connection with local associations. The current dynamic fosters their projects related to diversity, which are generally validated without much difficulty.

In contrast, Nantes is the city where libraries are least aware of local diversity, and the least willing to adapt to specific needs and demands. People with a migration background, whether French or foreigners, are still rarely considered as targets of public intervention. This is surprising, since local elected officials have taken a stand on diversity issues for years. The city was awarded the national Diversity Label in 2012 and 2017 for its personnel management policy, while the "Migration, Integration, Diversities" policy makes interculturality a priority. Nantes is also a part of the Eurocities network, whose Charter (Eurocities 2010) "recognises and values the contribution immigration and migrants have made to European cities". Yet, the local cultural policy proves to be ambivalent: on the one hand, it welcomes the contribution of new inhabitants coming from all over the world, but on the other it only values cultural diversity provided it fits into the local story conceived by public authorities. Amateur practices are encouraged, but artistic excellence is at the core of all prominent cultural institutions and events.

This logic appears even more accentuated in the case of libraries, which remain distant from commitments to diversity. Politicians involved in public reading policy do not aim to adapt libraries' offers accordingly: "We have a global [diversity] policy in the city, but here we are moving away from the realm of libraries. (…) We are often not the driving force behind all this, even if we have the responsibility to open the doors of our establishments" (interview Nantes, deputy mayor). Some managers of neighborhood libraries would like to take more account of the diversity of their audiences, but remain cautious. One reason is the reluctance of staff, who refuse to see their duties evolve towards a greater proximity with users through welcoming and counselling activities. If resistance to transformations in the professional role is a general tendency (librarians should not turn into "social workers"), it reinforces distance with a diverse audience and reduces the possibility of considering specific demands. The greatest openness to diversity is therefore expressed by the management of the network, even with some ambivalence. Taking better account of the diversity of users remains a work in progress: "A few years ago I would have told you that we are here for integration and a universal model. Now I think rather the opposite: a library for everyone. I think that's the future." (interview Nantes, Direction)

The case of Rennes presents an intermediate situation. In this city, public authorities and librarians are the most innovative in their relationship with the public. Libraries are very open to external interventions (by individuals or associations), and seek to combine traditional uses with new practices. Attention to diversity is also real, but concretizations are more partial and random. While responding to cultural diversity is presented as a commitment of the city, authorities oscillate between favouring integration or interculturality. Elected officials regularly celebrate the cultural wealth of the city, based on its population: "Just as France, Rennes must be thought of in the plural. Our city is blended and rich in its diversity. (…) Everyone must be recognized as unique and as a part of our common history" (Rennes 2015). The local cultural policy reflects these principles through two objectives: the support for the *Rennes au Pluriel* festival and for intercultural dialogue in immigrant neighborhoods (Rennes 2018). However, activities are confined to an annual cultural event and to a limited part of the local territory: they do not concern cultural policy as a whole.

A gap also appears between public statements and strategic orientations of the library policy. In the opening speech of a recent literary festival, the deputy mayor in charge of culture valued "the cultural diversity that underlies [the] common living in Rennes" (Careil 2019). But such principles do not appear in strategic documents of the Metropolitan Library, nor in those of the municipal network of libraries. Interviews with the management of the network confirm an interest in these issues and the possibility of carrying out related actions, but without making it a recurring line of intervention. It is in the activity of neighborhood libraries where the desire to articulate integration and socio-cultural diversity is the most clearly expressed. With regard to works in foreign languages, a director states: "These media allow the sharing of cultures (…) It is a desire on our part to fuel the desire to maintain cultural identity and memory. (…) The role of libraries is to reflect all cultures, to discover lesser known cultures or some lesser known aspects" (interview Rennes, branch manager 1).

Conclusion

This study started from the assumption that, contrary to national cultural policy that is linked to the "French integration model", cultural policies of big French cities might display a more open relationship to cultural diversity. Like in other countries, cultural policies may increasingly be mobilized to reconcile the homogeneity and cultural diversity of urban populations.

The result of the investigation is mixed: Library policies of Bordeaux, Rennes and Nantes fit well into the French national framework. Librarians altogether follow the paradigm of integration, as much in their general orientations as in the implementation of actions, at the network level and in neighborhood branches. Bringing the non-francophone populations to the understanding and practice of French is perceived as one of the essential missions. The ubiquitous means for learning French and the commitment to putting on French-language learning reflect the contribution of libraries to the construction of the French nation. Finally, as in national cultural policies, international cultural production is systematically integrated into collections and well showcased. But the situation is different for the cultures of migrant populations settled in these cities. In interviews, it was a recurring comment that it was imperative to avoid segmenting the offer, to constitute categories of users on an ethnic or cultural basis, because this would encourage stigmatization of users and contradict the republican ideal. Treating the public differently according to origin or belongings touches on a major political taboo in France. Librarians' limited awareness of the socio-cultural diversity of the public, result of the ban on specific data, restricts their ability to respond with targeted measures.

And yet, there is a real and growing attention to socio-cultural diversity in discourse and library activity, and this is also expressed through changes in the relationship with the public. Recognizing the cultural diversity of their audiences, some libraries develop multilingual collections by targeting the languages spoken by the city's population. Other initiatives include recognizing local cultural diversity, for example through exhibitions and public events that focus on the experiences and memories of immigrants . These actions aim to achieve a set of objectives, such as increased identification with the city, recognition of the diversity of the population, and attracting populations who do not usually come to the library. Analysis of the three cases showed greater openness in Bordeaux and Rennes than in Nantes. But even in the latter case, consideration of diversity was noticeable.

The national framework is not absent from the actions of the public authorities in these three cities, and its strength probably represents a French particularity. At the same time, while pursuing the universalist ideal of access to education, culture and citizenship, libraries are increasingly able to also offer services and resources for specific audiences. I therefore argue that local cultural policies, here public library policies, do not juxtapose the promotion of national unity and the recognition of diversity, but can combine both. Considering that the French model is not "a total structure of socio-cultural and normative meanings" which imposes itself on the actors, but "a discursive and normative field of struggles for legitimacy" (Bertossi 2012, 263), local culture policies seem to grant particularly wide scope for such struggles. Future research may want to explore whether these observations can be generalized.

Note

1. Immigrant background here refers to foreign birth (« immigré »), according to INSEE (National Institute of Statistics and Economic Studies) classification.

Disclosure statement

No potential conflict of interest was reported by the author(s).

References

Alba, Richard, and Jan Willem Duyvendak. 2019. "What About the Mainstream? Assimilation in Super-Diverse Times." *Ethnic and Racial Studies* 42 (1): 105–124.
Arnaud, Lionel. 2011. "Culture (développement Culturel)." In *Dictionnaire des politiques territoriales*, edited by Romain Pasquier, Sébastien Guigner, and Alistair Cole, 109–114. Paris: Presses de Science Po.
Association des Bibliothécaires de France. 2015. *Charter of the Fundamental Right of Citizens to Have Access to and Share Information and Knowledge Via Libraries*. Paris. http://www.abf.asso.fr/fichiers/file/ABF/biblib/charte_biblib_abf_uk.pdf.

Bereni, Laure, and Renaud Epstein. 2015. *Instrumenter la lutte contre les discriminations: le "label diversité" dans les collectivités territoriales. Rapport final*. Paris: Alliance de recherche sur les discriminations. (ARDIS), Région Île de France.

Bertossi, Christophe. 2007. *French and British models of integration Public philosophies, policies and state institutions*. COMPAS, University of Oxford, Working paper n°46.

Bertossi, Christophe. 2012. "French Republicanism and the Problem of Normative Density." *Comparative European Politics* 10 (3): 248–265.

Bordeaux. 2016a. *Document d'orientation culturelle*. http://www.bordeaux.fr/p82366/bordeaux-culture.

Bordeaux. 2016b. *Quinzaine de l'égalité, de la citoyenneté et de la diversité*.

Carbone, Pierre. 2012. *Les bibliothèques*. Paris: Presses Universitaires de France.

Careil, Benoît. 2019. "Rue des livres, une fête bouillonnante, joyeuse et interculturelle". https://elus-rennes.eelv.fr/ay-roop-un-cirque-jeune-poetique-audacieux-2/.

Chaudoir, Philippe, and Jacques de Maillard. 2004. *Culture et politique de la ville: Une évaluation*. La Tour d'Aigues: Éditions de l'Aube.

Cohen, Robin. 2007. "Creolization and Cultural Globalization: The Soft Sounds of Fugitive Power." *Globalizations* 4 (3): 369–384.

Delvainquière, Jean-Cédric, and François Tugores. 2017. "Dépenses culturelles des collectivités territoriales: 9,3 milliards d'euros en 2014." *Culture chiffres* 3 (3): 1–32.

Downing, Joseph. 2015. "Understanding the (Re)Definition of Nationhood in French Cities: A Case of Multiple States and Multiple Republics." *Studies in Ethnicity and Nationalism* 15 (2): 336–351.

Dubois, Vincent. 1999. *La politique culturelle. Genèse d'une catégorie d'intervention publique*. Paris: Belin.

Dubois, Vincent. 2015. "The Fields of Public Policy." In *Bourdieu's Theory of Social Fields*, edited by Mathieu Hilgers, and Eric Mangez, 199–220. Cambridge: Cambridge University Press.

Escafré Dublet, Angéline. 2014. *Culture et Immigration. De la question sociale à l'enjeu politique, 1958-2007*. Rennes: Presses Universitaires de Rennes.

Eurocities. 2010. *Charter on integrating cities*. http://www.integratingcities.eu/integrating-cities/charter.

Florida, Richard. 2002. *The Rise of the Creative Class*. New York: Basic Books.

Glasze, G., and A. Meyer. 2009. "Das Konzept der 'kulturellen Vielfalt': Protektionismus oder Schutz vor kultureller Homogenisierung?" In *Facetten der Globalisierung*, edited by J. Kessler and C. Steiner, 186-197. Wiesbaden: Springer VS.

Grodach, Carl, and Daniel Silver. 2012. *The Politics of Urban Cultural Policy: Global Perspectives*. London: Routledge.

Jacquet, Amandine. 2015. *Bibliothèques troisième lieu*. Paris: Association des Bibliothécaires de France.

Lahary, Dominique. 2015. "Les bibliothèques au risque des politiques publiques." *Bulletin des bibliothèques de France (BBF)* 5: 54–70.

Martin, Laurent. 2015. "Les politiques culturelles doivent-elles être multiculturelles?". https://chmcc.hypotheses.org/1494.

Martiniello, Marco. 2014. "Artistic Separation Versus Artistic Mixing in European Multicultural Cities." *Identities* 21 (1): 1–9.

Martínez-Ariño, Julia, Michalis Moutselos, Karen Schönwälder, Christian Jacobs, Maria Schiller, and Alexandre Tandé. 2018. "Why Do Some Cities Adopt More Diversity Policies Than Others? A Study in France and Germany." *Comparative European Politics* 17 (5): 651–672.

Masson, Philippe, Marie Cartier, Rémy Le Saout, Jean-Noël Retière, and Marc Sureau. 2013. *Sociologie de Nantes*. Paris: La Découverte.

Navarro, Clemente J., and Terry N. Clark. 2012. "Cultural Policy in European Cities." *European Societies* 14 (5): 636–659.

Négrier, Emmanuel. 2006. "Politique, culture et diversité dans la France urbaine contemporaine." In *Les métropoles au défi de la diversité culturelle*, edited by Bernard Jouve, and Alain Gagnon, 137–157. Grenoble: Presses Universitaires de Grenoble.

Oldenburg, Ray. 1989. *The Great Good Place: Cafes, Coffee Shops, Bookstores, Bars, Hair Salons, and Other Hangouts at the Heart of a Community*. Philadelphia: Da Capo Press.

Rennes. 2014. *Bibli Rennes. Orientations 2014-2017*. https://fr.calameo.com/read/004880416dcc6f7af07e2.

Rennes. 2015. *Rennes au pluriel. Programme (6-13 mai 2015)*.

Rennes. 2018. *États généraux de la Culture de la Ville de Rennes: Point d'étape sur la mise en œuvre des engagements*. https://metropole.rennes.fr/sites/default/files/inline-files/etats-generauxpointetape0118_.pdf.

Rennes Métropole. 2013. *Projet culturel communautaire*. https://metropole.rennes.fr/politiques-publiques/culture-education-vie-sociale/la-culture/le-projet-culturel-communautaire/.

Robert, Sylvie. 2015. *Rapport à Madame la Ministre de la Culture et de la Communication sur l'adaptation et l'extension des horaires d'ouverture des bibliothèques publiques*. http://bbf.enssib.fr/sites/bbf.enssib.fr/files/images/billets/septembre2015/rapport_sylvie_robert.pdf.

Servet, Mathilde. 2009. *Les bibliothèques troisième lieu*. Villeurbanne: Ecole nationale supérieure des sciences de l'information et des bibliothèques.

Starke, Virgile. 2015. *Crépuscule des bibliothèques*. Paris: Les Belles Lettres.

Vion, Antoine, and Patrick Le Galès. 1998. "Politique culturelle et gouvernance urbaine : l'exemple de Rennes." *Politiques et management public* 16 (1): 1–33.

Zielinska, Marie. 2001. *Celebrating 20 Years: A Concise History of the IFLA Section on Library Services to Multicultural Population*. International Federation of Library Associations and Institutions: The Hague.

The accommodation of Muslim body practices in German public swimming pools

Ines Michalowski and Max Behrendt

ABSTRACT

The renegotiation of secularity for Muslims has reached sports facilities such as swimming pools, where the human body is central and an element of cross-cultural contestation. The present study identifies factors that could explain intra-organizational variations in religious accommodation. Data from a survey of geo-located swimming pools in Germany ($n = 339$) shows that conflict among users becomes more likely if the variation in body practices, the share of right-wing populist votes and the population of immigrant background increases. On the organizational level, we find that 75 per cent of the pools in our sample allow the burqini while only 10 per cent provide separate swimming hours for women. Higher shares of right-wing populist (and to a lesser extent of conservative) votes in the organization's environment correlate with a higher likelihood of burqini bans. Our findings suggest that the relationship between organizational change and citizens' attitudes is loose at best.

Why should those interested in secularity be interested in religious accommodation for Muslims in German swimming pools? Following Gorski and Altınordu (2008) we assume that current regimes of state-religion relationship as they exist in Western Europe and elsewhere are the result of a historic and still ongoing process. Historically negotiated arrangements in Western Europe are mainly (though not exclusively) geared towards Christians and Jews. They are currently re-negotiated for growing secular as well as Muslim shares of the population. As has been argued elsewhere (Cadge et al. 2017), this process of re-negotiation differs across regimes of state-religion relationship *and* across types of organizations within such nationally defined regimes. The current study holds the type of organization (swimming pools) and the country (Germany) constant and instead seeks to understand what (local) factors may explain differences between individual organizations of the same type in terms of accommodation outcomes and user reaction towards accommodation.

In Germany, swimming pools are public organizations, mainly run by municipal authorities. School swimming lessons take place here and swimming pools facilitate sport and leisure activities for the local public. Swimming pools are secular spaces – at least in Germany, religious communities do not run swimming pools and have not done so in the past. Swimming pools are also places where the encounter of different body practices, possibly marked by religion, can be observed. Body practices can range from very prude to very permissive. Their degree of permissiveness can vary for example across individuals, social groups, religions or national cultures. Very prude body practices involve the total avoidance of swimming pools followed by swimming in gender-separated spaces only. For example, as late as 1959 some German Catholic priests intervened successfully against gender-mixed swimming (Pfaffenzeller 2019). Prude body practices comprise swimwear covering most of the body such as the Islamic burqini. Historically, one may think of the conflicts when women started to cut down on the length of their swimwear in the 1920s and when the bikini became popular in the 1960s. On the more permissive end of the scale, there is particularly revealing swimwear such as string-bikinis worn by women and men in mixed-gender pools. On this end of the scale, we also see body practices such as changing one's clothes in areas visible to the opposite sex, women sunbathing topless and the free-body-culture (FKK) of naked swimming and sunbathing traditionally prominent in some German regions.

Swimming pools are often presented as extraordinary in the sense that few other places exist where the sexes meet in such revealing clothing. This is particularly true in Germany where body practices in swimming pools are rather permissive or at least more permissive than in several other European countries. In internet sources,[1] European visitors and newcomers to Germany frequently express their bewilderment and shame after encounters with Germans showering naked and people sunbathing naked in public places. Thus, differences in body practices are easily observable across European nation-states – and they are even more pronounced when relatively conservative Muslims in Germany who do attend gender-mixed public swimming pools but only in body-covering swimwear are included in the comparison.

This article explores how and why swimming pools differ in their accommodation of conservative Muslim body practices and what factors (including the accommodation for Muslims provided by pools) might explain conflict between different types of users. Our data shows that the users and the broader environment were reluctant towards religious accommodation, drawing bright boundaries between Muslim and non-Muslim populations. The data also shows that the current state of the renegotiation of secularity in German pools is partially accommodating for observant Muslims. We discuss the nature of the claims as well as the mobilization of right-wing populist parties as potential explanations.

Theoretical perspectives on religious accommodation in organisations and body practices in swimming pools

A growing body of literature is following Bender et al.'s (2013) call to study religion outside of congregations and thus focuses on the negotiation of the role of religion in public organizations. Many of these studies, be they on prisons (Beckford and Gilliat 1998; Becci 2011; Jahn 2015; Martínez-Ariño et al. 2015; Harms-Dalibon 2017; de Galembert 2020), on the military (Bertossi and Wihtol de Wenden 2007; Hansen 2012; Bertossi 2014; Michalowski 2015), on hospitals (Bertossi and Prud'homme 2011; Cadge 2013; Bernardo 2018) or on the police (Thériault 2009; Gauthier 2011; Lillevik 2019) contain a reflection on the negotiation of secularity and religious pluralism in a specific organizational context. They show that there are important differences in the accommodation of religious pluralism not only across national but also across organizational contexts. For example, studies (for many see Griera et al. 2015; de Galembert 2020) discuss how a dominant professional group in the organization frames religion as functional or unfunctional in that particular organizational context thereby deciding whether or not it should be accommodated (e.g. religion may be presented as beneficial to the rehabilitation of prisoners but as an obstacle to scientific medical care in hospitals). Similarly, Adam and Rea (2018) who pool a broad range of public and private organizations under the label of "workplace organizations" find that organizational feasibility, continuous service delivery or the non-hindrance of customers are legitimate arguments used for or against religious accommodation in that particular context (for a comparative framework of organizations including such arguments about functional aspects of religion see Cadge et al. 2017, 5).

Yet, while cross-national and cross-organizational differences in religious accommodation are considered, differences across organizations of the same type located in one country have not been studied systematically, partially because of the qualitative nature of the existing case studies. When discussing the particularities of local strategic action fields (Crozier and Friedberg 1977; Fligstein and McAdam 2013), some studies argue that organizational decision-making on religious accommodation is based on pragmatism (Bertossi 2014; Harms-Dalibon 2017; Adam and Rea 2018) and highly dependent on how individual actors translate expectations that are addressed to them by the environment into organizational practices (de Galembert 2020; also c.f. Harms-Dalibon 2017, 17). The current study acknowledges such idiosyncrasies but still looks for more systematic factors that could at least partially explain local variation. Here, a study on the accommodation of religious pluralism in the rooms of silence of three Scandinavian universities, proposes local variations in the composition of users as one potential explanatory factor for variation in accommodation across local contexts (Christensen et al. 2018). Another study by Koopmans, Michalowski, and Waibel (2012) argues that citizenship rights for immigrants are more likely to be restricted in context with higher electoral success of right wing populist parties. We will pick up these ideas in our analyses of survey data on 339 geo-located German swimming pools. In particular, we ask what aspects of the organizational environment may have an influence on organizational decision-making with regard to Muslim accommodation and how the composition of the users may relate to conflict around organizational rules.

Next to theories on cross-national and cross-organizational differences, the sociology of migration produced theories explaining minority religious accommodation by focusing on the claims: Koenig for example (2005) differentiates Muslim minority claims according to their level of demandingness for the liberal state, speaking of claims for toleration, for autonomy, for tolerance and for equal participation in the organizational centre of the state. He argues that equal participation is the most demanding type of claim because it requires the state to consider religious and cultural identities in all organizational processes. Building on Statham et al. (2005), Carol and Koopmans (2013) classify claims for religious accommodation according to their level of obtrusiveness. The authors argue that claims become more obtrusive if they are not claims for parity but for special treatment, if they concern public institutions and in particular the personnel of these institutions, if they concern the religious practices of a small minority within the minority and if they require the rest of society to adapt their behaviour to accommodate the minority. Carol and Koopmans find that in countries which already provide more minority accommodation, claims tend to cover ever more obtrusive issues, thus following a logic of further differentiation and specification. In complementation of these theories one could, in view of the cross-organizational comparison, argue that claims for accommodation vary across organizations, in terms of content as well quantity: while studies of total institutions (Goffman 1961) such as prisons and the military have shown that these organizations are confronted with claims for accommodation ranging from Ramadan to dress and breaks, leisure organizations such as swimming pools receive more specific claims that relate – just like in hospitals and schools (the two other organizations studied in the larger project) – mainly to the question how the human body is displayed in public and regulated by the organization.

Thus, body practices are a central element of the negotiations over religious accommodation in public swimming pools because religions partially find their expression in body practices. Comparing Islam and Christianity,

Mellor and Shilling point out "[what … .] these two religions aim to achieve is the initiation of a process whereby bodies are made 'Christian' or 'Muslim'" (Mellor and Shilling 2010, 32). Examples that they give on the Muslim side are the body movements during prayer, the veiling of women and the use of prayer caps by men (Mellor and Shilling 2010, 31). Referring to other authors, Mellor and Shilling (2010, 34) state that "Islam is a religion whose resilience has in the past rested upon 'its essence as a way of life' embedded in physical habits and practices rather than contained within a cognitive 'belief system'". The more Weberian perspective of Philip Gorski (2003) assumes that religions vary in their degree of putting emphasis on and believing in the human capacity to control and discipline the body. Compared to Protestant Christianity, this belief in the capacity to control the body is weaker in Catholicism and even weaker in Sunni and Shia Islam which is why men and women are required to cover their *awra*.[2] Hard-line Muslim jurists insist that Muslim women should only swim in the presence of other Muslim women while comparatively more liberal jurists tolerate burqinis worn in mixed-gender pools (Shavit and Winter 2011, 270–1). Those women who wear the burqini can therefore be seen as social innovators from the perspective of conservative Islam. Some pool visitors in Germany, however, find burqinis difficult to tolerate. Although meant to hide the female body from the looks of non-related men, burqinis de facto lead to "a paradox hypervisibility" in German swimming pools (c.f. Karstein and Burchardt 2017, 213). Covering most of the body, burqinis may be (mis-)understood by other pool users as contradicting current trends of defining one's identity through investments in body capital, which promises success and can be reached through personal effort (Bourdieu 1982 cited in Gugutzer 2012, 289). Gugutzer (2012, 289) underlines the strength of such ideas by classifying body-optimising practices as this-worldly oriented, functional equivalents for religion. To the extent that burqini-wearing women are perceived as rejecting this trend, social boundaries are further enhanced.

The case

In Germany, swimming pools are public institutions. Municipalities are legally obliged to maintain public pools to allow school swimming lessons. Most public pools are governed by municipalities (81 per cent in our data set), tax-financed and open to the general public. There are different types of pools which to some extent attract different kinds of users. While some users seek a physical work-out, others – especially during summer – want to cool down and relax. Except for the recreation-oriented covered pools, open-air pools usually attract a much broader clientele than covered pools. Swimming pools are public places of socialization where different social groups meet. They are and most likely have always been places where individuals present their bodies and flirt (Kaschuba 2018). Open-air pools in Germany – this is substantiated by our analysis – are more permissive spaces than covered pools because people sunbathe on the lawns surrounding the wet area, some women are topless, and people sometimes change on the lawn where others can see them.

Swimming pools usually have a clearly-defined and well-limited space which everyone can access by paying an entrance fee. Although fees are on the rise, especially summer pools remain a comparatively cheap activity for those who cannot afford a vacation at the seaside (in the past an upper-class summer activity). In the twentieth century, swimming pools were also a venue of racist exclusion. In 1933, many German towns prohibited Jews access to public pools, and by 1937 such prohibitions were in place throughout Germany (c.f. Andryszak and Bramkamp 2016). In the US, Afro-Americans were excluded from public pools during times of segregation and de-facto excluded from swimming after desegregation (Zaubler 2015, 82) because public pools were then less well maintained and many better-off whites built private pools in their backyards (Smith 2012, 46). Smith (2012, 43) also underlined that "due to the intimate nature of swimming, public pools were enforced with the most stringent of segregation codes to prevent this race-mixing" and de-segregation was particularly slow.

In the clearly delimited area of the swimming pool, a different dress code applies than in most other public spaces. Beyond the changing rooms towards the wet area, showing a lot of naked skin is normal. Also, inside the pool and in particular inside the showers (note that in Germany, showers are gender-separated and many people shower nude) wearing covering clothes is easily perceived as a breach of norms. Most swimwear is more revealing than usual clothing. This first and foremost has a functional role since uncovering and tight-fitting swimwear facilitates swimming. The scarce dress in swimming pools, however, may also be an item of fashion and it can gain a sexual connotation when the body is exposed or observed. It is difficult to hide one's body in a swimming pool as even a T-shirt or a towel worn around the waist usually needs to be taken off when entering the water. Another particularity of German pools is that many pool visitors change in common changing rooms.

The pool regulates nudity. It formulates organizational rules that define what swimwear may be worn inside the pool. Furthermore, its architectural arrangements have an influence on how much nudity one encounters in a public pool. For example, gender-separated showers that are directly connected with gender-separated common changing rooms foster nudity more than gender-separated showers that are connected with gender-mixed single changing rooms. Swimming pools can also regulate whether naked swimming hours or areas for naked sunbathing exist and whether they offer separate swimming hours for women. The common prohibition to film and take pictures also falls under organizational regulations of nudity. Further-more, the swimming pool must regulate not only consensual intimacy but also cases of sexual harassment.

As mentioned above, most of the German pools are run by municipalities which are free to decide on the exact formulation of these rules. Rules can be changed through simple administrative decision as well as through political decision in the municipal council as was the case for some burqini rules. Such adaptations of pool rules can be influenced by the lobbying of Muslim and non-Muslim civil society organizations as well as by the umbrella organ-ization of all swimming pool operators, the German Bathing Society (*Deutsche Gesellschaft für das Badewesen*). Sociologists of organization assume that organizational change can flow from the organization itself, e.g. through the action of internal lobbyists (Dobbin, Kim, and Kalev 2011) and that it can also be initiated by the organization's environment (e.g. through legal changes, public debates). Such organizational change may find its expression in the change of both formal and informal organizational rules (Kühl 2015; Luhmann [1964] 1995). Unlike for example the military, swimming pools are intimately linked to their environment through the public and their municipal governance.

Hypotheses

Following Christensen et al. (2018) we assume that the users partially deter-mine how the framework for accommodation provided by the organization is lived in practice. It is thus not only important to study the pool rules on swimwear but also to take into account the permissiveness of the users' swim-wear. In fact, next to the formal organizational regulations, there is a lot of social regulation among users for example through the looks they carry on each other's swimwear and the complaints they make to the pool personnel about other users. We expect differences across pools in terms of the compo-sition of their users – some pools having a more homogenous and others a more heterogeneous population of users in terms of body practices. We expect enhanced conflict in pools with users with more heterogeneous body practices (H1). In a similar vein, we expect that a higher share of immi-grants (Muslim and non-Muslim) in the area around the swimming pool and thus by extension among the pool users increases feelings of alienation among certain visitors and thus leads to more complaints about Muslim body practices in swimming pools (H2). Referring to the literature on cross-religious differences in body practices, we also expect differences in com-plaints about the burqini according to whether a pool is located in a domi-nantly Catholic or Protestant region in Germany (H3). Relying on the literature about claims-making presented above we expect that burqinis are more likely to be accommodated than separate swimming hours for Muslim women (H4) since they can be framed as a parity of treatment while the latter involve special treatment for a small group and cut into access for the majority. We also assume that organizational rules influence the pool visitors' perception of social norms. This means that we expect pools which have explicitly allowed the wearing of burqinis for more than five years to receive fewer complaints about this swimwear (H5). With regard to the organizational environment we expect that an increased share of right-wing populist votes in the area surrounding the swimming pool leads to more complaints about Muslim body practices in swimming pools (H6a). Koopmans, Michalowski, and Waibel (2012) have shown that higher vote shares for extreme right-wing populist parties are positively correlated with a restriction of religious and cultural citizenship rights for immigrants. We thus expect that an increased share of right-wing populist votes in the area surrounding the swimming pool leads to less accommodation of Muslim body practices both in terms of swimwear and swimming hours (H6b).

Methods of data collection and analysis

This analysis is based on a survey carried out in cooperation with the German Bathing Society (DGfdB) among the roughly 5100 German swimming pools that are registered in a DGfdB dataset (www.baederatlas.de). 339 swimming pools participated in the survey (Michalowski and Behrendt 2020). Taking the 5100 swimming pools as the universe of cases, our sample is roughly representative of the swimming pools in Germany with pools in rural areas being slightly under- and larger pools that combine an indoor and an outdoor area and are located in densely populated areas being slightly over-represented. The survey asked a question about the pool's zip code. This allowed us to connect the dataset with standard geodata, e.g. on the population share with immigrant background and on voting behaviour. For most of our analyses, we excluded the questionnaires without zip code which reduced the sample from 339 to 323 cases. The questionnaire was filled in either by personnel working in the pool or by the pool operator. The questionnaire included questions about the permissiveness of the pool visitors especially regarding different body practices including swimwear, about pool rules and their implementation, about sexual harassment, separate swimming hours, and about the organizational structure.

We use complaints as indicators of conflicts about social norms. To better understand which factors increase the likelihood of complaints in particular about burqinis, on the one hand, and about particularly revealing swimwear on the other, we developed explorative models on the basis of our survey data. Our central goal was to identify general characteristics of the public that correlate with the likelihood of complaints. We differentiate between characteristics of the public that relate to a certain degree of permissiveness in showing one's body in public (swimwear, use of communal dress rooms, acceptance of children of the opposite sex in the showers) as well as characteristics of the public that relate to political preferences (voting behaviour) and immigrant background (regional share of individuals with immigrant background). Our dependent variable measuring conflict among users is an estimate of the number of complaints by pool visitors about other visitors provided by the person who filled in the questionnaire. For the model estimating the likelihood of complaints about the burqini, our dependent variable is "How often does your pool receive complaints by pool visitors about other visitors wearing a burqini?" (coded 0= never/rarely; 1= sometimes/often). For the model estimating the likelihood of complaints about pool visitors with particularly permissive body practices, our dependent variable is an index composed of the items:

> How often does your pool receive complaints about: (a) visitors wearing a string bikini?, (b) topless women?, (c) visitors getting changed in areas visible to the opposite sex (e.g. in front of the lockers), (d) visitors having physical contact in front of others, (e) children of the opposite sex in the showers?

The independent variables are identical for the two models and always scaled in four categories (never = 1; rarely = 2; sometimes = 3; often = 4). They first comprise the variable "Are there women wearing the burqini in your pool?" as well as the individual items measuring the permissiveness of the pool users (Frequency of … men in particularly revealing swimwear; women in particularly revealing swimwear; use of communal dress rooms; users getting dressed in areas visible to the opposite sex, e.g. in front of the lockers; users getting dressed on the lawn and women sun tanning topless on the lawn; note that the last two items were only asked in outdoor pools). For each pool, we calculated an average that was standardized from 0 to 1.

Both models control for the share of people with immigrant background among the inhabitants of the area in which the pool was located and for the voting behaviour in the area. The regional share of individuals with immigrant background was taken from the micro census 2017. It should be noted though that here data are provided for the level of districts comprising between one and five million inhabitants (former *Regierungsbezirke*), not municipalities. Voting behaviour was measured through party votes (*Zweitstimmen*) in the federal elections of 2017 on the level of *Kreise* and *Landkreise,* usually comprising between 50,000 and 500,000 inhabitants. We also use these variables on voting behaviour and share of immigrant population in further models to estimate the likelihood of burqinis being allowed in a pool.

Results: user behaviour and organizational rules

We present our results in two steps. First, we discuss results relating to the organization's public, i.e. the (potential) pool users. In a second step, we

focus on the pool rules, i.e. their adaptation as well as the potential consequences of such adaptations.

The users: complaints about burqinis and particularly revealing clothing

The survey's first section dealt with the permissiveness of the users. We chose
this topic to study how swimming pools adapt to increasing religious heterogeneity in the form of body practices marked by religion. Users may seek to
impose their own social norms, for example by complaining to the pool
attendant about the behaviour of other users.

Descriptively, we first of all see that only 7 per cent of the 339 pools frequently and 25 per cent sometimes count women in burqinis among their
guests. The other pools rarely (45 per cent) or never (21 per cent) have
women in burqinis among their guests. Almost all of the latter pools (86
per cent in case of "rarely women in burqinis" and 91 per cent in case of
never women in burqinis) say that they rarely or never receive complaints
about the burqini. Among the pools, however, where women in burqinis
are a more frequent sight, the share that rarely or never receives complaints
about the burkini is considerably lower (55 per cent in the case of "sometimes
women in burqinis" and 46 per cent in the case of "often women in burqinis").
In total only 32 per cent of the pools that participated in our survey declared
that they sometimes or frequently encounter the body practice of wearing a
burqini and 19 per cent declared that they sometimes or often receive complaints about the burqini. Remarkably, among the pools which sometimes or
often count women in burqini among their guests, only about half state that
they sometimes or often receive complaints while another half notice less
resistance against the renegotiation of secularity, i.e. the admission of a reli-
giously motivated piece of clothing in a public space.

Further statistical analyses show a robust, statistically significant correlation
between the number of burqini-wearing women in a pool and complaints
about women wearing a burqini (c.f. see the linear regression in model 1).
The model also shows that, when controlling for the number of burqini-
wearing women, the likelihood of complaints about the burqini increases
the higher the share of AfD votes in the 2017 parliamentary elections in the
region. This provides support for hypothesis H6a (Table 1).[3]

A region's confessional orientation (Catholic/Protestant) does not impact
the likelihood of complaints about the burqini (no support for H3), but
pools with more permissive users and pools in a region with a higher share
of immigrants are more likely to receive complaints about the burqini. In consequence, we find support for H2. We also see that pools which have more
particularly permissive and more particularly prude users than the average
are more likely to receive complaints about the burqini. Apparently, the

Table 1. Complaints about other pool visitors wearing a burqini.

Variables	Complaints about the burqini
Visitors wearing burqini (rarely)	0.0772*
	(0.0395)
Visitors wearing burqini (sometimes)	0.381***
	(0.0676)
Visitors wearing burqini (often)	0.458***
	(0.103)
Regional share of individuals with immigrant background	1.005***
	(0.361)
Index permissiveness of visitors	0.267**
	(0.128)
AfD party vote 2017	1.636**
	(0.816)
CDU party vote 2017	−0.431
	(0.434)
SPD party vote 2017	0.288
	(0.502)
Constant	−0.370
	(0.336)
Observations	313
R-squared	0.222

Note: Robust standard errors in parentheses ***$p < 0.01$, **$p < 0.05$, *$p < 0.1$.

encounter of the extremes does not foster a live-and-let-live-attitude (Table 2). In parallel, we calculated another model using the same explanatory variables to estimate their effect on complaints about particularly permissive behaviour, measured through an index. This model shows that complaints about particularly permissive behaviour increase when the number of women wearing a

Table 2. Complaints about the permissiveness of other pool visitors.

Variables	Model 1	Model 2	Model 3	Model 4	Model 5	Model 6
Visitors wearing burqini (rarely)	0.168***	0.169***	0.117***	0.114**	0.114**	0.111**
	(0.0485)	(0.0489)	(0.0454)	(0.0461)	(0.0464)	(0.0469)
Visitors wearing burqini (sometimes)	0.359***	0.360***	0.283***	0.277***	0.279***	0.272***
	(0.0557)	(0.0572)	(0.0539)	(0.0545)	(0.0562)	(0.0567)
Visitors wearing burqini (often)	0.422***	0.423***	0.382***	0.376***	0.378***	0.376***
	(0.105)	(0.106)	(0.0953)	(0.0952)	(0.0957)	(0.0970)
Regional share of individuals with immigrant background		−0.0358	0.384	0.319	0.320	0.276
		(0.260)	(0.257)	(0.297)	(0.297)	(0.297)
Index permissiveness of visitors			0.621***	0.620***	0.621***	0.598***
			(0.0934)	(0.0935)	(0.0935)	(0.0957)
AfD party vote 2017				−0.257	−0.246	−0.730
				(0.535)	(0.541)	(0.663)
CDU party vote 2017					0.0330	−0.207
					(0.305)	(0.379)
SPD party vote 2017						−0.540
						(0.417)
Constant	1.239***	1.246***	0.995***	1.044***	1.030***	1.304***
	(0.0396)	(0.0687)	(0.0724)	(0.127)	(0.177)	(0.282)
Observations	315	315	315	315	315	315
R-squared	0.135	0.135	0.241	0.241	0.241	0.245

Note: Robust standard errors in parentheses ***$p < 0.01$, **$p < 0.05$, *$p < 0.1$.

burqini increases. This provides support for H1 that the encounter of more heterogenous body practices (particularly prude and particular permissive) among pool users enhances complaints. At the same time – and different from complaints about the burqini – we find no significant effect of the share of individuals of immigrant origin in the region, nor of the right-wing populist vote on complaints about particularly permissive behaviour. It is important to note though that pools in which particularly permissive users are more numerous are also more likely to receive complaints about this particularly permissive behaviour. These findings suggest that there is limited habituation towards and acceptance of body practices falling outside the norm and that conflict increases if two body practices that fall outside the norm become more frequent in a pool.

Organizational rules: burqini allowances and separate swimming hours for women

Given the potential conflicts among users, one may ask how pool rules can alleviate or increase such conflicts. We first look at burqini admissions and prohibitions, then at separate swimming hours for women. Pools with naked swimming hours (FKK) only represent 7 per cent of our sample (25 pools) and do not differ systematically from the rest of the sample, e.g. in terms of burqini allowance. 75 per cent of the 339 German pools (255 pools) which participated in the survey allow the burqini. Only 32 pools, i.e. 10 per cent explicitly prohibit it while 52 pools (15 per cent) left this question unanswered – maybe because the situation is unclear (these pools did also not answer the question on the frequency of burqini-wearing women or stated that there are never or rarely women in burqini among the pool visitors). Among the pools that allowed the burqini and that answered an additional question about when the burqini was first allowed ($n = 195$), only 33 per cent had already allowed it in 2013 while in 2016, the year after the arrival of large numbers of refugees in Germany, 83 per cent allowed the burqini. By the end of 2016, the burqini allowance was also endorsed by the German Bathing Society, the umbrella organization of swimming-pool operators. This shows a clear change of organizational rules towards the accommodation of conservative Muslim users. In line with our hypothesis H6b, burqini prohibitions are more likely where the share of right-wing populist votes and – to a smaller extent – the share of centre-right Christian conservative votes is higher (c.f. see the linear regression in Table 3).

Pools with and without burqini admission do not differ significantly in terms of the share of the population of immigrant origin in their region, but pools with burqini bans obviously have fewer guests (wanting to) wear a burqini. These pools are also less likely to receive complaints about the burqini than pools with burqini admission. Interestingly, however burqini

Table 3. Influence of regional factors on burqini allowances.

Variables	
Regional share of individuals with immigrant background	−0.179
	(0.222)
AfD party vote 2017	−1.827***
	(0.582)
CDU party vote 2017	−0.833**
	(0.328)
SPD party vote 2017	−0.371
	(0.341)
Constant	1.505***
	(0.189)
Observations	273
R-squared	0.042

Note: Robust standard errors in parentheses ***$p < 0.01$, **$p < 0.05$, *$p < 0.1$.

bans do not fully prevent complaints: 25 per cent of the pools allowing the burqini and still 17 per cent of the pools prohibiting it sometimes or often receive complaints about the burqini. If we now compare the pools that permitted the burqini before and after 2013 we find, other than expected in hypothesis H5, no adaptation effect in the sense of a decrease of complaints about burqinis over time: even in the pools that were the forerunners of the currently wide-spread burqini admission, a higher number of women in burqinis goes along with more complaints about this piece of clothing.

Pools in our sample were more reticent to provide separate swimming hours for Muslim women. In general, public pools may either rent out opening hours to private associations, which may then offer separate swimming hours for Muslim women only, or they may offer separate swimming hours for women with or without adaptations for Muslim women. Our survey shows that only 32 of the 323 pools (10 per cent) offer separate swimming hours for women and among them only 7 state that these swimming hours are de facto intended for Muslim women. These 7 and further 9 pools have exclusively female pool attendants during these separate swimming hours. Given that the other half of the pools also employs male personnel, their offer is open only to a limited extent to conservative Muslim women. Thus, separate swimming hours for women do not necessarily seek to accommodate Muslim women. They are also not a new phenomenon: approximately one third of these pools already had separate swimming hours for women in 1999 and none of the pools that introduced such hours in the 1960s, 1970s, 1980s or 1990s has special hours for Muslim women. This is a newer phenomenon with the first separate swimming hours for Muslim women in our sample starting in 2003. Interestingly, six of the 32 pools with separate swimming hours for women declared that they introduced them in response to political pressure. Overall, this finding lends support to H4 predicting that swimming pools accommodate burqinis more frequently than separate swimming hours for Muslim women. This is in line with political claims theory predicting that claims for religious accommodation are less likely to be successful if they also require the general population to change its behaviour. Other than burqini admissions which only require a toleration of other practices, separate swimming hours for (Muslim) women are a claim for equal participation (c.f. Koenig 2005) which is highly obtrusive (c.f. Carol and Koopmans 2013) because it will require all men and potentially even non-Muslim women to renounce on swimming during those hours. The main argument used by the proponents of separate swimming hours for women is that this may well be the only way of letting conservative Muslim women participate in swimming and teaching those who have not been to school in Germany how to swim. The main argument used by opponents of separate swimming hours is that they separate citizens according to gender or even faith, thereby jeopardizing a common public good. Opponents of separate swimming hours for women also refer to a German federal administrative court ruling deciding that students must participate in mixed-gender swimming classes at school under the condition that the burqini is allowed.

Discussion and conclusions

The current study seeks to contribute to the existing literature on organization-specific approaches to religious accommodation by focusing on differences across organizations *of the same type* that are located within the same country. The article explored how and why swimming pools differ in their accommodation of conservative Muslim body practices and what factors might explain conflict between different types of users.

In terms of outcome-differences we looked at organizational rules relevant to accommodate conservative Muslims (i.e. burqini regulations and separate swimming hours for women) as well as at conflict among users (in particular at complaints about other users' body practices). In terms of potential explanatory factors, we looked at variations between users in terms of body practices (from prude to permissive), at organizational regulations, at the share of immigrants in the area surrounding the swimming pool, at Christian confessional distribution in the larger region and at the local share of right-wing populist AfD votes in the last federal elections 2017. We surveyed 339 geo-located German swimming pools about their users and their pool rules. Our survey is roughly representative of swimming pools in Germany, even though pools in larger cities are slightly over- and pools in rural areas slightly under-represented.

With regard to conflict between users we find that complaints about women in burqinis increase with the number of women wearing it. We also find, when controlling for the number of women wearing a burqini, that complaints are more frequent in pools located in regions that had higher shares of right-wing populist AfD votes in the last federal elections (support for H6a).

We also find support for H2, to the extent that a higher share of individuals of immigrant origin in the region surrounding the pool is positively correlated with complaints about the burqini, still controlling for the actual number of burqini-wearing women. Complaints about burqinis do not correlate with a region's Catholic or Protestant orientation (no support for H3) but they are more likely in pools where more users show a particularly permissive behaviour measured mainly in terms of swimwear and public nudity. This finding supports H1, predicting that greater variance in body practices increases conflict (rather than fostering a live-and-let-live attitude). Finally, with regard to users we find that pool rules only seem to have a limited effect on complaining behaviour because swimming pools that have allowed the burqini for five and more years do not experience a significant decrease in complaints about this piece of clothing. We thus find no support for H5. In terms of organizational rules, we find that burqini prohibitions are more likely in municipalities where the share of right-wing populist votes and – to a smaller extent – the share of centre-right Christian conservative votes is higher, providing support for H6b. The sample size was too small to observe similar effects on separate swimming hours for women. This relates to the fact that we found support for H4, predicting that swimming pools would be more likely to accommodate the less obtrusive burqini compared to the more obtrusive separate swimming hours for (Muslim) women that potentially require the majority to change its habits.

What do our findings tell us about potential explanatory factors of variations across different organizations of the same type? The existing literature as well as additional data currently collected in our project suggest that the idiosyncracies of local actor constellations are important for the final accommodation outcomes. If more and more pools today (inter alia because of legal pressures) include burqinis in their list of authorized swimwear, it still very much depends on the way this rule is implemented (maybe even informally), whether burqini-wearing women actually use the pool and how other groups of users react to this. Nonetheless, the present analysis has also identified systematic factors that can explain local variation in terms of conflict and organizational rules, namely the composition of users and the political environment. These can only partially be influenced by the organization itself. So, what can the organization do to facilitate social change? Our data suggests that formal organizational change does not necessarily lead to social change. If this was possible, one would expect pool users in pools that have allowed the burqini for more than five years to stop complaining about this piece of clothing. If social change could be enforced by social realities one might expect pool users in pools that frequently count women in burqinis among their users to get used to this sight and stop complaining about burqinis. Yet, none of this is the case. Burqinis are – unlike bikinis used to be – not just another provocative piece of swimwear. They are (mis-) understood as a marker of a bright group boundary between observant Muslims and increasingly secular Christians. Ezli (2014) pointedly argued that burqinis should not be understood as a sign of separation from society because conservative Muslim women wearing burqinis neither evade swimming pools, nor restrict themselves to female-only swimming hours. Yet, right-wing populist campaign posters showing bikini-wearing women and slogans such as "Burqa? We like bikinis – our land, our rules" use swimwear to make the social boundary brighter. Also current social trends of enhanced bodily fitness and beauty taking on quasi-religious forms of a marked individualist character (Gugutzer 2012) might enhance this social boundary. From this perspective, putting on a burqini can be understood as an expression of non-participation in the body cult and of belonging to a group that distances itself from individualism (Mellor and Shilling 2010) and favours practices considered emblematic of the legitimation of differences between the sexes (Karstein and Burchardt 2017). Yet, not all pools that frequently or sometimes have women in burqinis among their guests also experience widespread conflict. In more than half of these pools burqinis are apparently tolerated. This finding suggests that at least in some cases a fragile equilibrium of accommodating change for conservative Muslims in German pools may have been reached. In a next step, the BODYRULES project qualitatively explores how swimming pool guests legitimize their own body practices as well as their tolerance or rejection of other practices. This will help to better understand the nuances of the concerns and complaints pool visitors have about each other's body practices that are not captured in the current approach.

Finally, what can we say about the external validity of our findings on German swimming pools for other countries and organizations? Germany as a country-case is a liberal democracy, comparable for this purpose to other Western European countries that host large Muslim populations of immigrant origin. Although the public debate about Muslim accommodation in pools may have been more vivid in Germany than in some neighbouring countries, a quick research suggests that Austria, Belgium, France and the Netherlands also discuss burqinis and that there is variation in accommodation across pools within one country. Even in France where *laïcité* is frequently used as an argument to ban burqinis from public pools, some municipalities (e.g. Rennes) allow them. We therefore expect that our findings on the composition of users and on the political environment can be extended to other national contexts. Whether this is also true for other organizations will be studied in more detail in an upcoming comparison of swimming pools with two other organizations where the regulation of the human body stands central, namely hospitals and schools.

Notes

1. For many see: www.independent.co.uk/travel/europe/german-spas-the-naked-truth-6269555.html; www.allemagne-au-max.com/forum/la-nudite-en-allemagn e-vt15707.html; www.huffingtonpost.it/elena-cerizza/5-comportamenti-assurdi-nelle-piscine-tedesche-_b_7983090.html; www.vice.com/es_co/article/bm4gja/ en-berln-puedes-pasear-desnudo-en-un-parque-y-las-autoridades-no-te-dirn-nada, last consulted in August 2019.
2. With differences across legal schools, the male *awra* is usually defined as reaching from navel to below the knee and as including the entire body except for hands, feet and face in the case of women.
3. To avoid multi-collinearity, we calculated alternative models in which the centre-right Christian Democrats (CDU/CSU) were replaced with the liberal democrats (FDP) and the centre-left Social Democrats (SPD) were replaced with the Greens.

Acknowledgements

We would like to thank our colleagues at the WZB Berlin as well as our project partners Maja Apelt (University of Potsdam) and Liane Schenk (Charité Berlin) with their teams for comments on an earlier version of this paper. We also thank three anonymous reviewers for their helpful suggestions.

Disclosure statement

No potential conflict of interest was reported by the author(s).

Funding

The project BODYRULES was supported by the Federal Ministry of Education and Research (BMBF) [grant number 01UM1811BY].

References

Adam, Ilke, and Andrea Rea. 2018. "The Three "I"s of Workplace Accommodation of Muslim Religious Practices: Instrumental, Internal, and Informal." *Ethnic and Racial Studies* 41 (15): 2711–2730.
Andryszak, Lisa, and Christiane Bramkamp, eds. 2016. *Jüdisches Leben auf Norderney: Präsenz, Vielfalt und Ausgrenzung.* Münster: Lit Verlag.
Becci, Irene. 2011. "Religion's Multiple Locations in Prison. Germany, Italy, Switzerland." *Archives de Sciences Sociales des Religions* 153 (1): 65–84.
Beckford, James, and Sophie Gilliat. 1998. *Religion in Prison. Equal Rites in a Multi-Faith Society.* Cambridge: Cambridge University Press.
Bender, Courtney, Wendy Cadge, Peggy Levitt, and David Smilde. 2013. "Religion on the Edge: An Introduction." In *Religion on the Edge: De-Centering and Re-Centering the Sociology of Religion*, edited by Courtney Bender, Wendy Cadge, Peggy Levitt, and David Smilde. New York: Oxford University Press.
Bernardo, Luís António Pais. 2018. *Religious Diversity in the Portuguese Hospital Sector.* Berlin: Humboldt University Berlin.

Bertossi, Christophe. 2014. "French "Muslim" Soldiers? Social Change and Pragmatism in a Military Institution." In *European States and Their Muslim Citizens. The Impact of Institutions on Perceptions and Boundaries*, edited by John Bowen, Christophe Bertossi, Jan Willem Duyvendak, and Mona Lena Krook, 73–103. Cambridge: Cambridge University Press.

Bertossi, Christophe, and Dorothée Prud'homme. 2011. *La « diversité » à l'hôpital : identités sociales et discriminations*. Paris: IFRI.

Bertossi, Christophe, and Catherine Wihtol de Wenden. 2007. *Les couleurs du drapeau. L'armée française face aux discriminations*. Paris: Robert Laffont.

Cadge, Wendy. 2013. *Paging God: Religion in the Halls of Medicine*. Chicago: University of Chicago Press.

Cadge, Wendy, Mar Griera, Kristen Lucken, and Ines Michalowski. 2017. "Religion in Public Institutions. Comparative Perspectives From the United States, the United Kingdom, and Europe." *Journal for the Scientific Study of Religion* 56 (2): 226–233.

Carol, Sarah, and Ruud Koopmans. 2013. "Dynamics of Contestation Over Islamic Religious Rights in Western Europe." *Ethnicities* 13 (2): 165–190.

Christensen, Henrik Reintoft, Ida Marie Høeg, Lene Kühle, and Magdalena Nordin. 2018. "Rooms of Silence at Three Universities in Scandinavia." *Sociology of Religion: A Quarterly Review*. Online First. doi:10.1093/socrel/sry040:1-24.

Crozier, Michel, and Erhard Friedberg. 1977. *L'acteur et le système*. Paris: Editions du Seuil.

Dobbin, Frank, Soohan Kim, and Alexandra Kalev. 2011. "You Can't Always Get What You Need: Organizational Determinants of Diversity Programs." *American Sociological Review* 76 (3): 386–411.

Ezli, Özkan. 2014. *Baden mit dem Burkini in öffentlichen Bädern. Kulturwissenschaftliche Analyse und Dokumentation der öffentlichen Debatte in Konstanz*. Konstanz: Konstanzer Online-Publikations-System (KOPS).

Fligstein, Neil, and Doug McAdam. 2013. *A Theory of Fields*. New York: Oxford University Press.

de Galembert, Claire. 2020. *Islam et Prison*. Paris: Éditions Amsterdam.

Gauthier, Jérémie. 2011. "Des corps étrange(r)s dans la police ? Les policiers minoritaires à Paris et à Berlin." *Sociologie du Travail* 53 (4): 460–477.

Goffman, Erving. 1961. "On the Characteristics of Total Institutions." In *Asylums. Essays on the Social Situation of Mental Patients and Other Inmates*, edited by Erving Goffman, 1–124. New York: Anchor Book.

Gorski, Philip S. 2003. *The Disciplinary Revolution. Calvinism and the Rise of the State in Early Modern Europe*. Chicago and London: The University of Chicago Press.

Gorski, Philip S., and Ateş Altınordu. 2008. "After Secularization?" *Annual Review of Sociology* 34: 55–85.

Griera, Mar, Julia Martinez Arino, Anna Clot-Garrell, and Gloria Garcia-Romeral. 2015. "Religión e instituciones públicas en España: Hospitales y prisiones en perspectiva comparada." *Revista Internacional de Sociología* 73 (3). doi:10.3989/ris.2015.73.3.e020.

Gugutzer, Robert. 2012. "Die Sakralisierung des Profanen. Der Körperkult als individualisierte Sozialform des Religiösen." In *Körper, Sport und Religion*, edited by Robert Gugutzer and Moritz Böttcher, 285–309. Wiesbaden: Springer Fachmedien.

Hansen, Kim Philip. 2012. *Military Chaplains & Religious Diversity*. New York: Palgrave Macmillan.

Harms-Dalibon, Lisa. 2017. "Surveillance and Prayer – Comparing Muslim Prison Chaplaincy in Germany's Federal States." *Comparative Migration Studies* 5 (8): 1–22.

Jahn, Sarah. 2015. "Institutional Logic and Legal Practice: Modes of Regulation of Religious Organizations in German Prisons." In *Religious Diversity in European Prisons. Challenges and Implications for Rehabilitation*, edited by Irene Becci and Olivier Roy, 81–99. Wiesbaden: Springer VS.

Karstein, Uta, and Marian Burchardt. 2017. "Religion." In *Handbuch Körpersoziologie. Band 2: Forschungsfelder und Methodische Zugänge*, edited by Robert Gugutzer, Gabriele Klein, and Michael Meuser, 203–216. Wiesbaden: Springer VS.

Kaschuba, Wolfgang. 2018. "Interview." *Welt am Sonntag*, July 29.

Koenig, Matthias. 2005. "Incorporating Muslim Migrants in Western Nation States. A Comparison of the United Kingdom, France, and Germany." *Journal of International Migration and Integration* 6 (2): 219–234.

Koopmans, Ruud, Ines Michalowski, and Stine Waibel. 2012. "Citizenship Rights for Immigrants: National Political Processes and Cross-National Convergence in Western Europe, 1980–2008." *American Journal of Sociology* 117 (4): 1202–1245.

Kühl, Stefan. 2015. "Bensman, Joseph/Gerver, Israel (1963): Crime and Punishment in the Factory: the Function of Deviancy in Maintaining the Social System. In: American Sociological Review, Jg. 28, S. 588–598." In *Schlüsselwerke der Organisationsforschung*, edited by Stefan Kühl, 85–88. Wiesbaden: Springer VS.

Lillevik, Ragna. 2019. "The Political Accommodation of Military Turbans and the Police Hijab in Norway: Windows of Opportunity." *Journal of Ethnic and Migration Studies*. Online First. doi:10.1080/1369183X.2019.1675501.

Luhmann, Niklas. [1964] 1995. *Funktionen und Folgen formaler Organisation*. Berlin: Duncker und Humblot.

Martínez-Ariño, Julia, Gloria García-Romeral, Gemma Ubasart-González, and Mar Griera. 2015. "Demonopolisation and Dislocation: (Re-)Negotiating the Place and Role of Religion in Spanish Prisons." *Social Compass* 62 (1): 3–21.

Mellor, Philip A., and Chris Shilling. 2010. "Body Pedagocis and the Religious Habit: A New Direction for the Sociological Study of Religion." *Religion, State & Society* 40 (1): 27–38.

Michalowski, Ines. 2015. "What Is at Stake When Muslims Join the Ranks? An International Comparison." *Religion, State & Society* 43 (1): 41–58.

Michalowski, Ines, and Behrendt Max. 2020. Bodyrules - Swimming Pool Survey. Version 1.0.0. WZB Berlin Social Science Center. Dataset. https://doi.org/10.7802/1.2007

Pfaffenzeller, Martin. 2019. "Sittenstreit in der Provinz. Kein Freibad vor der Ehe." *Spiegel Online*, May 15.

Shavit, Uriya, and Ofir Winter. 2011. "Sport in Contemporary Islamic Law." *Islamic Law and Society* 18: 250–280.

Smith, P. Caleb. 2012. "Reflections in the Water: Society and Recreational Facilities, a Case Study of Public Swimming Pools in Mississippi." *Southeastern Geographer* 52 (1): 39–54.

Statham, Paul, Ruud Koopmans, Marco Giugni and Florence Passy. 2005. "Resilient or adaptable Islam? Multiculturalism, religion and migrants' claims-making for group demands in Britain, the Netherlands and France." *Ethnicities* 5(4): 427–59.

Thériault, Barbara. 2009. "Inquiring Into Diversity. The Case of Berlin Police Inspector Bobkowski." *German Politics and Society* 27 (4): 72–91.

Zaubler, William S. 2015. "Don't Dive in My Pool: Normalizing Segregated Swimming in Montclair, New Jersey." *The Concord Review* 25 (3): 63–100.

Index

Information within tables is indicated by a locator in bold text.